ACADEMIC WRITING CONSULTING AND WAC

Methods and Models for Guiding Cross-Curricular Literacy Work

THE HAMPTON PRESS SERIES
Research and Teaching in Rhetoric and Composition
Michael M. Williamson and *David A. Jolliffe*, series editors

Basic Writing as a Political Act: Public Conversations About Writing and Literacies
  Linda Adler-Kassner and *Susanmarie Harrington*

Culture Shock and the Practice of Profession: Training the Next Wave
  in Rhetoric and Composition
  Virginia Anderson and *Susan Romano*

New Worlds, New Words: Exploring Pathways for Writing About
  and In Electronic Environments
  John F. Barber and *Dene Grigar* (eds.)

The Hope and the Legacy: The Past Present and Future of "Students' Right" to
  Their Own Language
  Patrick Bruch and *Richard Marback* (eds.)

The Rhetoric and Ideology of Genre: Strategies for Stability and Change
  Richard Coe, Lorelei Lingard, and *Tatiana Teslenko* (eds.)

In Search of Eloquence: Cross-Disciplinary Conversations on the Role
  of Writing in Undergraduate Education
  Cornelius Cosgrove and *Nancy Barta-Smith*

Teaching/Writing in the Late Age of Print
  Jeffrey Galin, Carol Peterson Haviland, and *J. Paul Johnson* (eds.)

Rhetoric in(to) Science Inquiry: Style as Invention in the Pursuit of Knowledge
  Heather Graves

Revision Revisited
  Alice S. Horning

Multiple Literacies for the 21st Century
  Brian Huot, Beth Stroble, and *Charles Bazerman* (eds.)

Academic Writing Consulting and WAC: Methods and Models for Guiding
  Cross–Curricular Literacy Work
  Jeffrey Jablonski

Identities Across Text
  George H. Jensen

Against the Grain: Essays in Honor of Maxine Hairston
  David Jolliffe, Michael Keene, Mary Trachel, and *Ralph Voss* (eds.)

Classroom Spaces and Writing Instruction
  Ed Nagelhout and *Carol Rutz*

Unexpected Voices
  John Rouse and *Ed Katz*

Directed Self-Placement: Principles and Practices
  Dan Royer and *Roger Gilles* (eds.)

Who Can Afford Critical Consciousness?: Practicing a Pedagogy of Humility
  David Seitz

forthcoming

Toward Deprivatized Pedagogy
  Diane Calhoun Bell and *Becky Nugent*

Remapping Narrative: Technology's Impact on the Way We Write
  Gian S. Pagnucci and *Nick Mauriello* (eds.)

ACADEMIC WRITING CONSULTING AND WAC

Methods and Models for Guiding Cross-Curricular Literacy Work

Jeffrey Jablonski

University of Nevada Las Vegas

HAMPTON PRESS, INC.
CRESSKILL, NEW JERSEY

Copyright © 2006 by Hampton Press, Inc.

All rights reserved. No part of this publication may be reproduced, stored in a retrieval system, or transmitted in any form or by any means, electronic, mechanical, photocopying, microfilming, recording, or otherwise, without permission of the publisher.

Printed in the United States of America

Library of Congress Cataloging-in-Publication-Data

Jablonski, Jeffrey.
   Academic writing consulting and WAC : methods and models for
   guiding cross-curricular literacy work / Jeffrey Jablonski
      p. cm. -- (Research and teaching in rhetoric and composition)
   Includes bibliographic references and indexes.
   ISBN 1-57273-632-1 (cloth) -- ISBN 1-57273-633-X (pbk.)
   1. English language--Rhetoric--Study and teacing (Higher). 2. Interdisciplinary approach in education. 3. Academic writing--Study and
teaching (Higher). I. Title. II. Series.

   PE1404.J325 2006
   808'.042711--dc22

                                                        2005044797

Hampton Press, Inc.
23 Broadway
Cresskill, NJ 07626

For Colin and Bridget

CONTENTS

Acknowledgements   xi

INTRODUCTION   **1**

What this Book Is Not   6

Objectives and Method of this Book   6

Organization of the Book   10

Notes   14

1 RECONCEIVING THE INTELLECTUAL WORK   **15**
OF CROSS–CURRICULAR LITERACY SPECIALISTS

Cross–Curricular Literacy in Historical Context   15

Toward Understanding the Professional Knowledge Base   19
of CCL Specialists

Professional Reform and the Question of WAC Expertise   22

Notes   28

2 THE LIMITS OF COLLABORATION THEORY   **31**

The Traditional or Commonsense Collaborative Mode   32

The Collaborative Philosophy Mode   34

The Consulting Model of Collaboration   36

3 PROFILES OF ACADEMIC WRITING CONSULTING   **45**
PRACTICE

Constructive Reflection and Practical Inquiry   46

Defining Qualitative Interviewing   49

"But Isn't Interviewing Just . . . Talking?": The Validity   51
of Practitioner Prifiles

"Laurel": A Writing Center Director Who Defines   52
Collaboration According to Her Center's Mission
and the Faculty Member's Personality

"Patricia": A Researcher Who "Works and Publishes   61
    with Others"
"Roger": A Veteran Teacher Who (Tacitly) Knows the   69
    "Ecologies" of Collaborative Consulting Relationships
"Linda": A Cross–Curricular Writing Program Director   82
    Who Has Learned to Appreciate the "Tire-Kickers"
Conclusion: Intelligible Practices/Intelligent Practitioners   91
Notes   94

4 MODELS FOR ACADEMIC WRITING CONSULTING   97
A Framework for Writing Consulting   99
Reflective Inquiry and Discipline-Based Research Models   110
Conclusion   127
Notes   129

5 THE PROCESS OF ACADEMIC WRITING   131
   CONSULTING
Kuriloff's Five-Stage Model of Writing Consulting   132
Process Consultation and WAC: Addressing the Problem   135
    of Faculty Resistance
Building Theories of Academic Writing Consulting Practice   146
Notes   150

6 THE INTELLECTUAL VALUE OF CROSS–   151
   CURRICULAR LITERACY WORK
Locating WAC Work Within The "Usual Triad"   153
Patricia's Collaborative Service Ethic: "My Work Is of a Piece"   160
Roger's Cross–Curricular Links: "Part of the Mix"   164
Linda's Case for Tenure: "Living What You Practice"   170
Conclusion: Constructing WAC Scholarship   176
Notes   179

CONCLUSION: THE FOURTH STAGE OF WAC   181
Appendix A: Frontmatter to Roger's Evaluation Portfolio   191
Appendix B: Table of Contents From Linda's Promotion   195
    and Tenure Dossier
References   197
Author Index   211
Subject Index   215

ACKNOWLEDGEMENTS

I would like to thank the four writing specialists of this study who gracious-ly allowed me glimpses into their professional and personal lives. They sup-ported my project from the start by unanimously agreeing to participate, carving out time in their busy schedules for interviews, corresponding via e-mail, and verifying their transcripts and my drafts. They showed me their programs and institutions and practices. In this project I have argued the benefits of codifying experts' collective wisdom, but the language of methodology and case study can only convey so much of the privileged access that I have been granted by their generosity and candor.

As I mention in the opening chapter, Susan Leist deserves all the credit for introducing me to cross-curricular literacy work—and the challenges it presents. Her mentoring helped propel me to where I am today. I also thank Irwin Weiser, Shirley Rose, Graham Smart, and Tony Silva, whose feedback helped shape the project into its current form. David Jolliffe and Barbara Bernstein at Hampton Press have been wonderful to work with, and I appreciate their confidence in the book.

Lastly, I want to acknowledge the support of my wife, Stefanie, and her parents. I also thank my parents and brother. No written acknowledgement could fully "make whole again" their sacrifices on my behalf throughout my graduate training and early career at UNLV.

INTRODUCTION

As a new master's student at the State University of New York College at Buffalo (SUCB), I dogged my faculty advisor and mentor Professor Susan Leist from the first minute I met her about the possibility of gaining teaching experience. SUCB was a bit atypical as far as graduate programs go in that it had no means for supporting its graduate students through teaching assistantships. If I were to advance in the field of composition studies (although I didn't know it was called that at the time), I felt strongly about my need for some experience "thinking on my feet." Susan asked if I would be interested in working with Bill Lin, an assistant professor in the Computer Information Systems (CIS) Department, who had been asking for help teaching his upper division writing intensive (WI) course. Bill was among the many faculty on campus who had taken the preparatory summer workshop for WI course teachers, but who had also expressed reservations about the prospects of "teaching writing" and feelings of alienation from the supportive workshop environment. Of course, I agreed to participate, but had no idea what I was getting into. No idea.

The three of us spent the initial semester negotiating the roles and responsibilities of what we called our tripartite relationship. Bill would teach the course focused on networked systems design and assign a series of four WI projects. As the "rhetorician-in-residence," I would support Bill by tutoring referred or self-selected students, by helping Bill strengthen his assignments and clarify his grading criteria, by introducing writing strategies to his classes, and by researching writing conventions in Bill's emerging field of CIS. Susan, as the ad-hoc writing across the curriculum (WAC) director, would stay in the background, monitor our progress, and serve as an advocate for both Bill and me.

As I came to learn, we spent a lot of time that academic year reinventing some aspects of the wheel, but also charting much new territory as well, particularly at SUCB. Research *in medias res*, as it were, informed me that we were piloting a form of writing fellows program, a popular component for supporting students and faculty developed at some of the earliest WAC programs and spread to more than 100 colleges and universities by 1992 (Farris and Smith; Haring-Smith; Soven, "Curriculum-Based"). But being only recently introduced to WAC, I was acquainted with very little of the literature. Moreover, what research I conducted uncovered very little guidance on how to conduct such an ambiguous relationship. Bolstered by a semester of composition theory, I instead plodded my way using trial and error, common sense, and good faith. There were some harrowing early sessions where my enthusiasm may have threatened Bill's assumptions about my role. He was all for having a tutor dedicated to his students and for having a research assistant committed to investigating emerging standards of written communication, but he was less sure about having a graduate student from English assess the merits of his writing assignments and, in general, his pedagogy. As I recorded in a journal being kept to document our pilot, I confessed to Susan that I may have stepped on Bill's toes once or twice with some of my early assessments about his writing pedagogy. "I know," she replied. "Bill told me."

As the work of meeting with students progressed, and our dialogue about nonacademic writing became more engrossing for us both, the relationship became more informal and what I would now consider very collegial. I would drop by Bill's office once or twice a week, and our talk would range from specific students' writing, to our shared goals for research and assessment, to computers (Bill's area of expertise), to our personal backgrounds and planned futures. The success of the pilot program was evident to many—as we were careful to make known. Students wrote in evaluations how the class had helped them become better writers. Bill agreed to extend the relationship into the next semester. A grant was awarded by SUCB's Center for the Enhancement of Learning and Teaching to further articulate the program. Susan and I traveled to several department meetings on campus to describe our pilot program and recruit interested faculty. We presented our model at one institution-wide conference (with Bill) and another statewide. But the one measure of success that sticks with me most is when later, after I entered the PhD program at Purdue, Susan part jokingly, part regretfully shared with me how tough it was to find good writing fellows staff by relating Bill's repeated request, "Can't you get me another Jeff?"

Although Bill's comment is a personally rewarding testimonial to the efficacy of our working relationship, it also speaks to a number of concerns related to supporting faculty seeking to incorporate WAC principles into their pedagogies. If you'll bear with the self-aggrandizing move: Why *aren't* there more Jeffs—or Jills? In other words, how can Susan better ensure the continuity of her fellows program? How can she better recruit, train, and supervise effective writing fellows? The question can be framed beyond fellows programs, including the range of various components and models developed to implement WAC programs: How does one define and assess an effective relationship in cross-curricular contexts, where writing specialists of varying levels of experience and expertise must negotiate close working partnerships, for a variety of purposes, with specialists in other disciplines? What do you call "work" in such a context? Teaching or tutoring? Research? Service? Consulting?

At SUCB, I was in the midst of on-the-job training and wanted more guidance. Although I've since moved on to a tenure-track appointment at the University of Nevada, Las Vegas (UNLV), this early dissonance has stuck with me and shaped my career as a compositionist. I've been involved with cross-curricular literacy (CCL) initiatives ranging from a pilot science learning community at Purdue University, helping UNLV's College of Engineering integrate writing and speaking into its undergraduate curriculum, and working to integrate communication skills into UNLV's first-year experience program. All of these experiences involve working closely with highly educated individuals who nonetheless have very specific, often what would be considered narrow, views of writing and what it means for learners or newcomers to write effectively. Even the compositionist who doesn't self-identify as a CCL specialist will frequently have to deal with others not trained in composition. Richard Miller reminds us that compositionists will more than likely be called on to contribute leadership to their respective campus writing programs and campus-wide writing activities. When it comes to collaborating with others outside the field of composition studies, I have found the narrative of my early experience at SUCB to be a common story, an experience shared by many (oftentimes junior) writing specialists. Like myself, the so-called writing experts find themselves asking, Now what? *How do I start a conversation? How should I proceed? What are my goals?*

This book addresses such questions by providing theoretical models and practical methods for helping writing teachers and writing program administrators (WPAs) within postsecondary academic institutions conduct the interdisciplinary, collaborative consulting activities that are common to all CCL initiatives.[1] Since the early 1970s, writing specialists have worked across curricular boundaries in university-wide writing and faculty development programs to improve the communication skills of students and the teaching of those skills by faculty, typically under the auspices of formal or informal WAC programs (Maimon, "Preface;" Russell, *Academic Disciplines*; Thaiss, "Writing"). A central component to formal and informal

CCL programs is cross-disciplinary faculty development where writing specialists form close working partnerships with nonwriting specialists,[2] typically faculty in other disciplines such as philosophy or biology, who may be accomplished writers, but may not have the meta-language or "rhetorical knowledgability" to make the discourse practices of their field explicit to themselves and their students.[3] To conduct this work, writing specialists today have access to extensive writing in the disciplines (WID) research, anecdotal WAC program descriptions (e.g., Fulwiler and Young), and administrative knowledge (e.g., McLeod and Soven, "Developing"). What they have less access to, however, is a systematic body of knowledge on how writing specialists actually negotiate, sustain, and assess successful relationships in CCL contexts. In other words, interdisciplinary collaboration remains relatively underexamined in the published literature.

Although those in CCL studies implicitly recognize the importance of such relationships in initiating and sustaining faculty development (Soven, "Sustaining") and facilitating rhetorical inquiry (Bazerman), only a handful of published models exist as practical guides for conducting such relationships—either for facilitating pedagogy or for the purposes of studying some other element of writing or teaching (Kuriloff; McCarthy and Walvoord). Even fewer studies focus on the collaborative interaction itself (Kalamaras; McCarthy and Fishman, "Boundary;" Mullin et al.). What this amounts to is a body of WAC literature focused on collaboration as either a theory of learning for both students and faculty (e.g., Maimon, "Collaborative") or as a set of indirect accounts of interdisciplinary collaboration. Although there is a substantial body of theoretical and practical knowledge about administering WAC programs, there remains little discussion in the literature about how to conduct the day-to-day work of negotiating close working partnerships with faculty in other disciplines. Lucille McCarthy and Stephen Fishman note that "relatively little" has been said about collaborative relationships in the context of WAC ("Boundary" 422). George Kalamaras supports this argument when he notes that his role as consultant to a biology department had "been complicated by the lack of any substantial discussion in writing across the curriculum studies" addressing different aspects of being "such a liaison" (11).

I address this gap by using my notion of *academic writing consulting* as a lens for better understanding this key facet of CCL work. This book articulates the relationship between academic writing consulting and WAC (chapter 1), explores notions of "collaboration" in composition and rhetoric discourse (chapter 2), provides profiles of academic writing consulting practice (chapter 3), develops a theoretical model of academic writing consulting (chapter 4), examines the process of academic writing consulting, particularly how to deal with faculty resistance (chapter 5), and addresses the institutional barriers to such work by examining how the consultants profiled in chapter 3 constructed their work in annual evaluations (chapter 6). The book concludes with a call for further inquiry into methods for translating the specialized knowledge of composition studies to nonspecialists. Through theory-building and empirical illustration, this book deepens current understandings of how writing specialists collaborate with nonwriting specialists in academic contexts and provides a map for structuring successful collaborations in the future. The theoretical framework presented in the book is grounded by illustrative profiles based on qualitative interviews conducted as part of the research for this book. Because of its focus on both WAC theory and practice, this book should appeal to practitioners and researchers alike.

Such a book-length work is important because many of the latest university-wide reform initiatives are bringing a heightened focused on writing and communication skills at the postsecondary level. These initiatives include undergraduate assessment (O'Neill, Schendel, and Huot), engineering and scientific program accreditation (Williams), service learning (Jolliffe), learning communities (Zawacki and Williams), and computer-assisted instruction (Reiss and Young). The latest focus on postsecondary student literacy is spurring a new wave of collaboration between writing specialists and nonwriting specialists. Writing specialists are even assuming high-profile roles as directors or endowed chairs at freestanding centers or institutes for communication (e.g., Joe Harris at Duke, Chris Anson at North Carolina State University, and Steve Bernhardt at University of Delaware). The creation of such new programs, centers, and institutes also marks a resurgence of interest in CCL not seen since the initial rise of WAC programs in the early 1980s. As composition studies settles into the 21st century, it appears that CCL work—the activity of specialists in writing helping others teach and learn writing in academic contexts outside English departments—is thriving.

At the same time that CCL work flourishes, the founders of the WAC movement of the late 1960s are rapidly approaching retirement age. As McLeod suggests in "WAC at Century's End," the first generation of WAC program directors is literally graying. A whole new generation of writing specialists is finding itself asking questions about how to create CCL programs and, more specifically, how to conduct close collaborations with colleagues from across the campus. This fourth stage of WAC, as I call it (as I discuss in the conclusion of this book, the narrative history of WAC is generally framed as stages), is evidenced by many signs of increased interest among writing specialists in publications and other professional forums where CCL work is discussed. For instance, the National Writing Across the Curriculum Conference recently switched from a biennial format to an annual format. Another sign of this subject's vitality is the launch of the *WAC Clearinghouse*, a Web site devoted to the study of communication across the curriculum (http://wac.colostate.edu). Although many WAC programs have evolved into other entities, such as teaching and learning centers or communication across the curriculum programs, the popularity of new books such as *WAC for the New Millennium* (McLeod et al.) and the sustained reader interest in classic books like *Strengthening Programs for Writing Across the Curriculum* (McLeod; available online from the WAC Clearinghouse Landmark Publications in Writing Studies series: (http://wac.colostate.edu/books/landmarks.cfm) speak to the institutionalization of WAC programs and the durability of WAC as a reform initiative.

WHAT THIS BOOK IS NOT

This book is not intended as an explicit guide for nonwriting specialists teaching writing in their own disciplines. Generic WAC teaching methods have been codified in such texts as John Bean's *Engaging Ideas* (1996), Barbara Walvoord's *Helping Students Write Well* (1987), Andrew Moss and Carol Holder's *Improving Student Writing* (1988), and Art Young's *Teaching Writing Across the Curriculum* (3rd ed. 1999). Another resource for faculty in other disciplines is Chris Anson's *The WAC Casebook: Scenes for Faculty Reflection and Program Development* (2002). As its title suggests, the casebook includes scenarios that pose common WAC-related problems, prompts for analyzing the situations, and bibliographies for further reading. Such a text works well in faculty development workshop settings.

As I discuss in the chapters of this book, one of the problems with current approaches to WID research and WAC faculty development is that they presume that nonwriting specialists can apply these pedagogical guides, or our more specialized published scholarship, without much difficulty. But a mound of anecdotal evidence suggests the contrary. Faculty need help externalizing the discursive practices of their classrooms and disciplines, and they need help articulating methods for teaching them to others. This book is about developing guidance for the writing specialists who help faculty apply our disciplinary knowledge to new and highly situated contexts.

OBJECTIVES AND METHOD OF THIS BOOK

This book aims to focus attention on the interdisciplinary activities of CCL specialists by describing these collaborative activities in terms of existing scholarship, various theoretical lenses, and frameworks for assessing academic work. When taken together, the chapters explore the extent to which there *are, can be,* and *should be* systematic methods for informing writing specialists' interdisciplinary, collaborative activities with faculty in other disciplines in cross-curricular contexts. Specifically, the book addresses the following questions:

- What is the role of writing specialists in CCL programs and how do they apply theoretical knowledge in their day-to-day interactions with faculty and other professionals who seek our expertise in writing? (chapter 1)
- What is the relationship between academic writing consulting and CCL work? (chapter 2)
- What is the role of collaboration in CCL specialists' work? (chapter 3)
- What do CCL specialists know and do related to interdisciplinary collaboration, and what theories and methods guide them? (chapter 4)
- How do CCL specialists facilitate a relationship that leads to substantive change, one that helps the nonwriting specialist better understand the role and function of writing in particular settings and avoids its subordination? (chapter 5)
- How is CCL work valued, and how can one argue for its value? (chapter 6)

I liken my project's scope and design to Cynthia Lewiecki-Wilson and Jeff Sommers' "Professing at the Fault Lines: Composition at Open Admissions Institutions." The pair of researchers focus on the "social materiality" of teaching composition at 2- and 4-year open-admissions colleges in order to raise awareness of these marginalized sites of praxis. Lewiecki-Wilson and Sommers do this by provoking a "crisis of representation" for readers; they present "in vivid detail" images and stories of work at these sites so that they might "change views of the profession and redirect attention to work compositionists need to do for the future" (440). To gather these stories, the researchers conducted a range of face-to-face, phone, written, and e-mail interviews with nine colleagues who teach or have taught at 2- or 4-year open-admissions colleges. By integrating interviews with published data, including theoretical and historical studies, they address two goals: (a) to *describe* the teachers and students at such institutions and, importantly, (b) to "*make visible* what compositionists actually do at open admissions institutions" (445; italics added). In other words, Lewiecki-Wilson and Sommers' study was guided by two overarching questions: *Who* teaches and who learns writing at open admissions colleges, and *what* do compositionists actually do at these institutions?

The "answer" as represented by the participants' voices and the researchers' interpretations is this: Because they must continually argue the value of literacy to secure diminishing material resources, open admissions compositionists do a great deal of teaching and translating of disciplinary knowledge to nonspecialists. In the end, Lewiecki-Wilson and Sommers argue that a broadened conception of professional scholarship in composition studies is necessary if the translation work of open-admissions practitioners is to be recognized as valuable. The goals and conclusions of Lewiecki-Wilson and Sommers' study are very much in line with the goals of my study. Just as they sought to make visible the teaching of writing at open-admissions sites, the goal of this study is to focus attention on the interdisciplinary practices of CCL specialists. To clarify and give voice to who CCL specialists are and what they do, chapter 3 of this book presents illustrative profiles of four accomplished CCL specialists constructed from retrospective interviews. I collected information from four CCL specialists, selected both for their established scholarly record and their representativeness. Chapter 5, which applies the lens of consulting to the problem of dealing with faculty resistance, and chapter 6, which explores how CCL work is assessed and valued, are also based on my interviews with these specialists.

Another work influencing my approach is Ruth Ray's *The Practice of Theory: Teacher Research in Composition* (1993). Like Lewiecki-Wilson and Sommers, Ray is interested in the politics and disciplinary formation of composition studies. She makes an argument for how teachers can "'reclaim the classroom' through careful observation of and reflection on their own teaching." In the fields of professional education and teacher education, this practice has come to be known as "practical inquiry" (22). Ray synthesizes the British and North American teacher-researcher movements in education with feminist research methods in order to critique the rise of theory and research in composition and its concomitant de-valuing of practice and practitioner knowledge. She shows how embracing an epistemology which values teaching and practical inquiry can affect composition teacher-practitioners by contributing to "a sense of their own professionalism, status within educational institutions, and empowerment to effect change through a broadened definition of what it means to do 'research,' what constitutes 'knowledge,' and how teachers contribute to knowledge making in their fields" (72). To further support her argument, Ray includes studies of her own teacher research with K–12 in-service teachers and composition graduate students.

Of particular interest is her study of seven K–12 teachers participating in a National Writing Project professional development program. At the end of their in-service program, Ray conducted exit interviews and collected their final papers. Doing what she calls "retrospective analysis of their talk and texts," Ray describes the specific knowledge created by these teachers in terms of three types: personal, global, and local (82). Ray represents teach-

ers' understandings of their own knowledge-making activity. Like
Lewiecki-Wilson and Sommers, Ray finds it important to provide concrete
evidence of the kind of "work" that teachers do. In this case, the answer is
that teachers create knowledge that can be likened to traditional research
except that it is shaped more so by personal and local contexts than that of
the global professional community. Building from Stephen North and others, Ray provides the theoretical framework and rationale for studying composition teaching *practice* and viewing it as a legitimate form of knowledge-
producing activity at par with traditional research and theorizing. Ray studied the practice of composition generally and of secondary and graduate student teachers specifically. Lewiecki-Wilson and Sommers studied the practice of composition at open-admissions colleges. I aim to examine the practice of writing specialists in CCL contexts and to explain the professional,
scholarly nature of this activity. Although the whole of my study could be
considered practical inquiry, chapters 3, 4, and 5 use a combination of theory-building and case illustration, drawn from existing research and my own
primary research, to develop models for guiding CCL work.

I do not claim, per se, to be replicating the methods used by Lewiecki-
Wilson and Sommers, and Ray. However, I am certainly making a legitimacy argument by comparison, and my thinking about my own project has
been heavily influenced by their approaches. One would be hard-pressed to
find an extant characterization for their research. These studies might best
be called mixed-genre studies, incorporating elements of qualitative empiri-
cism, theory, reflective inquiry, and essayist/polemic argumentation. These
qualities attract me to their studies. Calls are increasing in composition studies for research to be situated, less driven by method and more responsive to
the agenda of the researcher and the context of the research (Blyler,
"Political Turn"; Mortensen and Kirsch; Sullivan and Porter). For Ray, the
problem domain of teacher research—individual, local classroom-based
inquiry—leads to a "methodological eclecticism" that is difficult to classify
according to traditional research genres. It invariably is manifested in "a
kind of hybrid text—part narrative, part case study, part experiment, part
ethnography, part discourse analysis" (93). This is because for teacher-
researchers, "validity is measured not so much in the adherence to formal
research procedures as in terms of what can be done practically and unob-
trusively in the classroom and *what would yield information of use to teachers and students working in similar situations*" (91-92; italics added).

I wanted to design a useful project within the problem domain bound-
ed by my personal/professional experience and my perception of a gap in
composition studies scholarship. I have given careful thought to how this
study addresses issues relevant to a broader, more general audience of compositionists and those interested in composition, but the principle audience
remains those interested in cross-disciplinary literacy work.

ORGANIZATION OF THE BOOK

Chapter 1 focuses on further contextualizing the project within historical and conceptual frameworks. After briefly reviewing the emergence of CCL programs as an education reform movement and sphere of intellectual and social activity in postsecondary education, I provide a rationale for studying academic writing consulting in more systematic ways.[4] Specifically, this rationale opens a space for examining the practical knowledge involved with academic writing consulting by critiquing what I call "missionary rhetoric" in WAC discourse, a paradoxical stance that eschews the writing specialist's expertise and thus far has limited inquiry into the writing specialist's unique role in cross-curricular writing program faculty development. Because of the WAC movement's faculty-centered, egalitarian roots, theorists have resisted putting writing specialists in an expert role. However, concepts from discourse on professional reform allow for a closer examination of the special forms of knowing employed by academic writing specialists. In keeping with the intent of this discourse, the discussion in this chapter is not about creating any sort of monopoly of expertise that perpetuates the academy's lack of commitment to literacy. Rather, my discussion aims at opening up a space for developing principles of good practice through systematic inquiry, principles that can guide future practice and practitioners.

Chapter 2 further establishes the need to explore academic writing consulting as a form of professional practice by discussing the limitations of prevailing conceptions of collaboration theory. By articulating three models of collaboration—the traditional/commonsense model, the collaborative philosophy model, and the professional consulting model—this discussion differentiates examination of collaboration as a general skill, such as interpersonal relations, or as an aspect of peer relationships, as in the case of student writing groups or collaborative research, from systematic inquiry into how writing specialists employ procedural knowledge to enact successful WAC-related faculty development. The discussion in this chapter points to the limits of current collaboration theory, including theories that ascribe to what I call the collaborative philosophy model, which many in composition studies would align with progressive conceptions of collaboration including those described by Lisa Ede and Andrea Lunsford. As I argue in this chapter, theories of collaboration that espouse nonhierarchical dialogue are inadequate for studying academic writing consulting activity, where frequently writing specialists must collaborate with nonwriting specialists in unequal power relationships.

Chapter 3 presents profiles of four writing specialists with experience doing CCL work, based on a series of retrospective interviews I conducted as part of the research for this book. These profiles help demonstrate the gaps, or underexamined knowledge, in the professional competencies of cross-curricular writing specialists. The four writing specialists studied admittedly paid little conscious attention to the social dynamic, ascribing variously to the commonsensical or philosophical models I describe in chapter 2. However, the interpersonal relations between the writing specialists and nonwriting specialists were central to their professional activities as academic writing consultants. As I argue at the end of this chapter, when codified as practice theories, these cases and others like them help contribute to methods for guiding CCL work.

Chapter 4 develops a typology of consulting models based on my reading of existing scholarship: the workshop model, the service model, the reflective inquiry model, and the discipline-based research model. I differentiate these models according to their aim, the role of the writing consultant, the methods typically used by the consultant, the role of the client (or nonwriting specialist), and examples found in the literature. These models help clarify what CCL specialists know and do. In particular, to achieve WAC ends, the writing specialist assumes a rhetorical approach, chooses among several methods (perhaps modifying existing methods or creating new ones), and uses them as tools to facilitate reflective inquiry into writing practices among particular faculty in specific contexts. This taxonomy also allows for the cataloguing of usable methods, which further articulates methods and models for guiding CCL work.

Chapter 5 addresses what the typology articulated in chapter four does not directly speak to: the procedural knowledge of the academic writing consultant. This chapter focuses on how consultants facilitate a consulting relationship that leads to substantive change, one that helps nonwriting specialists better understand the role and function of writing in their classrooms and avoids the subordination of writing. As I discuss in chapters 1, 4, and 5, not only do writing consultants seem to employ a certain "technical" or "content" knowledge of rhetorical theory and composition pedagogy, but they also employ a certain pedagogical content knowledge, the "blending of content and pedagogy into an understanding of how particular topics, problems, or issues are organized, represented, and adapted to the diverse interests and abilities of learners, and presented for instruction" (Schulman 8). What are ways that a consultancy framework can help codify this procedural knowledge and make it possible to present it as strategies or principles that can guide future practice? Chapter 5 addresses this question by looking more closely an episode mentioned in the profiles from chapter 3, applying Edgar Schein's process consultation theory to extend discussions of academic writing consulting.

Chapter 6 returns to discussing the intellectual character of academic writing consulting, an issue touched on in the last section of chapter 2. Industry and academic writing consulting activities are generally de-valued as (mere) service, especially in the humanities. Moreover, the literature of WAC raises issues about the institutional barriers to collaboration, namely the faculty reward system, the departmentalized structure of the academy, and the increasingly heavy workloads of faculty. Any discussion of CCL work must consider the institutional structures that discourage this type of work and that influence faculty priorities and values. In this chapter, I examine the extent to which the academic writing consultants profiled in chapter 3 experienced these institutional barriers in their own professional activity. I explore how CCL work is evaluated and how the writing specialists fit their faculty development activity into the tenure/job expectations of their particular institutions. After locating CCL work within traditional and contemporary frameworks for assessing faculty work, I examine how the specialists interviewed for this book justified their work at their institutions, which suggests strategies academic writing consultants can use to describe and document their work.

The conclusion discusses how CCL work relates to current discourse in composition and rhetoric on "going public," or translating disciplinary knowledge to nonspecialists in ways that improves discursive practices, social relations, and the status of composition studies as a discipline.

This book addresses a number of issues related to WAC interdisciplinary collaboration. Above all, it establishes that the interactions between writing specialists and faculty in other disciplines are much more complicated than the "brown-bag lunch" philosophy toward collaboration espoused in much WAC literature. It further suggests the limitations of the nonhierarchical, dialogical model of collaboration popularized by works such as Lisa Ede and Andrea Lunsford's *Singular Texts/Plural Authors*. By beginning to illuminate the epistemological, methodological, ideological, relational, and personal issues related to interdisciplinary collaboration in WAC contexts, this book suggests that frequently more than goodwill and good communication skills are needed when negotiating complex relationships forged in the ambiguous spaces across disciplinary ways of knowing and doing. This book articulates the professional dimension of this activity, brought about when writing specialists *focus* or *systematically reflect* on the role the collaborative dynamic plays in achieving WAC ends. For writing specialists to do their work better, more effectively, more ethically, there needs to be an elevation in the status of collaboration from a transparent or invisible "skill" to a complex activity that requires systematic reflective practice.

This work contributes to the knowledge base of composition studies by codifying common CCL practices and representing them for the benefit of future practice and practitioners. For an area of composition studies that specializes in studying the socialization of disciplinary ways of knowing and acting, it is ironic that the experiences and relationships that generate these theories are themselves left unexamined. WAC has historically provided "service-learning" opportunities for graduate students and undergraduates in the form of curriculum-based tutoring programs. What WAC hasn't provided is a strong theoretical and practical foundation for sending would-be writing specialists (as tutors or consultants) into the "strange lands" of the disciplines. The book speaks to the need for training/professionalizing writing specialists for CCL work brought about by the "graying" of the first generation of composition scholars. Those interested in CCL need to start thinking of ways to train the next generation of writing specialists. This book would be a useful text in various composition theory, WPA, and WAC-related courses. The vicarious experience and frameworks for approaching collaboration presented in the book can be used to help undergraduate tutors, graduate students, and writing specialists attend to the social dynamics of their CCL work.

This book also points to ways writing specialists might reconceive of their professional identity. By foregrounding the intellectual and disciplinary character of CCL work, writing specialists can potentially make their work more recognizable, and by implication, more valuable to others in composition studies, English departments, and across the university. The study addresses the question of how the intellectual work of program administration, faculty development, team teaching, and academic/community outreach can be documented and described for the purposes of promotion and tenure, the institutional reward system that most agree reflects the values of the academy and determines what work is valorized and what is marginalized. Without institutional and departmental support, the emerging call to apply humanistic knowledges outside narrow disciplinary confines by academic activists like Elaine Showalter, Cary Nelson, Peter Mortensen, and Ellen Cushman will never take shape. In this vein, the study informs discussions of re-evaluating the scholarship of teaching and service in English studies/composition studies and higher education. Theorizing CCL work necessarily requires engaging not only WAC discourse, but also broader discourses that socially, materially, and ideologically construct the milieu within which CCL specialists must work. Critiques of academic being and doing in the face of sweeping changes in global and national socioeconomic systems are leading to dramatic reform proposals. CCL work, historically nontraditional and interdisciplinary, seems well suited for, if not prescient to, the changing nature of academic work in the 21st century. That is, if writing specialists choose to engage these discourses.

NOTES

1. Following David Russell, I use *cross-curricular literacy* (CCL) as an umbrella
    term referring to writing that occurs in academic contexts outside English depart-
    ments. Although I consider *writing across the curriculum* (WAC) to be a similar-
    ly inclusive concept, not everyone shares this view. Many, for instance, distin-
    guish between WAC and writing in the disciplines (WID). Moreover, many peo-
    ple in and beyond composition studies misunderstand the scope, aims, and meth-
    ods of WAC, as Susan McLeod and Elaine Maimon asserted.
2. One must be cautious when naming the counterparts with whom writing spe-
    cialists collaborate. The often used term *content* instructor is problematic. It
    suggests a naïve dualistic split between content and language, denying the epis-
    temic dimension of language and reinforces traditional assumptions of lan-
    guage as transparent medium of pre-existing knowledge (see Kaufer and
    Young). It also implies that the writing specialist has no "content" area of his
    or her own. "Discipline" instructor is similarly problematic because it rein-
    forces the low status of composition, that it is not a discipline, thus not wor-
    thy of serious intellectual attention. I prefer to use "faculty in other disci-
    plines" or "nonwriting specialists." Referring to faculty as "nonwriting spe-
    cialists" is not to deny their expert status as highly technical communicators
    within their specialized fields; rather, it is to suggest that they may lack writ-
    ing specialists' theoretical and practical understanding and technical language
    for externalizing such discipline-specific practices. Nor is the term intended to
    deny their expert status as teachers and learners. One drawback of using the
    term *faculty* is that it obviates the increasing complexity of roles and occupa-
    tions assumed by individuals within academic institutions. When I use faculty,
    I assume that although most WAC relationships involve supporting tenure-
    line members of academic departments, it is also likely that CCL specialists
    will form partnerships with other members of academe, such as admissions,
    counseling, and faculty development personnel, adjunct instructors, and grad-
    uate and undergraduate students.
3. Segal et al. offer a lucid discussion of the ends of written communication
    research. They build on Anthony Gidden's notion that social structures are pat-
    terns of social knowledge that are reproduced daily by "knowledgeable agents,
    not simply by institutions." Thus, rhetorical knowledgeability is the awareness
    of how discourse operates to structure and constrain social activity and to
    "know enough about [these] discourse practices to know when to revise them—
    and when to protect them. . . . The consciousness of language that our rhetori-
    cal investigations offer can provide practitioners with a new or unfamiliar criti-
    cal perspective on their discourse and create opportunities for professional com-
    munities to change or modify language practices deliberately and thus bring
    about change. . . . Rhetorical knowledgeability may be a danger to immediate
    efficiency, as self-consciousness may 'disrupt' normal operations; yet it is also,
    in the long term, not only advantageous, but also necessary" (76-77).
4. CCL and the WAC movement have influenced K–12 contexts, too, primarily
    through teacher-training programs such as the National Writing Project. My
    project focuses on CCL in postsecondary contexts, however.

1

RECONCEIVING THE INTELLECTUAL WORK OF CROSS-CURRICULAR LITERACY SPECIALISTS

So how do writing specialists find themselves to be "traveling rhetoricians," Judy Segal et al.'s name for composition teacher-researchers working across disciplinary boundaries? In this chapter, I trace today's CCL programs from the emergence of WAC, the most recent higher education reform movement aimed at expanding the contexts of writing and literacy instruction beyond first-year writing courses in English departments. This discussion establishes two central assumptions of WAC: (a) that all faculty share responsibility for teaching general and discipline-specific literacy, and (b) that WAC is fundamentally a faculty-centered, not student-centered, movement. Following from these points, I recast the activity of academic writing consulting in the name of faculty development as a from of expert practice and argue that looking analogically at discourse on professional knowledge, such as teacher knowledge, helps further articulate the "gaps" in CCL specialists' professional knowledge, or what current discourse on WAC theory and practice overlooks.

CROSS-CURRICULAR LITERACY IN HISTORICAL CONTEXT

There have been several narratives constructed of the history of the WAC movement (Fulwiler "Quiet;" Maimon, "Past, Present, and Future," "Preface;" McLeod, "Defining;" Russell, "American Origins;" Thaiss, "Writing"). In a series of articles and a book, *Writing in the Academic Disciplines, 1870-1990: A Curricular History*, David Russell broadens the

15

scope of histories of writing instruction beyond departments of English and the ubiquitous first-year writing course ("American Origins," "Lessons from the Past," "Historical Perspective," "James Fleming Hosic"). Russell wondered why, as in the case of the WAC movement, writing instruction had never been considered the purview of faculty in all fields. As he found out, it had. From the classical era to the British recitation system adopted by early American colleges, the liberal arts curriculum had always relied on a system of education grounded in a common curriculum and rhetorical training. Virtually all faculty participated in assigning and assessing student oratorical and compositional skills. According to Russell, this changed when the German research model of specialized education and elective curricula contributed to the erosion of responsibility of faculty across the disciplines for evaluating students' communication skills. Russell identifies the conflicts inherent in this academic disciplinary organization regarding the nature of writing, its acquisition and instruction, and the relationship between language and the structuring of mass education. He does this to illuminate the theoretical and historical divisions over the who, where, why, when, and how of writing instruction. Since the turn of the 19th century, American education systems have placed the responsibility for teaching writing outside the disciplines, including that of English studies, which until recently was focused on the study of literary texts. Largely unexamined assumptions about the nature of writing, influenced by positivistic modes of thought and the increasing need for specialization, contributed to disciplinary and professional lack of rhetorical self-consciousness. Writing became tacitly understood as either *transparent*, a set of elementary transcription skills for putting pre-existing ideas—like scientific knowledge—into words, or as *belletristic*, the product of genius or inspiration rather than the "mundane social and professional activity of the disciplines" ("American Origins" 24).

According to Russell, WAC can be linked to earlier reform efforts aimed at correcting the limitations of the disciplinary construction of the modern academy. These reforms include the Correlation movement of the 1930s, which sought to unify public school curriculums with what would now be considered interdisciplinary "core classes" (*Academic Disciplines* 209-221), and the Communications movement of the 1950s, which concentrated the "four skills" of listening, reading, speaking, and writing in "speech-English" freshman courses (*Academic Disciplines* 256-261). Both of these movements prefigured various general education, core, or communication curricular requirements. Most were built on progressive-era philosophies of student-centered, liberal education. Most reforms also sought to address dramatic increases in enrollments brought about by social changes, such as the post-World War II influx of GIs when higher education enrollments tripled between 1945 and 1949.

In the late 1960s and early 1970s, another series of dramatic changes to the structure and social role of mass education contributed to faculty and public perception that students were somehow less prepared than their predecessors for the literate tasks of college and beyond. These "social upheavals" included the establishment of open-admissions policies aimed at racial and class integration, the proliferation of regional postsecondary institutions, the corporatization of academic administration, and the increased government involvement in higher education. In a passage worth repeating, David Russell contextualizes this sociohistorical exigence for WAC:

> In the early 1970s, these social and institutional factors produced the widest social and institutional demand for writing instruction since the mass-education system had founded composition a century earlier to solve the problem of integrating new students into academia. An outcry against "illiteracy" in the 1970s, like those of the 1870s, 1910s, and 1950s, coincided with the attempt to broaden access to schools and colleges for students who had previously been excluded from them; though the 1970s crisis, like its predecessors, almost ignored the complex political issue of raising social expectations and focused instead on the popular issue of declining standards. . . . The national press greeted with shock and indignation the release of the 1974 National Assessment of Educational Progress (NAEP) results on writing ability. . . . [The report] showed an apparent decline in some areas of secondary students' performance since the first test administered in 1969. Newsweek's 9 December 1975 cover story, "Why Johnny Can't Write," brought to a head the national discussion . . . over literacy, particularly writing instruction, with its inflammatory conclusion: "Willy-nilly, the U.S. educational system is spawning a generation of semi-literates." (*Academic Disciplines* 275-276)

Grassroots collectives of faculty and "top–down" campus committees formed to deal with this latest "literacy crisis" or "writing problem." Writing specialists at a handful of colleges and universities tapped into the British education reform movement known as Language across the Curriculum and the North American revival of rhetoric and composition as an academic discipline. The earliest approaches to WAC involved what has come to be known as writing-to-learn pedagogy. Important studies like those of James Britton et al., Janet Emig, and Mina Shaughnessy were used to justify cognitive, expressive, and social approaches to writing, which incorporated strategies such as ungraded writing and peer review as tools to aid learning in any classroom. To disseminate these pedagogical practices and composition theories, schools sponsored faculty retreats and seminars like those at Beaver College, Pennsylvania; Carleton College, Minnesota; Central College, Iowa; and Michigan Technological University. Other schools instituted college-wide curricular requirements such as writing intensive courses in the major and "mid-career" or "junior-rising" writing proficiency exams. Local chapters of the National Writing Project were organized with federal funding to further introduce WAC approaches to secondary and postsecondary teachers. Writing specialists began sharing scholarship on "WAC programs" and "WAC theory" at professional conferences.

Beginning in the mid-1980s, a body of what Russell refers to as sociorhetorical research further established the social dimensions of writing, that "writing (and rhetoric) is deeply embedded in the differentiated practices of disciplines, not a single elementary skill" learned early on and once and for all (*Academic Disciplines* 15). Derived from this WID research was a second pedagogical approach to WAC known as learning to write, which focused on helping students understand how to write like engineers, or scientists, or humanists through the design of discipline-specific writing tasks. By the late 1980s, more than 50% of postsecondary institutions had developed college-wide writing programs administered by WAC directors/committees and staffed by composition faculty, graduate students, undergraduate fellows, and faculty in other disciplines (McLeod and Shirley). As a sphere of intellectual and social activity, WAC has come to exist in various programs and curricular entities, in faculty development centers, and in various local, regional and national networks of specialized academic communication. There is an annual national conference, a national Board of Consultants of the National Network of WAC programs, a professional listserv, and journals, such as *Across the Disciplines* and *The WAC Journal*. Evidencing WAC's existence as a field of inquiry and action, Anson, Schwiebert, and Williamson's annotated bibliography inventories more than 1,000 WAC-related publications, circa 1993 (xi). WAC exists as interdisciplinary workshops on writing and teaching writing, as WI courses, as linked and adjunct courses, and (when informed by WID) as advanced writing classes in English departments focused on business, science, social science, engineering, and technical writing. It exists in perhaps its latest manifestations as electronic communication across the curriculum (Reiss and Young), assessment (Yancey and Huot), and living/learning communities (Zawacki and Williams).[1]

Thus, because writing can enhance learning of any subject, and because it is central to the social activities of disciplines and professions, including their construction of knowledge, their patterns of communication, their distribution of authority, and their members' socialization/acculturation, proponents of WAC assume that writing belongs to the whole curriculum, and that it shouldn't be limited to one course or one conception of writing. This assumption leads to what Russell characterizes as the cross-curricular or interdisciplinary nature of WAC initiatives of various kinds, involving interaction of specialists in composition and specialists in other disciplines to varying degrees. As Peshe Kuriloff notes, "nearly every [WAC] program . . .

depends at least in part for its success on collaboration among writing consultants and non-writing teachers" (134).

It is important to remember that all CCL initiatives seek to improve student literacy (literacies, really) through faculty development. Many WAC programs, according to Toby Fulwiler, mischaracterize this aim by prioritizing student-centered goals:

> The writing across the curriculum programs that I am most familiar with are faculty-centered. That is, these programs identify the instructors of a given institutions as: (1) the primary agents of instruction, creators of both knowledge and attitude toward learning; (2) the determiners of writing assignments, including the nature, purpose, frequency, and kind of writing asked for; (3) the key audience for whom students write those assignments and whose expectations the students must fully understand in order to write successfully; and (4) the respondents and correspondents from whom students hear regarding the quality of the ideas as well as the quality of the language in which those ideas are expressed. ("Evaluating" 65)

WAC programs are faculty-centered because, as Susan McLeod observes, "improvement in student writing as a result of a particular program, while it certainly occurs, is almost impossible to measure." Instead, WAC specialists work to improve student writing "by working to change university curricula and faculty pedagogy, which in turn have an effect on student writing" ("Foreigner" 112). Consequently, in addition to being composition teachers (teaching writing courses traditionally in English departments), CCL specialists are also cross-curricular WPAs and cross-curricular faculty developers. The CCL specialist frequently assumes the role of consultant working to help others integrate CCL practices into their existing theoretical, practical, and pedagogical frameworks. Although there has been much called-for discussion as to the nature of this role, particularly regarding its ideological thrust, the consulting dimension has nonetheless become a defining feature of WAC-inspired CCL work.

TOWARD UNDERSTANDING THE PROFESSIONAL KNOWLEDGE BASE OF CCL SPECIALISTS

WAC's roots have been traced back to the 1970s, to places like Beaver College, Pennsylvania, where WAC began when faculty from across the small college came together for "nonhierarchical exchange" on the issue of improving student writing (Maimon et al., "Beaver College" 159; see also

Maimon, "Preface"). In "The Future of WAC," this narrative was re-cast by
Walvoord through the lens of social movement theory, further solidifying
the historical origins of WAC as a grassroots, bottom–up, faculty-centered,
and faculty-owned movement. But, as the story goes, WAC went the way of
most educational trends and became institutionalized, developing sem-
blances of disciplinarity that threatened WAC's egalitarian, predisciplinary
roots.[2] The early collegial conversation, according to the narrative, reified
into the overzealous and uncritical application of composition pedagogy
(developed for the first-year writing course) to other disciplinary contexts.
As WAC spread, programs were increasingly driven by top–down mandates
and directed by WAC administrators, the one or two writing experts presumed to be "in the know," as Maimon et al. put it. These writing experts
thusly delivered with evangelical zeal WAC pedagogical strategies to faculty often positioned as "novices," or at least as those who were "naïve" about
writing ("Beaver College" 159; see also Bergmann).

A discourse emerged within WAC critiquing this so-called missionary
stance and questioning the presumed expert status of the WAC specialist
(Farris; LeCourt; Peritz). This missionary rhetoric, as I call it, can be traced
in part back to Catherine Blair's classic essay wherein she argued English
departments and, presumably, specialists in English language study "should
have no special role in writing across the curriculum—no unique leadership
role and no exclusive classes to teach—not even freshman composition"
(383). Blair argues that "the predominance of the English department's single point of view in designing and running a writing program would not be
dialogue but what Freire would call 'oppression'" (386). She draws upon
Bakhtin and Freire to develop the conversation metaphor as a means to
recover writing from its association with English departments, locating her
WAC program instead in an interdisciplinary committee that "determines
policy for the program and coordinates its activities" (387).[3] But embedded
in Blair's essay is also a paradox of this discourse, one that simultaneously
denies and authorizes the writing specialist's role. Blair's dialogic WAC program is collaboratively administered and presumably "staffed" by faculty
teaching WI courses. But these faculty are "aided by consultants hired to
support faculty efforts."

> With the consultants as facilitators, the faculty meet to train each other,
> support each other's efforts, and help each other solve problems cre-
> atively. Their disciplinary perspectives enlighten each other. *Since the
> consultants are outside the faculty power structure, they can help without
> unbalancing the dialogue. Their job is to promote dialogue among the
> disciplines.* And their research and experience can be a vehicle through
> which expertise in the teaching of writing from scholarly journals, pro-
> fessional associations, and other writing environments enters the cam-
> pus community. They can make available a full selection of teaching

methods which the faculty choose from and adapt to the needs of their own classes and disciplinary context. And these methods can come not only from the English department's experience with teaching writing but also from other areas in which writing is taught. (388; italics added)

The quoted passage, particularly the section in italics, speaks to the ambiguous role of the WAC specialist. At the same time, it acknowledges that the WAC specialist does make a particular contribution. Despite her missionary rhetoric, Blair admits that writing consultants are experts who employ some body of knowledge and skills in the service of improving student writing and faculty teaching. According to Blair, when supported by such specialists, faculty from other disciplines come to appreciate writing-based pedagogies and contribute to professional writing scholarship. However, to preserve WAC's egalitarian philosophy, Blair de-professionalizes writing specialists within her program. In other words, in her move to democratize WAC, she disenfranchises writing specialists, relegating them to the status of semi-professionals occupying support staff roles (with lower status, and likely receiving lower pay, less security, etc.).

This paradoxical denial of the writing specialist's expertise pervades WAC discourse. Karen Wiley Sandler echoes this paradox in her essay offering advice to WAC administrators: "I am charged with the well-being of the program and know more about running it than most on our campus, *but I cannot (and should not) lead it*" (51, italics added). In her essay, "Getting Started," Walvoord cautions that workshop leaders or "initiators" should never view themselves as the only experts or as the only teacher in the group, but rather as a "colleague in mutual exchange, where everyone learns and everyone contributes" (14). However, these initiators must also position themselves as writing specialists "with their own kind of insight" who must "enter as participants in the dialogue" and "provide resources," for "teachers always need help with new research and theory about writing, thinking, and learning" (14, 16). Walvoord and her colleagues indicate this approach is influenced by WAC's "egalitarian philosophy" inspired by the National Writing Project which "deliberately eschews leaders" (*Long Run* 5).

The cultivation of this egalitarian philosophy has contributed to an ethos among CCL specialists, represented by the stance of Walvoord and others, that eschews the writing specialist's expertise. This has left largely unexamined the paradox concealed by a rhetoric that preserves the early egalitarian philosophy and denies the professional role of the writing specialist in cross-disciplinary writing programs.[4] Instead of recognizing the development of a particular theory of program administration[5] or consulting, as I'm arguing, this denial of expertise obviates much of the professional knowledge amassed by CCL scholar-practitioners and prevents further inquiry into how this role—and the social status ascribed to this role—can be enhanced. In the next section, I examine how CCL specialists can benefit from reclaiming their expertise through the discourse of professionalism and professional reform.

PROFESSIONAL REFORM AND THE QUESTION OF WAC EXPERTISE

In exploring the professional dimension of CCL specialists' work, I am not suggesting that the CCL community engage in a project of traditional disciplinary formation or professionalization. There is a lively discourse on professionalizing writing specialists and WPAs in composition studies (e.g., Hansen; Healy; Hult). John Trimbur observes that accompanying the benefits of disciplinary status are problems of power and internal differentiation. In other words, although composition studies may have asserted its legitimacy as a discipline and thus gained to some degree the entitlements afforded a discipline—writing departments, tenure-lines, graduate programs, majors, journals, and so on—it has also exacerbated the disenfranchisement of part timers and graduate students and created its own "stratified" professional class system of "insiders" and "outsiders." Trimbur calls these dilemmas the "contradictory politics of professionalization" ("Writing Instruction" 142). I believe a similar resistance to differentiation underlies the missionary rhetoric of WAC, particularly the strong reservation over the possibility of creating a new monopoly of expertise that ignores the knowledge of faculty in other disciplines' and perpetuates their lack of felt responsibility for literacy instruction and acquisition.

WAC is the historical antecedent to several progressive-reformist educational movements aimed at reversing the modern academy's increasingly specialized disciplinary and curricular organization, including the relegation of responsibility for writing instruction to English departments. But to resist this disciplinary organization is to ignore what Russell identifies as the "fundamental organizing principle of modern academia, the compartmentalization of knowledge" manifested as academic specialization: "it was the ever-increasing specialization of knowledge (and, with it, of discourse) that allowed modern academia to create new knowledge so effectively and rapidly. . . . [These] divisions are not only inevitable but also, if we understand them correctly, invaluable . . ." (*Academic Disciplines* 11, 33). Russell has observed that because WAC programs associated with progressive-reformist philosophies—those that implicitly seek a "return to a homogeneous academic community"—go against the grain of the higher education system and modern society, they risk succumbing to the "subtle unraveling effect of academic politics" ("Historical Perspective" 66). That is, Russell's history of cross-curricular writing initiatives shows that those programs farthest outside the complex organizational structure of the university were those most likely to eventually fade. And just as interdepartmental curricular programs are at risk (or risk being marginal), so too are members of the academic community who fail to exert their professional status as experts.

WAC's egalitarian philosophy, which denies writing specialists' expertise in favor of "nonhierarchical" collaboration, is in this sense a form of anti-professionalism, a position that is ultimately irreconcilable with the organizational structure and values of higher education. Stanley Fish defines anti-professionalism as "any argument or attitude that enforces a distinction between professional labors on the one hand and the identification of what is true or valuable on the other" (89). Fish asserts that anti-professional critiques, which posit professions as valueless, self-serving institutional structures, actually operate within the historically and politically contingent contexts of the very professions they decry. They are thus "the strongest representation within the professional community of the ideals which give that professional community its (ideological) form" (106). Rather than blame professions as some ahistorical evil, Fish argues, critics should instead work to revise professional practices. In terms Fish might agree with, arguments for the interdisciplinary status of WAC programs (e.g., Mahala; Mahala and Swilky) are not antithetical to disciplinary organization—and not much of a radical departure from disciplines—but rather part of the historical construction of disciplinary ideology. Exploring the connections between WAC's egalitarian philosophy, the status of WAC as a discipline (or inter- or transdiscipline), and its relationship to other disciplines is beyond the scope of this inquiry. However, I assume that a specialized body of knowledge exists about writing and writing instruction and that specialists in this field are often called on to contribute their expertise to cross-curricular writing initiatives. I am more concerned with further articulating this body of knowledge, so that the role of writing specialists in cross-curricular writing programs can become more recognizable and, when aligned with the structure and values of the academy, more valuable.

For Louise Smith, the reservation to assert disciplinary expertise reflects nothing less than a "professional anxiety of influence and of influencing" among English studies faculty (394). In the classic exchange between Smith and Blair over who "owns" WAC and where WAC should be "housed," Smith comes down on the side of specialization, asserting that WAC will thrive only where writing specialists take leadership roles. Although she agrees with Blair that this role should be in "initiating and sustaining dialogue throughout the curriculum," she refuses to equate "dialogical" with "egalitarianism," asking "why must participants in egalitarian dialogue deny their various expertise?"

> The sooner we admit our expertise in the study of the construction and
> reception of texts (both literary and non-literary, written by profession-
> als or students) and our expertise in composition theory and pedagogy,
> the more eager our colleagues will be to converse with us, knowing
> we're equally interested in their expertise and that we cheerfully recog-
> nize some overlap between theirs and ours, overlap that makes WAC
> feasible and fun. (Smith 391)

Like Smith, I do not think the CCL community should assert its disciplinarity (read as "cognitive exclusiveness") at the expense of its inclusive literacy mission and its clients, faculty and students. But I do want to explore
the possibilities of professionalism for gaining a better understanding of
CCL means and ends. On the one hand, fully exploring the boundaries of
who can be a "WAC specialist" is beyond the scope of this project. Clearly,
nonwriting specialists integrate CCL knowledge and pedagogy with their
existing knowledge, becoming specialists in their own right. On the other
hand, as Blair and Smith both show, individuals trained in composition studies and/or communication fields typically administer and staff cross-curricular writing programs (along with faculty in other disciplines), serving as
knowledgeable writing specialists in teaching and consulting roles.[6] That is,
their "subject area" expertise or professional training is presumed to include
writing theory and practice. These are who I refer to as academic writing
consultants.

The lens of professionalism can encourage us to think more systematically about how to do the work of facilitating dialogue on writing, teaching,
and learning across the disciplines. This line of inquiry can be aligned with
the teacher-research movement in composition studies and in education.
This movement can be subsumed under the broader movement that Donald
Schön calls the "reflective turn," whereby researchers seek to systematically
articulate expert practice (*Reflective Turn*). This is a movement not so much
to monopolize expertise as it is to recover ways of knowing suppressed or
marginalized within the existing intellectual formations of the disciplines
and professions. In the professions, this is a move to recover practical arts
from the prevailing technical rationalist paradigm (Schön, *Reflective
Practitioner*). In academia, it is part of the broader critique of the politics of
theory and research (Ray). In academic contexts, the reflective turn also has
implications for improving the material conditions of practitioners within
various occupations, particularly education. But the reflective turn according to Schön, "carries with it an intention to make the study of practice useful to practitioners" (*Reflective Turn* 10). Practical inquiry aims to codify
the experientially based wisdom of expert practice and develop principles of
good practice that can guide future practice and practitioners.

Moreover, theorizing academic writing consulting as a form of professional practice opens up the possibility of thinking analogically from the

scholarship on teacher knowledge to its implications for understanding what academic writing consultants know and do. In "Knowledge and Teaching: Foundations of the New Reform," Lee Schulman, education researcher and current president of the Carnegie Foundation, synthesized the then growing interest in improving teaching as an activity and a profession through the traditional model of professionalization. Policymakers and teacher-educators turned their attention to articulating "what teachers should know and know how to do" so that it can be more effectively taught, learned, and evaluated. This line of inquiry looks at the "intellectual basis for teaching," including the sources of that knowledge, and how that knowledge is systematically enacted in pedagogical practice. As Schulman writes: "The advocates of professional reform base their arguments on the belief that there exists a 'knowledge base for teaching'—a codified and codifiable aggregation of knowledge, skill, understanding, and technology, of ethics and disposition, of collective responsibility—as well as a means for representing and communicating it" (4).

To begin with, we might say that what Lee Schulman claims to be received views of teacher knowledge could also hold for writing consulting:

> Teaching [is commonly viewed as] little more than personal style, artful communication, knowing some subject matter, and applying the results of recent research on effective teaching. Only the last of these, the findings of research on effective teaching, is typically deemed a legitimate part of a [teacher's] knowledge base. (6)

Schulman argues there are limitations to this view, namely that it denigrates the complexity of teaching, contributing to its low status and leading to invalid measures of teacher competence. This view, as discussed in chapter 2, evokes naturalized attitudes about practice. For the writing specialist, this translates into a view of collaboration as an *invisible* dimension of interpersonal relations, a dimension not open to critical scrutiny much less professional development. In this context, an appropriate mix of personality types, work habits, and matching levels of individual motivations are assumed to determine successful working relationships more than anything else. However, the few published accounts of WAC collaboration show that there are many challenges to negotiating close working partnerships with faculty in other disciplines. Just as teachers martial all of their professional and personal knowledge to teach, writing specialists draw from a range of knowledge and skill to facilitate their cross-disciplinary activities.

The application of this argument to CCL contexts becomes apparent when—again, thinking analogically—we look at Schulman's categories of teacher knowledge:

- *Content knowledge,* the accumulated literature and studies in a subject area.
- *General pedagogical knowledge,* those broad principles and strategies of classroom management and organization that appear to transcend the subject matter.
- *Curriculum knowledge,* particular grasp of the materials and programs that serve as "tools of the trade" for teachers.
- *Pedagogical content knowledge,* that special amalgam of content and pedagogy that is uniquely the province of teachers, their own special form of professional understanding.
- *Knowledge of learners* and their characteristics.
- *Knowledge of educational contexts,* ranging from the workings of the group or classroom, the governance and financing of school districts, to the character of communities and cultures
- *Knowledge of educational ends,* purposes, and values, and their philosophical and historical grounds. (8)

Schulman adds that among this knowledge-base, pedagogical content knowledge is "of special interest" because it

> identifies the distinctive bodies of knowledge for teaching. It represents the blending of content and pedagogy into an understanding of how particular topics, problems, or issues are organized, represented, and adapted to the diverse interests and abilities of learners, and presented for instruction. *Pedagogical content knowledge is the category most likely to distinguish the understanding of the content specialist from that of the pedagogue.* (8; italics added)

Schulman's distinction between content specialists and teachers, I believe, is an accurate description of the difference between the "discipline-oriented" research tradition of WID and "education-oriented" tradition of WAC and, more pointedly, the difference between the WID researcher and the writing consultant-practitioner (Bazerman and Russell). Essentially, the WID research tradition is premised on the assumption that "detailed [content] knowledge [of disciplinary discourses] which people can incorporate into their daily literate interactions" is foremost what writing specialists need in order to help faculty (Bazerman 211). Yet, as Shulman's schema shows, although disciplinary content is an important source of practitioner knowledge, other sources include local contexts and curricula, research on teaching, learning (and we could say, consulting), and practitioners' own experientially based procedural knowledge.

Mainstream WID researchers seem to be reaching this same conclusion, but in a roundabout way. According to Judy Segal and her colleagues, sociorhetorical inquiry is not making as much of a difference as it should —

or worse, the more critical interpretations are being outright rejected. They call the later occurrence "backlash critique," where many academics and professionals "find it difficult to hear the more critical aspects of our rhetorical analyses, others are simply not interested, and still others are actively resistant to anything perceived as ideological" (81). The problem for Segal et al. is that the researchers haven't figured out how to "talk with the scientists and practitioners in other disciplines who are threatened by or contemptuous of the analyses we offer" (82). Segal et al. advocate for an activist ideological stance that compels them to use their interpretive methods to understand professional discourses and increase the rhetorical knowledgeability and, hence, agency of the professionals themselves. To enact this "self-evidently beneficial" standpoint, they propose professional writing research take a more participatory, action orientation and that writing specialists adopt a teacherly stance:

> If we intend to make a difference, we must find a position between the [passive] descriptive stance of the traditional anthropologist and the evangelical zeal of the missionary. We hope that the proper label for that position is "teacher"—not just any teacher, but a thoroughly informed, ideologically critical, and most important, respectful teacher, a teacher who wishes to connect with, but not necessarily to convert, her "students" [i.e., academics and professionals] in the professional communities. (83)

Walvoord might argue that assuming the role of "teacher" and positioning faculty as "students" risks objectifying faculty and reproducing the problematic assumptions inherent in her "conduit" and "convert" models of WAC, where faculty are made the objects of writing specialist defined goals ("Conduit"). However, I agree with Segal et al.'s teaching metaphor. Such a stance is sensitive to the professional knowledge of writing specialists, part of which is knowing how to translate disciplinary knowledge in ways that are "thoroughly informed," "ideologically critical," and "respectful." Of course, Segal et al. argue that we have not been doing a good enough job of translating our knowledge, which is the point of my study, further articulating methods and models for accomplishing this. The ethical position of Segal et al. recovers much of the denial of expertise found in WAC missionary rhetoric and reflects a growing ethos among CCL specialists to assert their professional status as change agents (Kalamaras; LeCourt; McCleod "The Foreigner"). But to evoke the metaphor of teacher brings us back to the question: What is the specialized body of knowledge—following Schulman's notion of *pedagogical content knowledge*—that "expert" CCL consultants possess?

NOTES

1. Learning communities are becoming increasingly popular with deans and other upperlevel university administrators. However, some of the earliest WAC programs (e.g., Elaine Maimon's Beaver College program) incorporated "clusters" of courses grouped around common themes or texts and wherein students wrote projects satisfying requirements for multiple classes (see Russell, *Academic Disciplines* 284). Russell also notes how WAC has become "part of the general rethinking of pedagogy and assessment, as institutions [seek] to increase 'student involvement in learning' . . . through faculty–student mentoring programs, offices of faculty development and teaching, 'freshman experience' programs . . . and a host of other programs" (*Academic Disciplines* 290).

2. For David Russell, a central tension inherent in disciplinary communities is their need to balance the tension between exclusion and inclusion or, more specifically, issues of disciplinary excellence (i.e., restricting who can be a member based on merit and cognitive exclusion) with issues of social equity (i.e., allowing freer access to its knowledge and, in the case of most professions, social status built on cognitive exclusivity) (*Academic Disciplines* 20-30). The institution of WAC is imbued with a similar tension, comparable to the centuries-old debate over the province of rhetoric, as to who can teach writing. To correct modern historical problems with literacy acquisition and instruction, WAC aims at inclusion. However, it also paradoxically constructs an exclusive role for the writing specialist. While resolving this tension is beyond the scope of this inquiry, I do intend to further articulate the unique contribution of the writing specialist to cross-curricular writing programs.

3. The institutional location of a program indeed speaks volumes and although Blair essentializes English departments and conflates distinctions between institutional structures and social actors, she rightly argues WAC should be located outside the English department. Perhaps the central tenant of WAC is that, following the exposition of its key terms, writing instruction belongs to the whole curriculum, not just English departments (i.e., WAC shouldn't be "located" in any *one* department).

4. Mary Minock is one possible exception. "A paradox in our position [as WAC administrators]," she observes, "is that our genuine wish to listen and respect our colleagues, coupled with our lack of institutional power, conflicts with the high visibility of our assignment, since we are often hired as WAC directors to be agents of change. And if our simple best instincts about writing tell us that faculty will sustain that change if they work from shared inquiry, we are nonetheless hired because we are expected to know. . . . The paradox of our position makes it crucial that we introduce and sustain an adequately theoretical conversation that allows the insights of all faculty to be exchanged and modified" (506-507). Her essay examines how this is possible in the context of a WAC seminar.

5. In discourse on writing program administration, scholars examine ways leadership and administration can assume more collaborative, nonhierarchical rela-

tions among program administrator and teaching staff (see, e.g., the Spring 1998 special issue of *Writing Program Administration*).

6. If the WAC director has no training in rhetoric, according to McLeod and Soven they should be given time, "at least a semester (preferably a year)" to study other programs, ask advice of other WAC specialists, and gather WAC scholarship (27).

2

THE LIMITS OF
COLLABORATION THEORY

Does current collaboration theory provide a sufficient body of specialized knowledge capable of guiding CCL work? Collaboration has become a fundamental WAC principle, and collaborative learning theory is among the most commonly invoked discourses justifying WAC programs. This is represented most clearly by Elaine Maimon's "Collaborative Learning and Writing Across the Curriculum." For Maimon, "whenever [WAC] is more than a catch phrase, collaborative learning plays a part" (9). She identifies collaboration as a means of faculty development (in workshops fostering faculty conversations about writing), as a pedagogy (in classrooms using peer review, audience analysis, and student acknowledgments), and as a rationale for better cooperation among levels of education (in partnerships between colleges and school districts). Maimon identifies what one might call several sites of WAC collaboration. However, she doesn't push much past the conversation metaphor as a conceptual lens for enacting these broad mandates. Christina Murphy, in her comprehensive, critical review of social constructionist theory, likens this faith in the power of collaboration to the "Jeffersonian ideal of democracy," the belief that "truth will win out if all groups are allowed their say and will reason together toward consensus. Whether, in actuality, this principle of the Jeffersonian ideal will work in educational settings, social constructionism has yet to prove to many theorists' satisfaction" (31).

As I argue in this chapter, prevailing assumptions and attitudes about collaboration, particularly regarding collaboration among enfranchised members of academic institutions, generally lead to reductive views of collaboration as either a basic people skill or a personal relationship that either works or doesn't, depending on the social actors' personalities. Moreover, I hold that our scholarly understanding of collaboration vis-à-vis the writing classroom exerts a heavy influence on our own collaborative behavior. These prevailing assumptions limit our ability to pay closer, systematic attention to collaboration in CCL faculty development activity. To demonstrate this claim, I first consider two prevailing modes of collaboration, what I call the *commonsense mode* and the *collaborative philosophy mode*. I contrast these modes with the *professional consulting mode*, which includes more formal approaches to supporting faculty and researching disciplinary discourses. These modes variously close off or open up the possibility of systematic inquiry into academic writing consulting. Each reflects implicit or explicit assumptions guiding relationships between writing specialists, faculty in other disciplines, students, writing program staff, and so on. This discussion also allows for a review of the important studies relevant to interdisciplinary collaboration mentioned in the introduction.

THE TRADITIONAL OR COMMONSENSE COLLABORATIVE MODE

This model views collaboration as an *invisible* dimension of interpersonal relations, an aspect considered not open to critical scrutiny much less professional development. In this context, an appropriate mix of personality types, work habits, and matching levels of individual motivations are understood to determine successful working relationships more than anything else. In their research of workplace collaboration, Lisa Ede and Andrea Lunsford found that social interactions tended to manifest themselves in what they considered a hierarchical mode, which is "carefully, and often rigidly, structured, driven by highly specific goals, and carried out by people playing clearly defined and delimited roles" (133). Thus, when not conscious of the social dynamic, individuals generally assume product-oriented and goal-driven postures.

When left unexamined, collaboration can also be looked on with distrust, even disdain. Evoking Cartesian assumptions of individuality, originality, and authorship, collaboration for some undermines the author-function, what Foucault names as the social and material implications ascribed to linking individuals with texts. For the most part, the traditional faculty-reward system, particularly in English departments, confirms this view, treating collaborative publication as a less reliable—and less significant—measure of an individual's scholarly contributions (see Ervin and Fox; Roen and Mittan; Sullivan for more discussion of institutional barriers to collaborative work in the humanities). Collaboration could also be considered not worthy of serious intellectual inquiry, a "people" skill that one either possesses (or doesn't), has an inclination toward, or no interest in—an attitude toward collaboration that could be likened to Gail Stygall's critique of the ideology of "gentlemanly amateurism" cultivated in English departments regarding administrative knowledge. This tradition, grown from the German ideal of the independent scholar, holds that being a good department chair is more a matter of possessing "good communication skills," having "an open door," and "providing open forums for intradisciplinary discussion" than the employment of "research and theories of administration strongly linked to disciplinary knowledge" (12). It is not much of leap to read "being a good collaborator" over this statement and find many who would agree.

Commonsense approaches to collaboration are often instantiated in research about collaborative scholarship. Geraldine McNenny and Duene Roen's first "principle" of "successful scholarly collaborations" is representative of this lore of working together: "Choose collaborators carefully. Shy away from working with those who are egotistical, irresponsible, selfish, lazy, or too busy to carry their share of the load. If you have any doubts about a potential collaborator, work on a small project together to test the waters" (305). Viewed through the lens of Ede and Lunsford's hierarchical mode, these traits represent difficulties or "problems" to be overcome (133). In the case of McNenny and Roen's first principle, the solution is to avoid difficulties altogether. Of course, McNenny and Roen join others, like Ede and Lunsford, who evoke social constructivist and collaborative writing theories to argue for the communal nature of scholarship and its recognition in the faculty-reward system. McNenny and Roen go on to articulate five principles, including "develop procedures for raising and resolving conflicts" and "establish an ethical framework" (for attribution and editorial control). Although these offer insight into how to conduct working relationships with other faculty, it is reasonably safe to assume negotiating such guidelines will probably be made much easier after their first principle has been met: work with conscientious (i.e., not lazy, not egotistical, etc.) partners. In short, they make a valuable contribution to notions of collaboration (outside the classroom), but I cite their "commonsense" principles to exemplify the limitations of such a perspective. Often, institutional arrangements do not afford the luxury of the work-with-your-mirror-image approach to collaboration. CCL specialists are rarely able to choose their faculty partners so carefully.

Collaboration has been systematically addressed by fields such as interpersonal psychology and interpersonal communication. Measurements such as the Myers–Briggs personality type scale are often used in business settings to manage effective teams (see, e.g., Allen et al.; Galegher, Kraut, and Egido; Kelly; Knapp and Miller). However, this line of inquiry has more or less been ignored, one could even say discredited, in composition studies since

the field's turn away from cognitive studies of writing. Paying little conscious attention to the social dynamic is adequate for guiding first-stage
WAC efforts. For WAC administrators, first-stage programs have generally
enjoyed the benefits of high cooperation from cadres of self-selected faculty participants. However, shortly after the collegial glow of the first-stage
workshop wears off, come questions of how to "support" faculty, how to
maintain "enthusiasm," how to deal with "resistance," and how to "sustain"
the program with middle- and late-adapters. Somewhere between the success of early relationships and the failure of later ones lies the possibility of
re-thinking the collaborative dynamic as a key element in effecting/of effective WAC relationships. And as Trimbur and others have argued, unexamined or overly narrow views of collaboration ignore the shaping influences
of context and of the interactants' subjectivities on collaboration and overlook how individuals' fluid and sociohistorically shaped perspectives based
on identification with and attribution to existing categories such as race,
class, and gender influence social relationships ("Consensus").

THE COLLABORATIVE PHILOSOPHY MODE

Both the traditional mode and the collaborative philosophy mode share the
tendency to *take the social interaction for granted*. But whereas the first
model could be said to ignore the collaborative dynamic, the second model
is characterized by a willingness to work together. Adherents to the collaborative philosophy tend to be more conscious of the social dimensions of
activity, including writing, and work to incorporate such principles into
their practice. The collaborative philosophy mode is characterized by mutual learning, mutual effort, nonhierarchical or reciprocal relations, and a willingness to explore. This mode can be likened to Ede and Lunsford's "dialogic mode" of collaboration:

> [The] dialogic mode . . . is loosely structured and the roles enacted with-
> in it are fluid: one person may occupy multiple and shifting roles as a
> project progresses. In this mode, the process of articulating goals is often
> as important as the goals themselves and sometimes even more impor-
> tant. Furthermore, those participating in dialogic collaboration general-
> ly value the creative tension inherent in multivoiced and multivalent
> ventures. What those involved in hierarchical collaboration see as a
> problem to be solved, these individuals view as a strength to capitalize
> on and to emphasize. In dialogic collaboration, this group effort is seen
> as an essential part of the production—rather than the recovery—of
> knowledge and as a means of individual satisfaction with the group.
> (133)

This mode, which Ede and Lunsford attribute to a feminist epistemology, is often valorized for its potential to subvert power relations, empower the disenfranchised, and suggest ways to resist conventional assumptions about writing/authorship/social relations.

My use of *philosophy* is based on the distinction that Richard Fulkerson makes between "philosophy" and "theory." Fulkerson asserts that any full theory of composition, held tacitly or explicitly, has a philosophical component, a procedural component, and a pedagogical component. The philosophical component constitutes a general commitment to what is good, or what are appropriate ends. Fulkerson refers to this as one's axiology, or "value theory conceived generally" (410-411). Thus, a full theory accounts for how to achieve desired ends (the procedural component), and how to instill these procedures in others (the pedagogical component). Fulkerson's notion of axiology suggests one might believe collaboration is "good," but not have a conception of how to achieve it. Fulkerson contrasts his use of philosophy with James Berlin's use of ideology, which he feels too imprecise a taxonomic concept for theories in writing. Both employ them similarly as a "belief in what is good," but Fulkerson's discussion helps support conceptual distinctions I am making between implicit assumptions of collaboration and more explicit procedural knowledge of collaboration. In other words, our field has developed complex theoretical and practical assumptions about collaboration (particularly as they apply to pedagogy), but as individuals we may still overlook how these values apply (or are played out) in working relationships outside the classroom.

In composition studies, collaboration has become, in the words of John Trimbur and Lundy Braun, "conventional wisdom" (31). It has become so fundamental as to become an ideological assumption, a dominant or "natural" system of beliefs and practices. This philosophy is represented in Maimon's sweeping connection of collaboration theory with WAC principles and in the egalitarianism espoused in the foundational narratives of WAC's emergence as a grassroots, faculty-centered education movement. Those ascribing to the collaborative philosophy tend to hold stronger assumptions about what is and isn't collaboration. So much so that if a relationship is not dialogic, if it fails, it is viewed as *not* collaborative. For some, not all co-labor is collaborative. The collaborative philosophy, in other words, is limiting in explaining interactions where the spirit of negotiation breaks down, where individuals hold differing assumptions of collaboration, and where notions of peership are complicated by the institutional contexts of work. As Russel Durst and Sherry Cook Stanforth point out, "Collaboration which 'comes' naturally may sound promising, but if it ignores or dismisses what can be 'unnatural,' unpleasant, problematic, or institutionally difficult . . . then important aspects of collaborative work may go unexamined" (74). Even well-informed compositionists might overlook how the contexts of their work obviate collaboration (e.g., McNenny and Roen's first principle and their advice about working only with those who have the "time" to work). As scholars have observed, structural forces constrain, discourage, and often prevent collaborative work (Burnett and Rothschild-Ewald; Ervin and Fox; Kuriloff). In short, collaborative theory and good intentions might not be enough to facilitate working relationships in CCL contexts, where the traditional structures and values of the academy work against dialogic modes of collaboration.

THE CONSULTING MODEL OF COLLABORATION

If collaboration in the context of WAC has often been (implicitly) associated with a general skill, such as interpersonal relations, or with peer relationships, as in the case of student writing groups or collaborative research, it has also, as Maimon, Bruffee, and others have suggested, been conceived as a central tenet guiding much WAC theory and practice. Collaboration in CCL contexts oftentimes becomes more formal and, to a degree, more institutionally sanctioned. The CCL specialist often assumes the role of a consultant helping others modify their assumptions about writing and adopt WAC pedagogy. This activity typically occurs when the writing specialist works with faculty as they apply what was learned in a WAC workshop or when the writing specialist provides leadership or expert advice to campuswide writing initiatives.

Existing conceptions of consulting in the discourse of WAC remain largely focused on program administration issues and typically fail to focus specifically on the nature of the collaborative interactions themselves. A useful distinction might be to view consulting within WAC variously as a *stage* (a way to start or sustain a program), as a *component* (as one part of a multifaceted WAC program) or as an *activity* (the act of a writing specialist "consulting" with a nonwriting specialist). Consulting blurs into WPA when issues of interdisciplinary program development and maintenance are involved. For example, recognized expert "WAC consultants" such as Barbara Walvoord, Tori-Haring Smith, and Toby Fulwiler visit incipient programs to conduct workshops or otherwise help local administrators develop and sustain these programs. These WAC specialists and others have contributed to a body of scholarship theorizing and describing program administration, which includes design, implementation, and assessment issues (e.g., McLeod and Soven; Walvoord et al.; Yancey and Huot). Consulting blurs with *collaborative research* when these interdisciplinary relationships lead to or are motivated by publishable scholarship.

Russell and others refer to the "consultant model" of WAC, distinguishing these types of approaches from others such as writing center models, advanced writing models (writing courses designed by writing specialists for specific fields like business, social sciences, etc.), and the most prominent model, faculty workshops ("Historical Perspective" 60; see also McLeod, "Defining" 23). Among the earliest descriptions of interdisciplinary writing consulting is Catherine Lamb's 1983 essay, "Initiating Change as a Writing Consultant." Lamb stresses the one-to-one nature of her "low-cost, flexible" WAC consultancy model: "the individualized nature of [the consultant's] work provides insight into how writing is actually used in courses and the writing problems instructors themselves have. In this sort of non-threatening atmosphere, the possibilities for significant change in the teaching of writing are enhanced" (297). Using a language of consulting, Lamb weighs the advantages and disadvantages of the "need" to "sell" her "services." On the one hand, faculty came to value her input; on the other, she feared being seen as the one responsible for writing instruction. In another early article on WAC consultancy, John Dick and Robert Esch describe their "systematic procedure and leading questions to make communications with colleagues in other disciplines more manageable" (179). Their procedure begins with *investigation* of the discursive conventions of the target field by studying published scholarship, requesting writing samples, and interviewing faculty. Dick and Esch's specific heuristics/guiding questions help writing specialists and faculty plan writing-based pedagogies.

In what has been called the "rhetoric of inquiry" movement within WAC scholarship, many have argued that writing specialists must demonstrate ethnographic sensitivity to disciplinary issues of content and context when working with colleagues across the curriculum (Farris; Kirscht, Levine, and Reiff; Peritz; Waldo, "Inquiry"; Young, "Impediments"). Reflecting on their pilot WAC program at Carnegie Mellon, David Kaufer and Richard Young raise many questions about the nature of writing consulting, including how participants' assumptions about writing and expertise influence such collaborations. After being rebuked by a biologist for suggesting the students use their biology lab notebooks for journal writing exercises, Kaufer and Young realized they had to change their approach from being missionaries introducing writing-to-learn methods to being anthropologists "investigating the culture of academic biology" (82). The writing specialists "immersed" themselves in the biology course, taking notes about what went on in the lectures and labs; collecting syllabi, assignments, and lab reports; and conducting surveys and taperecorded interviews with the biology professor and her students. In another example of ethnographic approaches to WAC consultancy, George Kalamaras describes the ideological conflicts he faced trying to change assumptions about writing and knowledge construction in his 2.5 years consulting for the Biology Department at

Indiana University-Purdue University at Fort Wayne. Taking a research approach, Kalamaras positioned himself as both a "participant-observer" and "student-learner" investigating the discipline's language practices by participating in the biology courses, the labs, and other coursework. The main challenge he discovered was reconciling his critical agenda (of empowering students and creating institutional change) with the "service" expectation of his biology colleagues. In the end, Kalamaras found this process of "inner dialogue" a productive source of insight. Strategies such as negotiating, modeling, and creating situations for collegial discussion and reflection became central practices for him. Kalamaras notes the lack of published guidance in the literature, and his report—as a conference presentation— partly supports the proposition that such systematic reflection on WAC specialists' work remains undervalued—or at least not widely disseminated.

The limitation of most WAC studies is that they conceive of interdisciplinary collaboration as a research *method*, but not as an appropriate research *object*. Lucille McCarthy and Barbara Walvoord argue persuasively for the need to move beyond the "first-stage" workshop models to actually investigate the kinds of teaching and learning that occur in disciplinary classrooms. While they expound on collaborative approaches to research, it is invariably aimed at facilitating the study of writing, discourse, disciplinary socialization, and the like. That is, collaboration is used as a method for studying other objects. There are a handful of studies of faculty resistance to implementing WAC pedagogical strategies that implicitly look at collaboration as a factor influencing the extent to which nonwriting specialists adopt WAC. However, the object of these studies remains the amount of "change" in individual pedagogy, not the collaborative dynamic (Lemke and Bridwell; Swanson-Owens; Swilky; Young, "Impediments"). It is Swilky who suggests that factors such as "personality, assumptions, beliefs, and institutional conditions affect teachers' decisions about pedagogical priorities" and that WAC specialists might work more closely—and for an extended duration— to support teachers integrating WAC strategies into their existing frameworks (59). But as Walvoord et al. so astutely observe, these studies, focused on WAC outcomes, objectify the teachers, ignoring their individual agency, and, more importantly for the purpose of my study, the role of the writing specialist in fostering change.

There have been a few important studies that explicitly observed the role of collaboration in WAC. In a series of groundbreaking collaborative studies, Lucille Parkinson McCarthy and Stephen M. Fishman explore their negotiations over authority in classroom-based research and collaborative scholarship (see also Fishman and McCarthy). In "Boundary Conversations," McCarthy and Fishman conducted what they called a "twin study" of student literacy in Fishman's philosophy course and of their own interdisciplinary collaboration. Reminiscent of the travel metaphor popularized by McCarthy ("Stranger"), their study uses the central image of "boundary conversations" to describe the learning experiences of Fishman's students and the pair of researchers themselves, learning forged from the interactions (in the form of conflicts) between students' and teachers' "ways of knowing," the tensions created when one's "values, beliefs, and experiences must engage another set of values, be they disciplinary or individual" (423). A key to student learning in Fishman's course was how each negotiated his or her stance between personal and academic languages, the degree of success that each managed at juxtaposing several competing epistemologies, such as the students' own "subjective knowing" based on personal experience and the "constructed knowing" required by philosophy discourse, a weaving together of personal and disciplinary perspectives (447).

Turning their naturalistic lenses onto their own relationship, McCarthy and Fishman concluded that their own process of collaboration was similar to the learning experiences of Fishman's students. The early stage of their relationship was focused on getting the other's perspective, or "working to articulate our positions, identify our disagreements, and create a common language for talking about them," as McMarthy and Fishman later recounted in a methodological article about their boundary conversations study ("A Text" 165). Similar to Ede and Lunsford's dialogic mode, the two continually questioned each other's personal and professional perspectives. They read scholarship in each other's field to better understand these ways of knowing, resulting in the construction of a "shared language" within which to more clearly define their differences ("Boundary" 462). Their study suggests that "to understand an academic's approach to instruction and research means knowing more than his or her discipline" ("Boundary" 463). Collaborators' "autobiographies," one's experiences as a student and one's professional "initiations and preferred epistemological stances," are important sources for explaining patterns of interaction, negotiations over authority, and ways of "listening" ("Boundary" 463-464). McCarthy and Fishman's reflection suggests effective CCL specialists must also gain insight into their counterparts' views toward disciplinary initiation, views of authority over the specific project (such as the role of the writing specialist), and views of disciplinary practices (such as preferred methodological approaches).

In "A Text for Many Voices," McCarthy and Fishman discuss how naturalistic assumptions compelled them to reveal the process of knowledge construction and representation in their classroom research. This led to reflexivity over negotiations of power/authority and necessitated a new "academic textual form" for representing such work. Adding an account or "story" of their collaboration, what they considered a form of John Van Maanen's "confessional tale," became an important goal of the boundary conversations study. Such a story rendered "explicit the assumptions about reality, knowledge, and method which shaped the collaboration" ("A Text"

169). By externalizing their assumptions, they made them open to more critical scrutiny and revision. A key insight of McCarthy and Fishman's work
is that collaboration does not always mean that there is an equal power relationship at play. Significantly, McCarthy and Fishman came to understand
that this complexity required more systematic attention, or what they called
"inquiry into collaboration" ("A Text" 172). Similarly, Russell Durst and
Sherry Cook Stanforth viewed "the negotiations over power and authority
in a collaboration between colleagues at different levels of the academic hierarchy" as one of the central tensions of teacher-research, one that necessi-
tates explicit interrogation throughout the relationship, because lines of
power are dynamic and constantly changing (62). These studies further con-
firm the limitations of both the common sense and collaborative philosophy
models of collaboration.

McCarthy and Fishman's boundary conversation study and subsequent
retrospective analysis ("A Text") reveal in rich detail the complexity of interdisciplinary collaboration. Their accounts suggest such collaboration is
time-consuming and requires flexibility: "negotiation about the relationship
. . . is a continuing process. It cannot be settled once and for all at the start
of work together" ("A Text" 172). They also suggest that personal and professional dimensions of work/life are difficult to separate during the process
of forging a relationship, an issue often overlooked in collaboration theory
according to Christina Murphy. The research also provides insight into how
academic writing consulting might usefully be constructed as rigorous intellectual work.

In "Constructing Each Other: Collaborating Across Disciplines and
Roles," Joan Mullin, Neil Reid, Doug Enders, and Jason Baldridge present
a similarly heteroglossic account of their experiences negotiating roles and
assumptions during one tutor-supported WI geography course at University
of Toledo administered by Mullin, taught by Reid, tutored by Enders, and
taken by Baldridge. They focus on (a) *how collaboration works* and (b) how
"*balances* were or were not struck within the contexts [they] worked and as
a result of the *perspectives* they held" (153; italics added). Using excerpts
from interview records, journals, and individual reflections, Mullin and her
colleagues illustrate how collaborants' previous experiences shape their
assumptions about disciplinary perspectives, motivations, and purposes.
They also illustrate the importance of "being aware of" or examining the
"projected and assumed" roles of oneself and the others. A previous tutor,
who did not take an active role with his pedagogy or students, shaped Reid's
expectations about Enders' role. At the same time, Enders, who felt conflicted about his roles as tutor and teacher, pledged to monitor his own perceived
conflicting agendas (to assess the course's fit to the attached-tutor program,
to be a nondirective tutor, to be a directive teacher). Mullin realized that
even though she felt herself appropriately "orchestrating" the collaboration

(in line with Ede and Lunsford), she learned initial meetings were not enough to establish roles and expectations. Grading and evaluative criteria became the "central issue" during the course, as Enders and Reid negotiated Enders' responsibility beyond the narrowly confined focus on mechanics originally assumed by Reid.

Mullin et al. learn that negotiating roles is "no simple task," for "layered amid expectations are the images we take on and project within our classes." It also takes much time and dialogue to "iron out" roles in such collaborative situations: "The missteps—those that resulted from what was spoken, not spoken, not learned, or not fully articulated—continued throughout our conversations and written responses about the class. *But all these misses seem a necessary part of the process of engagement*" (157; italics added). They conclude that, in order to foster a "culture of reflectivity," it is important to encourage face-to-face and e-mail conversations that facilitate negotiation over authority and examination of assumptions about "writing, terminology, and disciplinary expectations" (169-170). The WAC director, the instructor, and the tutor facilitated their negotiations through initial and recurring meetings that continually established roles and expectations (Mullin saw her role as protecting the tutor from abuse and encouraging discussion of pedagogy). The teaching assistant (TA) tutor kept a journal, which included conversations with Reid and the students, and reflections of class observations. Mullin hand-recorded interviews about teacher, TA, and student experiences. Finally, Mullin collected written reflections by Reid and his students to "questions posed by the group during meetings" (152).

The findings of Mullin and her colleagues are very much in line with McCarthy and Fishman. Both teams address the complexity of collaboration in WAC contexts. Both address how previous experiences (personal and professional) shape assumptions about disciplinarity, writing, and teaching/learning, as well as how such assumptions influence the negotiation of roles in existing relationships. Although McCarthy and Fishman focused more on conflicts inherent in individual epistemological and disciplinary perspectives than Mullin et al., both stress the need for engaging in dialogue and negotiation. Both are aware of the power dynamics inherent in collaborative arrangements crossing institutional boundaries. Mullin et al.'s study relies heavily on assumptions I've associated with the collaborative philosophy model. The difference between their stance and the collaborative philosophy, however, is the conscious attention that Mullin et al. paid to these dynamics.

Most WAC studies are co-authored or resultant from teams of teacher-researchers, but are they collaborative? In published research reports, we seldom learn of how authors negotiate their projects with participants. As McCarthy and Fishman have argued, traditional research genres and modes of representation mask the social construction of knowledge. Traditional research reports do, of course, have references to how "we" collected X, and how "we" learned Y. But are published reports *prime-facie* evidence of successful collaborations? Walvoord argues that much research in WAC has *not* been collaborative, that it has ignored the agency of teachers, given them little voice in public representations, and made judgments about their adoption of or "resistance" to researcher defined strategies. In other words, research studies of WAC outcomes generally report on how WAC works from the point of view of the WAC director, making faculty the objects of WAC agendas. When faculty are given voice, it has tended to be represented in the form of "testimonials" of conversion to WAC strategies and WAC philosophies. The narratives are cast as "how WAC helped Jane see the light," often ignoring how pre-existing personal and professional backgrounds and complex career trajectories shape faculty choices (see Walvoord "Conduit"; Walvoord et al.).

Constructivist and critical/feminist approaches to research seek to give back agency formerly invested solely in the objective researcher assuming a foundationalist stance. Walvoord suggests that studies that put faculty in the roles of "creators" of what counts as good teaching, "collaborators" in terms of what counts as good WAC programs, and "client-customers" in terms of what counts as effective WAC services dramatically alter how CCL specialists understand their role and their relationships with faculty ("Conduit"). Our postmodern understanding of knowledge-making (from individual and group acts of composing to larger discourse communities) has steadily influenced what we look at when we study *with* teachers and students in WAC contexts. Among the reasons few studies of collaboration exist in the context of WAC is that these relational dynamics have always been taken for granted, viewed as a commonsensical dimension of achieving other WAC objectives, like "training" teachers how to use journals, studying how professionals write to other professionals, or assessing how well WAC programs work. A constructivist framework asks for a different ideological stance toward faculty development, discipline-based research, and program assessment. This stance has opened up the possibility of focusing on how the social interactions between writing specialists and other faculty influence the changes CCL specialists hope to foster (i.e., increasing the academy's sensitivity to the rhetorical constructedness of discourses and improving the teaching and learning of these discursive practices).

Another important aspect of academic collaboration often overlooked is the institutional constraints that shape the choices faculty make about their work. Central to this study's argument is that collaborative consulting activities have been consistently undervalued in the traditional reward structure of the academy. As Kuriloff notes,

> The department-based authority structure that characterizes most
> American colleges and universities today restricts many WAC activities

to the margins of the curriculum. Formal collaboration and team teaching suffer from marginalization and have proven difficult to institutionalize. (149)

Russell corroborates this observation in the conclusions of his extensive historical studies of cross-curricular writing instruction; for the WAC movement to overcome the failures of previous reform initiatives, it must be "structurally linked to the values, goals, and activities" of the academy and its disciplines (*Academic Disciplines* 302).

Any discussion of interdisciplinary collaboration must examine the institutional structures that discourage this type of work. Elizabeth Ervin and Dana Fox present a compelling critique of not only the prevailing Cartesian epistemological attitudes toward collaboration but of the discursive structures and physical structures that "suppress and discourage scholars from working collaboratively" (55). Analyzing not only the published scholarship on social construction and collaborative writing, but also their own experiences as graduate students in composition, the institutional policies surrounding their study (e.g., academic honesty, dissertation production), and the "rules of the game" as modeled by the faculty socializing them into their profession, Ervin and Fox determine that "while academe has finally acknowledged that collaboration exists, it has not yet recognized its scholarly legitimacy, nor has it developed structures to reward collaborative work" (59). For them,

> At every point in the academic program, students and faculty are discouraged from seeking support and sharing ideas, and they are encouraged instead to pursue projects independently and competitively. Consequently, while discussions of the importance of collaboration are necessary and useful, the time for real change has arrived. We've done enough rethinking, renegotiating, and reconceptualizing; now we need to revise. (Ervin and Fox 69)

In their study of academic collaboration Ann Austin and Roger Baldwin report that postsecondary institutions pose unique barriers to collaboration, ranging from promotion and tenure procedures to lack of designated time and travel money for collaborative work, especially for colleagues who reside at geographically disparate institutions (67-74, 83-89). Although these studies highlight the contextual constraints on academic collaboration, they tend to focus on *intra*disciplinary work, leaving room in this discourse for a discussion of WAC interdisciplinary contexts.

Broader discourses in higher education have begun to address the system of faculty reward built on independent, discipline-based research. Ernest Boyer's *Scholarship Reconsidered* is credited with focusing the debate about the mission of higher education by arguing for a redefinition of the concept of academic work to include alongside the traditional scholarship of *discovery*, the scholarship of *integration, application*, and *teaching* (see also AAUP Committee; Diamond; Glassick et al.). The MLA Commission report, "Making Faculty Work Visible," brings this discussion within the context of English studies and composition studies (see also "ADE Statement"; Gebhardt). It coincides with arguments for new standards of scholarship and professionalization advanced by writing program administrators (Bullock; Council of WPAs; Hansen; Hult; Roen; Rose and Weiser). The essence of this discourse is that the traditional academic value system has privileged research, the production of disciplinary knowledge, at the expense of other missions of higher education. This value system has become so ingrained as to render, in the words of the MLA Commission, relatively *invisible* work that, by virtue of not producing easily quantifiable scholarly products, falls under the categories of teaching or, in particular, service. In the face of received views of administration as managerial, as drawing from no specialized knowledge, as producing no new knowledge, WPAs have argued the work of curriculum development, teacher training, program assessment, and so on involves application and integration of knowledge(s) and often produces new knowledge at both local and disciplinary levels. This discourse on intellectual work suggests ways to argue within the existing institutional structures (e.g., promotion and tenure committees) for valuing academic writing consulting activity and, like WPAs, for arguing professional identity.

The rest of the chapters in this book explore the professional dimension of collaboration, which grows from systematic reflection on the role the collaborative dynamic plays in academic writing consulting practice. Although there is a fair amount of theorizing about collaboration—learning theory, research methodology, team-teaching—it has yet to be fully applied to CCL contexts. McCarthy and Fishman and Mullin et al. offer examples of reflective stances encouraged by constructivist, feminist, and critical research ethics and the teacher-research movement in composition studies. Teacher-research aims to elevate the status of teaching by aligning classroom teaching with the rigor of traditional research. It encourages self-consciousness, reflection, and ethnography-based empirical observation in the service of improving individual and collective understanding of pedagogy. The key to teacher-research is the reflective stance assumed during the process. In the context of CCL work, this stance can influence how writing specialists approach their roles as faculty developers, program administrators, and composition teacher-researchers. One dimension of this work is the social negotiations writing specialists must enact to achieve WAC ends (most typically, improving student writing, usually through faculty development). The ability to effectively translate our disciplinary knowledge to nonspecialists is more than a transparent or invisible "skill" but rather a complex activity that requires systematic reflective practice.

3

PROFILES OF ACADEMIC WRITING CONSULTING PRACTICE

Although the road of interdisciplinary collaboration and writing consulting might be said to be reasonably well trodden, the people who have traveled it, the places they have been, and the knowledge they have gained are less well known. Approaching academic writing consulting as professional practice opens up new avenues for developing methods and models for guiding CCL work. In this chapter, I profile four CCL specialists, focusing on their perceptions of the kinds of interdisciplinary collaborations they engage in and how their institutional contexts affect this activity. Influenced by a number of different conversations—WAC, teacher-research, collaboration theory, intellectual work, academic professionalization, higher education reform, and more—I set out to codify academic writing consulting practice. The four descriptive profiles follow the research tradition of presenting images of writers such as those in Lisa Ede and Andrea Lunsford's study of workplace collaboration and Gesa Kirsch's profiles of women academic writers. My writing, literally and figuratively, of their stories is inescapable. These profiles are, as Ede and Lunsford argue, "crafted visions, not slices of life, or raw moments of reality." But Ede and Lunsford believe such images are valuable because they can help us better understand how writing works and "how to make it work more effectively" (43).

In this chapter, then, I first discuss the qualitative interviewing method I used to construct these profiles and justify my focus on the subjective reality of the CCL specialist, rather than the intersubjective reality of the consultant and nonwriting specialist, as a useful and valid way of better understanding CCL practice. Following this discussion, I present four profiles that depict the tacit knowing-in-action of expert academic writing consultants. As I argue at the close of this chapter, these cases help contribute to methods for guiding CCL work.

CONSTRUCTIVE REFLECTION AND PRACTICAL INQUIRY

I conducted 10 interviews with four participants, who were chosen based on their CCL experience as evidenced in their scholarly publications, conference activities, and electronic listserv activity. These four WAC specialists were selected partly for their established scholarly record related to the subject, partly for their representativeness, and partly for their accessibility:

- Laurel:[1] an accomplished writing center (WC) director at a large northeastern land-grant university. Although Laurel didn't participate in the full interview process, she helped me hone my protocol and probe assumptions about what "counts" as collaboration.
- Patricia: a prominent WAC scholar who has established some of the earliest WAC programs. At the time of the study, Patricia held a joint appointment as an English Department member and administrator of a teaching and learning center at a prestigious private university in the midwest. Her research and service have made significant contributions to the field of WAC over the last three decades.
- Roger: a long-time lecturer teaching at a private west coast university. Roger works within a progressive program that supports a broadened conception teaching practice. Roger's nontenure track position, his cross-disciplinary work, and his institutional location all add a markedly different point of view from the three other participants.
- Linda: another reputable WC and WAC director at a southeastern urban university. In an electronic discussion list, she characterized much of her work as consulting. This made her inclusion in the study attractive.

The interviews produced just over 14 hours of interview tapes and more than 100 pages of single-spaced interview transcripts. Once past my initial experience of data overload, I found—and continue to find—the transcripts to be rich sources of experiential wisdom, what Kathleen Yancey refers to as the "texts" of these participants' reflections on their past CCL work.

In *Reflection in the Writing Classroom*, Yancey traces the convergence of the reflective turn in education and composition studies. For Yancey, "members of the educational establishment" have embraced the "underlying promise" of reflection as a means to bridge the theory and practice binary which has ignored the experientially-based and situated knowledges of practitioners at the expense of researcher defined and generated theory (7-8). Yancey explores the potential of seeing individual "teaching and learning *practices* as a source of knowledge, a metaphorical text that can be systematically observed, questioned, understood, generalized about, refuted—in a phrase, *reflected upon*" (126).

In the relative absence of systematic accounts of how writing specialists conduct their consultancy work, collecting such "texts" of CCL practice emerged as an important warrant guiding my methodological approach. Collecting and interpreting texts of consulting practice can be likened to research on teacher knowledge in education. As Lee Schulman writes,

> One of the more important tasks for the research community is to work with practitioners to develop codified representations of the practical pedagogical wisdom of able teachers. . . . As we organize and interpret such data, we attempt to infer principles of good practice that can serve as useful guidelines for efforts of educational reform. (11)

And just as Donald Schön developed his conception of professional practice using "compelling case rhetoric," or concrete examples accompanied by critical analysis, I set out to codify selected CCL specialists' *reflections-on-action*. According to Illene Harris, reflection-on-action occurs *after* the action; it refers to subsequent analysis brought about by some "puzzling, interesting, or troublesome phenomena, by problems that elude the ordinary categories of a practitioner's knowledge and appear as unique or unstable, and by the need to articulate or codify the bases for practice, most typically by the need to teach aspiring practitioners" (31). I wanted to provoke such occasions for reflection and for education. I wanted to ask expert practitioners about past experiences leading to their tacit theories, or practical knowledge, about academic writing consulting.

In her theorizing of reflection's role in the teaching and learning of writing, Yancey likens reflection-on-action to her concept of *constructive reflection*. Following Schön, Yancey posits three modes of student reflection on writing and learning to write: reflection-in-action, constructive reflection, and reflection-in-presentation. Yancey's reflection-in-action by student writers (and writing teachers) is the Schön-inspired decision-making process of "reviewing and projecting and revising" during a specific composing event (13). Reflection-in-presentation "appears as a formal reflective text written for an 'other,' often in a rhetorical situation invoking assessment" that occurs following individual or multiple composing events (13). Constructive reflection is the oftentimes tacit process by which individuals generalize from specific experience and develop prototypical models for application to future situations. This is the process by which the writer develops the "understandings and strategies that accommodate themselves to another rhetorical situation" (51); it is the "cumulative effect of reflections-in-action on multiple texts" (50) and "what the student 'takes' away from a writing task, what he or she may be able to transfer reflectively" (56). Yancey also adds an important dimension to this kind of practical theorizing. For her, constructive reflection contributes to the identity formation of the writer through "the process of developing a cumulative, multi-selved, multi-voiced identity, which takes place between and among composing events and the associated texts" (14). In other words, students' identities as writers are shaped according to the extent to which they can see themselves generalize across situations.

According to Yancey, constructive reflection is a distinct reflective skill that can be developed. She discusses several ways this can be accomplished in a writing classroom. As Yancey puts it, "constructive reflection can be 'staged.' That is, we can ask students to articulate what they are learning; ask them to express the tacit; ask them to bring it to the page so that we have *a good verbal description*" (60). By fostering a culture of reflectivity, the writing teacher can facilitate occasions whereby the student begins to make connections between particular acts of composing and general rhetorical strategies. She likens this process of prompting or "staging" constructive reflection to the moments of situational "talk-back" (Schön *Educating*) during reflection-in-action:

> The talk-backs . . . [or, the problems experienced during specific composing situations] . . . also provide a place where students may contemplate their writing practices over time, where they may discern patterns in multiple texts, where in reviewing these multiple texts they see themselves as writers with practices and habits that transcend specific texts. *Working in the particular, they mark and map the general.* (59; italics added)

In the writing classroom, students learn how to be strategic writers through *practice*, that is, a systematic process of reflection-in-action and *staged* constructive reflection.

Yancey's discussion of developing constructive reflective skills resonated with my interest in codifying experientially based knowledge. Like Schön's notion of reflection-on-action, constructive reflection is more than articulating absolute "principles" or "maxims" based on experience. Constructive reflection is not, in other words, practice divorced from theory. It is, rather, the process and product of critical reflection across specific acts (of writing or, in my case, writing consulting) and more general strategies for acting. I needed a method that could provide a form of "talk-back" stimulus to elicit participants' constructive reflections. It was why I chose qualitative interviewing, a form of unstructured interviewing that allows for the exploration of context-specific meaning during a particular conversation between researcher and participant.

DEFINING QUALITATIVE INTERVIEWING

For Steinar Kvale, "conversation is an ancient form of obtaining knowledge" and the qualitative interview represents the relatively recent awareness of the theoretical and methodological bases for using interviews to understand social phenomena (8). Interviews can provide access to external conditions, in the form of accounts of events only witnessed by those interviewed, but also provide information about internal conditions, about people's perceptions and their interpretations of their perceptions. Qualitative interviewing methods such as account analysis and life history represent methods that "acknowledge a person's ability to monitor, comment on, and criticize his or her own actions in retrospect" (Debs 247). It allows access to decisions actors make during social activity, such as choices made during the writing process or in collaboration with other writers. In their review of interview methods, Andrea Fontana and James Frey link the emergence of critical ethnography during the mid-1980s with the awareness of the value-laden nature of interview research. Critiques of traditional structured research methods established the discursive nature of interviews, positing that all interviews are context-bound regardless of efforts to control the instrument, the interviewer.

In qualitative interviewing, the interviewer explores topics using open-ended questions, without "imposing any a priori categorization that may limit the field of inquiry" (Fontana and Frey 56). This technique is variously identified with qualitative, informal, unstructured, in-depth, or ethnographic field interviewing. The central difference between traditional interviews and qualitative interviews is the stance of the interviewer. In unstructured interviewing, the interviewer is guided by a desire to understand rather than explain. So, the interviewer feels compelled to "deviate from the 'ideal' of the cool, distant, and rational interviewer" (Fontana and Frey 57). The fundamental question changes for the researcher from "What really happened?" to "What happened that was meaningful to this person?" (Debs 247). The interviewer can explore questions of the moment, raised in the context of the on-going conversation with the respondent. The interviewer can also answer respondent questions or modify semistructured questions accordingly. This "open" stance allows interviewers to explore complex issues through the meaning that people attribute to their lived experience. Qualitative interviewing involves less interplay with an immediate social context than ethnographic approaches, but it allows people to contribute their perspective in addition to the researcher-observer's. As Kvale writes, "qualitative interviewing is the construction site of knowledge" (2). It embodies the social, symbolic, contextual, dialogic, and narrative construction of meaning between individuals qua language.

As I discussed earlier, I see qualitative interviews as instances of *staged constructive reflection* designed to prompt critical reflection on past practice. Interview transcripts can be examined for evidence and illustrations of individuals' consulting practice. The transcripts can be read, much like any text, for participants' reflections-on-action, typically in the form of storied accounts of meaningful past experience. These accounts can yield evidence of "practice theories," or the models, principles, maxims, and/or frameworks developed by practitioners over time based on experience. According to Ilene Harris:

> Practice theories result from analysis and codification of expert practice, in particular the practical knowledge embedded in therein. These practice theories incorporate principles for potentially generalizable strategies and techniques, rationales for strategies, . . . and decision parameters for implementing the strategies in practice. (34-35)

By asking participants to recollect specific situations and the meanings they attribute to these experiences, the qualitative interviewing procedure can potentially access a continuum of participants' practical knowledge, ranging from their knowing-in-action (their tacit or unarticulated theories of practice) to their explicit practice theories. As Harris writes, "In reflection, the knowledge implicit in action is delineated, criticized, restructured, and [later] embodied in further action" (31). Qualitative interview reflections are indicative of a complex interplay across this continuum of reflective practice. At times, the individuals I interviewed were very certain of their tactics and, without much hesitation, could articulate them as principles. This is evidence of a practitioner's own awareness of practice theory, developed from constructive reflection. On the other hand, the four participants often struggled to make sense of decisions represented in their own stories of past practice. My questions often prompted this uncertainty and subsequent "delineation" and "restructuring." However, through the dialogic construction of knowledge during the interview (and even after, in postinterview member checks), interview subjects came to articulate and better understand their tacit knowledge as more explicit practice theories.

"BUT ISN'T INTERVIEWING JUST . . . TALKING?": THE VALIDITY OF PRACTITIONER PROFILES

Qualitative interviewing research assumes that participants' perspectives are reliable and valid accounts of experience and that interviewing "provides access to the context of people's behavior and thereby provides a way for researchers to understand the meaning of that behavior" (Seidman 4). Although ethnographic-like observation provides access only to people's behavior, interviewing provides access to the understanding that people ascribe to that behavior. The work of McCarthy and Fishman and Mullen et al. helps establish the complexity of the intersubjective relationship between CCL specialists and nonwriting specialists. The profiles in this chapter, on the other hand, present only the subjective reality of the CCL specialist. Is this approach fundamentally flawed? Given my previous discussion of constructive reflection, I hope the reader will agree that the answer is "no." Although there is much that can be learned from examining the negotiations over assumptions about roles, disciplinarily, and methodology, as McCarty and Fishman and Mullin et al. illustrate, my focus in this chapter is on practical inquiry. That is, I aim to develop a better understanding of CCL work by codifying expert practice. My chosen method for codifying CCL practice is qualitative interviews and the discursive profile.

For Irvin Seidman, the problem of validity is different for qualitative interviewing than in experimental studies. Interview participants must consent to be interviewed, so there is "always an element of self-selection in an interview study" (44). The researcher's means for external validity then become twofold: (a) the interviewer calls to the audience's attention connections among the experiences of the individuals participating in the study; and (b) the interviewer, by presenting the participants stories in depth, "open[s] up for readers the possibility of connecting their own stories to those presented in the study" (45). The interviewer's job, according to Seidman, "is to go to such depth in the interviews that the surface considerations of representativeness and generalizability are replaced by a compelling evocation of an individual's experience" (44). Through the researcher's carefully crafted research account, the reader potentially comes to *connect* with the subject of the report:

> In connecting, readers may not learn how to control or predict the experience being studied or their own, but they will understand better their complexities. They will appreciate more the intricate ways in which individual lives interact with social and structural forces and, perhaps, be more understanding and even humble in the face of those intricacies. Understanding and humility are not bad stances from which to try to effect [social] improvement. (45)

This was the general approach I assumed for my practical inquiry project, one I associate with critical and teacher-research standpoints. The validity of teacher-research is measured in terms of what yields "information of use to teachers and students working in similar situations" (Ray 92).

One important decision to make when representing qualitative interviews is whether to preserve the original speech, including pauses, false starts, and slang, or to translate the spoken word into more standard forms of written English (see Weiss 192-193). In transcribing my interview tapes, I followed what Kvale characterizes as a dialogic approach to transcription. Instead of viewing transcription as a "bastardization" of the oral event, a "hybrid" between the more or less private, face-to-face discourse and the written text created for later public consumption, Kvale suggests that the researcher ask, "How do I analyze what my interviewees told me in order to enrich and deepen the meaning of what they said?" (183). Using this approach, my foremost concern was putting the interviewees' reflections in a formal written style that would honor their perspective and not detract from its representation through some perceived lack of grammatical correctness, coherence, or formality. The dialogic approach locates transcription as another key site of co-construction between researcher and participant. The transcript becomes not an end in itself, but a means to achieving understanding between research and participant. I invited participants to add to the transcripts, extend their conversation, correct their own representation, and verify my transcription.

Finally, in keeping with informed consent procedures, all identifying information, such as names and institutional affiliations, has been changed to allow the participants to speak freely and to protect them and the people they discuss from personal or professional harm. While using pseudonyms risks objectifying the participants, their own desire for anonymity took precedence. I have learned a great deal from my conversations with these participants, and I have shaped my purpose as relating that knowledge— what I have learned—to the four participants and to readers of this study.

"LAUREL": A WRITING CENTER DIRECTOR WHO DEFINES COLLABORATION ACCORDING TO HER CENTER'S MISSION AND THE FACULTY MEMBER'S PERSONALITY

"Your massively huge and important question is," Laurel asked hypothetically to herself, "Is that collaboration? That's an extraordinarily good question. I guess it crosses collaboration, but you can't really say it's collaboration until they come to you." Laurel was speaking of the most common form of interaction she and her WC staff has with faculty across her campus, a subject she introduced as I explained my project to her. Laurel sees herself primarily as a WC director who administers a well-established center housed in the English department of a large northeastern public university. She may not identify completely with WAC—she's not, for example, "the" WAC director—but her work administering a highly visible WC often forces her to consider her center's relationship to WAC goals. There is no officially sanctioned, university-wide WAC program at her university. In the absence of a formal WAC program, Laurel sees her WC as an "informal" site of faculty development. According to her, the WC tutors work with students who are often struggling with poorly designed assignments. "Students come in from all over campus combating un-writable writing assignments." The best way she's found to improve this situation is to "make contact with people," to go out and work with faculty and help them with assignment design. But faculty sending students to the WC and possibly assenting to an hour-long workshop or a visit from a WC representative did not seem to meet Laurel's own conception of collaboration. She offered an alternative scenario to further explore her own thinking:

> The department head of Physical Therapy[2] is both a concerned teacher and a concerned administrator. I talk about Physical Therapy in really friendly terms because they've been fun to work with, partly because they've done so much work on their own. Because the national centers for accreditation are now emphasizing communication skills, they've . . . really gone out and prepared themselves. The department head came here, and said, "Would you look over these assignments?" He already knew a lot of what he wanted to do because he actually, as an administrator, oversees a bunch of graduate students who are introducing writing into their courses. So, we began meeting and working out course assignments. Students started coming to the lab, and then he would come back afterward for feedback: "How are the students responding to these assignments? What difficulties did you see?"
>
> That I would classify as collaboration. That's great. We sat there and talked together. I had to understand how physical therapists think, what kind of writing they have to do. And we would spend a couple hours over each assignment because I really never thought about what the problems of physical therapy writing are, and he had to define them for me. And I didn't have to do a lot work on my side to define a lot of the writing concerns. He understood, for example, audience because that's part of their concern; physical therapists have multiple audiences to write to.
>
> I would call that an instance of collaboration, in a broader term—and this is where there's an informal working together, not a formal working together. Nobody sets these things up. I would contrast that with either formal WAC collaborations where you actually work with faculty at the earlier stages when they're designing assignments or with an engineer who says, "Oh, we have to send these people to you because

they can't write; We're going to assign the papers and you tutor." We have no input into what's going on and they have nothing set up in their department for anything different.

This is a snapshot of Laurel's constructive reflection during the course of our interview. In the midst of delineating for herself what counts as collaboration, Laurel drew a line between what she considered to be formal collaboration institutionally sanctioned and supported by WAC programs and the "informal" contacts she has with faculty through volunteer, outreach workshops, and consultations aimed largely at pre-empting difficult tutoring sessions brought about by poorly constructed assignments. Both could be considered forms of collaboration but of a different kind. As for instances where tutoring services are expected by faculty or departments without much in return by way of changed attitudes or practices, Laurel was quite certain this did not count as collaboration. Distinguishing between what was and wasn't collaboration, and between formal and informal collaboration, became the focus of our shared exploration of meaning during this particular interview. The two predominant themes that emerged were (a) how the institutional context of her WC shapes the nature of her collaboration with faculty in other disciplines, and (b) how individual personalities, partly determined by institutional context, also affect her collaborations with faculty.

Laurel established one of the earliest WC and helped establish the professional network of communication among WC specialists, including the National Writing Centers Association. She has authored numerous books, edited collections, and articles on the subject. She's made scores of national presentations, led dozens of workshops, and consulted widely. But locally, the scope of her interdisciplinary collaboration is constrained by the institutional location of the WC and its historically ill-defined mission: "Part of the situation here in the writing center is no one has ever defined for us what are mission is. Do we work with composition? Do we work with the school of liberal arts? Do we work with everybody in the university?" Without a WAC program, the English Department provides most of the writing instruction on campus through a large, multifaceted writing program that includes first-year composition, advanced composition, business and technical writing, and a writing major. Most of the 10 schools on the campus of more than 35,000 students require majors to fulfill writing requirements via these service courses. So, of the more than 6,000 students annually who come through the WC, most are taking required writing courses taught by English Department staff. However, the center's records show that a percentage of the remaining students seek help with writing assignments from courses across the university. Faculty who use writing in these latter courses do so primarily out of their own personal pedagogical goals. Despite the lack of a formal WAC program, Laurel and her staff see collaborations with faculty across campus as an extension of their literacy mission:

All the people in here are really good people and respond to any student needs. So, everything coming in the door, we say, "Oh sure, I can help with that." Which is a little too much, but we don't want to be the ones who define who we help. . . . If someone is going to send students in here, we can't effectively help unless the assignment that brought them in here is fairly decently constructed. So, if your effort is to try to save the student, and hope that they're writing *a lot*, part of what you always want to do is create more effective teaching situations. What went through my mind [with the Physical Therapy case] is: "Here's a great opportunity, because they might be sending people in here, and here's a person who seems genuinely interested." It seemed just right. And we did work with some of their students, and I think they've pretty much gotten it on their own. They seem to be doing pretty well by themselves. I haven't had any contact with them in the last year.

Laurel used the case of the physical therapy collaboration to illustrate her point about how supporting faculty is "not part of her job," ancillary but oftentimes necessary to accomplish the end of improving student writing abilities, which is generally understood to be the primary mission of the WC. Laurel contrasted this "informal" extension work with more formal, institutionally authorized collaborations, be they arising in the context of a formal WAC program or collaborative research project among peers. In this context, her approach to interdisciplinary collaboration was one of "Let me talk to this person and see what we can do and how we can keep them from over-straining the writing center's facilities." An overarching concern of hers was for not taxing the resources of her center. She cited the axiom in WC discourse that a center's efforts should match its resources, and not take on, in Stephen North's words, the "whole institution's (real or imagined) sins of illiteracy" ("Writing Center" 17). This concern subtlety influences her interaction with faculty, another instance of how the local institutional context structures collaborative interactions between writing specialists and faculty in other disciplines. The result in Laurel's case was an ambiguous stance toward writing consulting that continually tried to balance the needs of the WC with the needs of the faculty.

It was important, then, that faculty "came to her," as she said, given the lack of clear mandate and support for this kind of work.[3] And for Laurel, the individual personality of the faculty member was a major determinant of whether or not she engaged in what she considered collaboration or a lesser form of interaction, what she called "providing resources." This distinction emerged as I questioned Laurel about what goes through her mind as she's approached by someone like the head of the Physical Therapy Department. As we teased out how Laurel defined "personality" and its role in her stance toward collaboration in the context of WAC-related faculty support, she seemed to connect two key elements to her own conception of personality:

(a) the extent to which the faculty member assumes the *institutional and disciplinary identities* seemingly determined by the local context, and (b) the *perceptible motivation* of the faculty member. For Laurel, the institutional identity aspect of personality is manifested in how faculty members exercise the power ascribed to them by their institutional positionality. Although hierarchies may always be present, individuals have some agency in determining the application of that power, as Laurel illustrated with the case of the department head:

> Gosh, it's so personality bound. I was impressed that a department head comes running over, and says, "Would you help me, please," sits down, apologizes for taking your time, and leaves. That's not a department head stance, normally. I was impressed by that. I didn't have any obligation to him. I think the only thing I responded to was, "That's terrific! That is really incredible, and I really like this guy!" He became my model when I talked to other people, I think because his unassuming sense and his unwillingness to even suggest a power dynamic. And I think the only reason I knew he was a department head is that he was trying to explain he was representing a lot of people, all of whom would not descend on me, but that he would be the person to take the word back. And so I don't think he sees a power dynamic in such situations because of his personal modesty.

In "Constructing Each Other," Mullin et al. illustrated how previous experiences shaped collaborators' assumptions about collaboration. In the above-quoted passage, Laurel indicated how the department head became "her model" when she talked with other people. For Laurel, collaboration begins with a willingness of the person to work together. "Given the personality of this man, our interaction was non-hierarchical." In line with the collaborative philosophy mode described in chapter 2, Laurel saw this as an instance of collaboration because there was "mutual learning" and "mutual effort":

> I thought he had all the right interests, the right motivation, and willingness to work. He was nice to talk to, and he came here and began to understand that there really were people who like to talk about writing and that we could help him. I think it went from an initial "how can we help each other," to a much more active kind of helping. He kept coming back with drafts of re-written assignments—*the department head!*

This was significant for Laurel, given that she felt her campus culture was particularly hierarchical, where faculty often seemed to prefer to work with other faculty.

Invariably, this dimension of personality can also contribute to a lack of collaboration or a failure to collaborate. Laurel gave an example of an electrical engineer she had recently worked with to illustrate how she understood individual personalities as "contextual within an institution":

> A man in Electrical Engineering was convinced that writing is important because he came from the business world where he was making large sums of money, so he has good credibility with his students, and he says, "You have to be grammatically correct!" He sent me a couple of e-mails, came over here, and I couldn't quite figure out what we were going to do together. He was going to send all of his students here, and we were to mark the grammar. So, I thought maybe we could talk a little, and I could explain to him that that's not what we do and how that doesn't really help the students. But he was convinced that they had to improve their grammar. . . .
>
> He became the laughing stock of this place. He talked for about two hours as the staff went back and forth. *He never heard what I said.* He talked and he talked and he talked. There was no collaboration. He simply unloaded on me all his problems and why he can't do this and why he can't get the money for people to grade his papers. I would try to explain, and he would come back with what he said. I thought that we had moved an inch or two toward his understanding what was possible outside his class, and then that semester he essentially sent in a lot of students to have their papers graded. And then the staff would send the notes back saying, "Well, we don't grade, but we're happy to help them learn how to proof-read." It took a lot of unpleasantness before we finally got to understanding each other.
>
> That was a lack of collaboration. What made him the scourge of the writing center was his close-mindedness, an inability to open up to some thinking that we were trying to suggest. The whole staff became resistant to working with him. And why should they have an unpleasant tutoring experience? Why should the student come in and have an unpleasant experience? No one's solving anything; we're spinning our wheels. And we couldn't handle the growing size of the course. It was mushrooming to multiple sections, hundreds of students. We had to eventually just close the door. Some of the students came in here for the right reasons, and a little bit of grammar I suppose got cleaned up and explained. But we were getting nowhere.
>
> So, I really want to distinguish the role of personality. . . . I think it runs the gambit: there would be a continuum of people who are willing to open up the examination of their field to the implications that a writing person would try to suggest. They can become very excited about it. . . . There are other people who honestly consider writing nothing more than correcting grammar, because no one has suggested anything more. They might be opened to thinking about it, if they had the time. . . . Other people come in with a sense that, *they are the content teacher*. The power structure between us, no matter what their academic status, is

quite different altogether. In these cases, the writing center becomes subservient because writing is subservient in their eyes.

In the case of the electrical engineer, personal goals and motivations, institutional power relationships, assumptions about disciplinary status, and attitudes toward writing are interwoven in a complex mesh that in common-sensical collaborative models are often construed as constitutive of individual personality. Indeed, personality is often used as an umbrella term to explain a constellation of motivations and behaviors. Individuals may hold differing conceptions of personality. Some people's motivations, as Laurel was careful to qualify, are also shaped by their workload and career exigencies:

> There are some people who would like to collaborate, but their lives are overwhelmed by their jobs and their need as faculty to spend their time on their own research. I've met some people frustrated by their inability to carve out time to collaborate. There's some really good people I've met—sometimes on the phone, sometimes because I've gone to their classrooms to talk to them or their graduate students—who would really like to do something, and they have that kind of sad look in their eye, that sort of, "God, if I could only have a semester off to work on this" feeling. So, there's failure of collaboration in a good sense when they seem to understand what they would like to do, but can't figure out how to do it.

This seems to be the case of Laurel herself and, more concretely, her center's resources. Although she is quite clear in asserting that her WC is a resource for both students and faculty, the major budgetary allocation is for tutoring and supporting students who come through the center.[4] Without institutional support, important WAC-related faculty support and faculty development cannot take place.

Laurel emphasized that she felt her example of the electrical engineer "fell off the bad continuum," and that she didn't think he "came up often as a type." Yet, some aspect of his "personality" made him closed to understanding Laurel's perspective. The interview with Laurel does not allow complete access to what personal assumptions or institutional forces were shaping the electrical engineer's behavior, but in the context of the research university, some form or another of closed-mindedness as Laurel defines it is not uncommon. It is partly why Laurel distinguished between informal relationships where faculty members assume a service mentality—where they want help improving student writing or integrating more writing into their teaching, but for a number of reasons want "someone else to take care of it"—and more formal, engaged relationships where faculty are more open to exploring their attitudes about writing, teaching, and learning. It suggests the writing specialist working either formally or informally can look to better understand the underlying forces shaping faculty behavior. As I suggested in chapter 2, there are limits to the collaborative philosophy. What we may be quick to dismiss as "closed-mindedness" is likely a complex of motivations only accessible through, in McCarthy and Fishman's words, inquiry into collaboration.

Indeed, Laurel's reflections suggest the importance of exploring assumptions about collaborative activity itself. When I asked Laurel to reflect on whether she ever self-reflexively thought about collaboration as she worked with the electrical engineer, she answered:

> I think I made the assumption early on that collaboration isn't something everybody wants to get involved with, that some people have a natural hierarchy that they're predisposed to seeing. Inevitably, you think that you want to help them widen their horizons, but there has to be a compelling *need* for them to want to widen their horizons. I think maybe I have an assumption, and I guess I did not reflect on this—this is a huge question—Is everybody open to collaboration? Would you say that all people willingly come to a situation where there could be collaboration or are some people uncomfortable with collaboration?
>
> It's a philosophical stance, I think, and I guess I'm not sure whether I made some assumption about the electrical engineer's unwillingness. I thought we had other problems that were more immediately pressing. I didn't think about these things because I kept thinking that what we really needed to do is to talk about what writing really is, but I couldn't find a way for him to listen to me. Feeling defeated about that, I never thought about the issue of collaboration. I felt defeated that we could not talk about the subject that we needed to talk about, i.e., what is writing, and how do people learn to write better? When it became clear that that door was closed, I guess I gave up.
>
> So, that's not an ethical questions, as much as a failure to help somebody see something? Rather than a failed relationship, I didn't do something right because he never understood, and never opened up to thinking about it. And then you have the larger question, When someone tries to teach someone else something or open up the door, who is the failed person, the person who won't listen or the other person who tried to open the door?

In her comfortable "tutor mode," Laurel was satisfied with answering my questions with more questions. But the issues she raises are worth considering in the context of interdisciplinary collaboration. The sort of disposition or willingness to talk about writing that Laurel spoke of as a hallmark of collaboration has always been an invisible aspect of WAC, particularly as defined through the lens of movement theory (Walvoord, "Future"). Only until writing specialists are confronted with a difficult relationship or scenario does the social dynamic of collaboration become more visible. These are the "talk-back" moments in collaborative consulting that writing specialists can, through reflective practice, become more attuned to.

Laurel admittedly invested considerable effort trying to help the electrical engineer, and looking back, she is unduly hard on herself, a professional humility most compositionists can relate to. "I spent a lot of time," she said, "trying to write e-mails—he preferred to communicate by e-mail. My husband calls me the eternal optimist, and I think it's maybe a personality flaw! At some point you have to cut your losses and quit. I probably took longer than I should have." She regretted that there were now "hundreds of electrical engineering kids in whatever this huge course was that [she] didn't know what was happening to them." Her personal feelings of frustration and loss are difficult to separate from her professional persona.

To encourage further constructive reflection, I asked her what she thought she would do differently:

> I would have like to have met with the people involved in the course. As we learned from him, it proliferated; there were other people now involved. I never met the department head. I asked to come over there several times because the department head seemed to be driving some of these things. I sent him a letter. I sent him an e-mail. I called. I never met him in person. He never responded to me, never answered my letters. I never learned the whole set-up over there. I always felt like it was a very blind situation. . . . So I think what I would do differently is wait until I could get a better sense of the context of what was happening. It was like there was a wall between me and what was happening over there.

Laurel's profile suggests the underlying complexity of the relationships between writing specialists and faculty in other disciplines and between WAC programs and the rest of the academy. Clearly, Laurel was constrained by her own institutional positionality. In the absence of a formal WAC program, she carefully and cautiously assumed partial responsibility for broadening the contexts for writing instruction at her university. But as she pointed out, institutionally sanctioned collaboration is very different than those acts that come from "the goodness of everyone's heart." Without compelling reasons to change, the level of interaction necessary to foster substantive change in attitudes about writing, teaching, and learning requires more interaction than the informal workshops or consultations Laurel can reasonably provide. It also requires material resources to support CCL specialists as they go "into the field" to gain the necessary contextual understanding.

Laurel was very cautious about assuming what Susan McLeod calls the role of the "Peace Corps volunteer":

> Some administrators think that program development is simply service. Funding isn't necessary—all one needs is an enthusiastic volunteer, someone who will see the need for change and work for the sheer love of it. WAC directors cast in the role of Peace Corps volunteers are expected to do their job with no released time, no funding for workshops, no administrative support. They are supposed to cobble together a program, making do and doing without, working on less then a shoestring. ("Foreigner" 110)

McLeod urges WAC specialists to simply refuse being forced into this role, but rather to negotiate with administrators for at least a modest budget to support the formal faculty development activities necessary for fostering WAC goals. But Laurel's case shows how difficult it is to close the door of her center, so to speak, to the faculty and students who come knocking. These are the personal/professional dilemmas not easily captured in rigid theoretical taxonomies and prescriptive principles. In the case of the Electrical Engineering Department, there was much context that Laurel was not given access to, and the effort to integrate writing failed for reasons we will likely never know. But as Laurel's stories of Physical Therapy and Electrical Engineering demonstrate, substantive engagement is possible— indeed, often desired—but generally discouraged by the structure and values of the university, which are often reflected in individual personalities and played out in one-to-one interactions.[5]

"PATRICIA": A RESEARCHER WHO "WORKS AND PUBLISHES WITH OTHERS"

Patricia's story takes us considerably closer to formal, institutionally sanctioned CCL work. It can perhaps be counted among the archetypal WAC stories. The central image she has of herself is as a change agent and a resource provider: "I try to bring needs and resources together, and that's what I've done all my life. That's to me the essence of my job as a reformer." She has a philosophical position that predisposes her to CCL work and has steadfastly held on to values born of her early academic experiences:

> I value the quality of my relationships with colleagues very highly. I value loving what I do. And I value doing the kind of work that makes a contribution to people who are actually doing the work of the world. . . . I like to collaborate, and I know how to do it by now.

Patricia's story nearly parallels the history of WAC's development as a reform movement and academic field. Indeed, it is difficult to unravel her personal account from the field's metanarrative. During her nearly 30-year academic career, Patricia has directed four faculty development programs at both college- and state-wide levels. She has worked at four institutions ranging from a small private liberal arts college to mid- to large-sized public and private research universities. She has published several key WAC books and articles, many of them co-written by academics with specializations in fields outside English. She has also directed the writing of more than 15 grants in her career, many of them from prestigious private and government institutions. Since the late 1970s, she has conducted upward of 30 workshops a year at all types of institutions and professional associations. Reflecting current trends in higher education and "the way of WAC," as she put it, Patricia now directs an interdisciplinary center for teaching and learning at a large university.

Patricia started her career "all-but-dissertation" (A.B.D.) at a small private college in the south. Working in a close-knit collegial atmosphere significantly shaped her attitude toward collaboration throughout her career. To explore the nature of her work and her professional preparation, I asked Patricia to describe how she originally became involved in WAC and how her start was related to the historical narratives of WAC's emergence as a grassroots movement:

> There was a cohesion of events. One was that the faculty were complaining to us that although the students had passed an English course, they couldn't write. So, "Johnny can't write, Jane can't write" was certainly the underlying social condition, and people were upset about that. What could we do? Nothing concrete was being done—except to complain to the English department. The second thing that happened was some time become available in my schedule because my literature class did not make. . . . I was terrified that my department head would make me take one of the other comp. sections. I would have three sections of comp, 75 papers a week, plus the so-called world lit. class, which had 45 students in it. And I would die. [laughs]
>
> So, I thought, "What could I do so that my department head wouldn't do that?" I came up with this idea that we would get some colleagues together and talk about what was happening with student writing in our classes. So we advertised it. Fourteen people were interested in it. They gathered every Tuesday afternoon for a semester. We made a pot of coffee, some brought cookies by turn, and we started talking about student writing. There were no materials. There was Mina Shaughnessy's *Errors and Expectations*, but it was so full of grammatical terms that didn't mean anything to faculty members outside of the discipline—except for its attitude. Its attitude was that this is neither hopeless nor inscrutable, that these are learners and they can be studied and their behavior has

patterns. And that they deserved to be respected for the heroic efforts they are making. They're not stupid, and they're not problems. They're people learning and this is our job and we can do this.

And so we did. First we wrote a couple of little grants and then we got a big National Endowment for the Humanities (NEH) grant. The writing of those grants was collaborative. We formed a collaborative committee, the Writing Council, which oversaw the writing across the curriculum program and had people on it from across the disciplines. That Writing Council met frequently, and all major policy decisions were made there. We got a little grant to help us with some more extensive workshops. I got some release time. We got a grant for beginning the writing center and hired someone on soft money to start that. I had already started that out of my back pocket, but now we got somebody who knew what she was doing. And then when the grant ran out, her position was made permanent, so we had a writing center director. Then we got the big NEH grant. That was for much more extensive summer workshops. We got a grant to reach out to K–12 teachers and started doing teacher training for them. At that point I left [after being recruited to start a new WAC program at a mid-sized university in the east]. . . .

So the collaboration that went on at that college, I would say, had several aspects. First of all, when we got that first group together it was a widely multidisciplinary group of faculty, and although I was the convener, it was highly collaborative. We viewed ourselves as a group of colleagues meeting together to talk about a common problem. And it was very clear that the people in the group were each experts on teaching and writing and learning in their own disciplines. What we did was to bring in samples of student writing in our classes, and assignments that we were giving, and we read some things that I could find, and we talked about them. But I certainly was not the expert. And out of that group emerged several recommendations. One was first initially for another similar workshop the next year, which I did for 12 more faculty. Now we had 24 faculty out of a total faculty of 65. There was more than a third of our faculty at that point who had been through this semester of discussion.

Grant writing and proposal writing became a focus for our collaborative effort. One thing we did was get a proposal through the faculty senate that each major would certify its students as possessing the requisite writing, speaking, and reading skills necessary to function effectively in that discipline. So each department had to define for itself what those standards were, and it would assess its students against its standard. It was a very early precursor to the assessment movement, only we would never have called it that at that point. Each department, though, had responsibility for defining what it wanted. So, you can see at this very collegial, small place—which had about 1,000 students at that time—a highly collegial environment, a faculty that was used to working well together, a very high faculty governance tradition, a tradition of trust between faculty and administrators, and a tradition of doing things together. In a sense, the whole college in those days was a collaborative effort. I've never seen anything like it, the collegiality that existed there. It was a wonderful, wonderful start to my academic career. And those kinds of collegiality and collaboration have influenced everything I've done since then.

Collegiality and collaboration indeed are the thematic patterns that stand out in this narrative. The axioms in WAC discourse that faculty workshops be relaxed, informal, nonhierarchical are represented in Patricia's story as a reflection of her college's culture, where not only faculty governance is valued, but teaching and service as well. WAC is an extension of these values. To some degree, the collegial axiology of WAC emphasizing grassroots faculty ownership has its roots in the cultural values of the small liberal arts colleges where WAC was born. The epistemology of faculty governance, of democratic leadership of the college, is reflected in this principle. Faculty across disciplines at small liberal arts colleges tend to have more shared identity as teachers invested in the institution. This shared identity transcends the loyalty to disciplines that marks academic work at larger sized, research-oriented universities. The collegial axiology has also been a source for many of WAC's inherent tensions, particularly given the disciplinary construction of the modern academy and the increased emphasis placed on publication for measuring faculty productivity at all types of institutions.

Another theme is the collaborative production of local knowledge. In her case, Patricia was supported as the "convener" of the workshops, although she started the WC "out of her own pocket." The faculty were all volunteer participants, doing service out of a shared sense of purpose and for personal growth. Because there were few WAC resources at the time, she and her colleagues focused on developing materials. They turned to soft money grants as a means to support the development of these materials. While always focused on improving individual teaching, initially the program's "shared" purpose was manifested most visibly and concretely in developing workshop materials and securing grants. Internal curriculum proposals also involved the whole college and individual departments in collaboratively participating in dialogue on standards of writing, speaking, and listening skills, discourse that, once written into curricular policy, created significant and lasting institutional change. Patricia's case demonstrates how writing consultancies aren't limited to one-to-one interactions, but often involve teams.

At the beginning of the 1980s, from the small liberal arts college, Patricia went to a mid-sized university on the west coast to initiate and direct a WAC program. There, she further formalized many of her collegial values into WAC practice. She described how she brought the pedagogical materials developed in the workshops at her former institution to the new program in the form of a book manuscript:

The first thing that I did was to organize a group of faculty colleagues from various disciplines to read the manuscript and critique it for me. In other words, I asked them to take the role, not of learners in my "class," not of students in my "class," but as faculty colleagues who were asked as co-experts to critique this manuscript. It's a common role for faculty of equal status to play with one another, and the assumption behind it is the reader has the expertise to respond as a scholarly colleague offering suggestions. I was putting what was principally my writing out there for them to critique, and they were suggesting how I could make it better, given their own expertise and experience with writing.

This positioning of faculty into familiar roles and shared identities is a significant insight, a practice linked to the earlier WAC movement, one that goes against the grain of still-current WAC discourse that suggests disciplines are isolated islands with distinct and often incompatible languages and cultures. Patricia brought her materials developed at the college in the form of a booklet and asked the new group of faculty to help her test, revise, and extend these resources. By inviting faculty to essentially critique her work, she brought them into a collaborative mode, risked how they would receive her and her work, and encouraged a research perspective. This research emphasis was also manifested in a grant to study writing in disciplinary classrooms. Writing specialists were paired with disciplinary faculty in team-teaching relationships. These relationships put faculty in the role of scholars, another identity comfortable to academics. They also focused attention on producing research articles and led to several publications.

Taking a research approach has always been an "important emphasis" of Patricia's: "I always focus on some product that has a payoff for everybody in the group and whose demands give structure to what you're doing." The faculty meet around an "object," which subsequently produces "lots and lots" of discussion. A research approach also focuses attention on student learning, a significantly different emphasis than on changing "someone's teaching," something Patricia commented WAC has often tried to do. A collaborative research approach positions faculty as scholars, shifting the focus to a shared purpose of "producing scholarship on pedagogy and student learning, building understanding among faculty members, and enhancing collegiality." Moreover, a research emphasis often generates "goodwill" and leads to more "determination" to see a project through to completion: "it helps keep people's attention fixed on something where they have something to gain personally." For Patricia, the difference between collaborations focused on producing a quantifiable object like an article or a book and collaborations focused on improving someone's teaching, which is not as clearly measurable as a product, is the myriad body of untold stories of failed collaborations.

This research approach was most clearly manifested in another strategy, a series of collaborative research projects set in disciplinary classrooms and supported by grants:

> The next thing that happened at that west coast university is that two other faculty, a writing person and a historian, wrote a big NEH grant, which provided for other similar cross-disciplinary collaborations. Those collaborations paired a writing teacher with a faculty member in the discipline for one year. They were supposed to work together in whatever ways made sense to them. But it was not the kind of deal where the writing teacher was just in charge of the grammar and punctuation. These were two faculty members of equal status, and they were expected to work together as equals and to learn from each other. So the writing people needed to know how students would be using their writing in other settings and the people in the other settings needed to know what was being taught in the writing courses. So, I was paired in two different years with two different faculty members. Each time I was the one who suggested that we try to get a publication out of it. To me, classroom research is a very, very wonderful basis for collaboration, because together you are researchers looking at the classroom.

One strategy that emerged from these collaborations was a "written agreement" between her and her partner(s) that structured the roles, rights, and responsibilities of everyone in the collaboration. Something akin to but apart from a research prospectus or informed consent form, these written agreements identified who was to contribute in what capacity. Not only did this practice build in agency for the teacher(s) whose disciplines were being studied (by ensuring their active role and status as co-writer) but it also helped "break the project down into its component parts."

Another collaborative project involving Patricia was the founding of a statewide version of the National Writing Project. She and two other writing specialists, one from a high school and one from another college, began a faculty development program targeted mostly at K–12 teachers, co-directing the project and collaboratively writing grants to sustain it. As she put it, the program "just went whoosh." They expanded their workshops, sponsored conferences, and hosted writer's workshops for outstanding student writers. Here again, Patricia put into the practice the principles of (a) focusing projects through collaborative writing, and (b) positioning faculty in familiar roles and shared identities, that of experts and researchers. Patricia added a new role, that of spokesperson:

> One of the things that we did at the college and university level was to form a pool of presenters who would go around to different schools in teams and make presentations. That was very successful. And those pre-

senters included faculty from a variety of disciplines. The whole philosophy of the Writing Project was that you make people experts as soon as you can—experts and spokespeople. You don't just treat them as students or learners or people who are doing it wrong and need to have the right brought to them. . . . That just cuts faculty out of the expertise role. That's what they're trained for, that's what they like, and that's what they do. So we made experts out of people as quickly as we could, and we eventually had literally scores of people who would give workshops at the K-12, college, and university levels.

Patricia's reflections help ground the development of WAC as a (sub)field of composition studies in her subjective experience. She talked about the divisions she witnessed in WAC discourse as it matured:

> Anne Ruggles Gere in an old book, *Roots in the Sawdust*, in the preface makes one of the earliest distinctions that I know of between WAC and WID. I think it is a very wrong and misleading distinction that she made there. I was angry at the time, thinking she's just going to divide us in ways that are untrue and unhelpful. I still believe that. I believe that the real subject of inquiry is, if you want to focus on writing, is "How does writing function?" and "How is it learned in all of its many contexts?" WAC as a scholarly discipline is the study of writing in its many contexts. Broadly, we're all studying literacy and learning. Because we're writing specialists, we're focusing on writing as part of that larger picture. . . .
> The study of the writing that takes place in other academic disciplines besides first year composition is certainly an ongoing study. I mean, I'm reading a manuscript now that has just been sent to *Research in the Teaching of English*, and it's work very like the work that I did over a decade ago. As I was reading this article at home this morning, I was thinking, "Man, this is so different in just ten years!" You just have no concept of how different the works cited list is now, because there's this enormous field now. It just looks so different; the whole feel of the thing is so different. There's this whole body of theory that the writer now has to deal with that we didn't have to deal with because it wasn't there.

Her story also shows the melding of personal/professional goals with her program development activities. She started out with "a foot in two camps," as she called it—literature and composition. Her first workshop was partly a survival tactic. At the beginning of her career, Patricia was justifiably concerned about her workload and proposed a professional development seminar to both stave off another labor-intensive writing course and address a pressing concern among her colleagues. These two factors refute the notion that early WAC was somehow a product of missionary zeal to disseminate composition pedagogy. Indeed, the origins of the nonexpert, facilitator role in WAC discourse are as much tied to the lack of a body of knowledge as a particular ideological stance. When I asked Patricia to comment on why she assumed a nonexpert stance early on, she replied:

> Yes, that was a stance that I deliberately took, but it was also true because I had been trained in literature, not in writing. I had never had a course in composition pedagogy or anything, or WAC—*we didn't call it WAC at that time!* I taught writing because everybody in that English department taught writing; we all did our share. There was no composition expert. There were no composition experts at that time. There wasn't a PhD program that I knew of anywhere, not in an English department. I was working on my PhD and doing a dissertation on modern British literature. So I was no expert.

Patricia became an expert as she helped facilitate the development of shared local knowledge on teaching and writing through workshops and collaborative research projects. The early book of resources was published in her name and "counted for something" in her career trajectory. Indeed, "maintaining just a fine publishing schedule" was how she preserved her values. As the field of WAC became more recognizable and widespread, her reputation grew on the basis of her WAC work. After moving to the mid-sized university in the 1980s, she stopped publishing in literature altogether. From directing the WAC program and statewide Writing Project, she moved on to direct a large WAC program at a public research university in the midwest. A few years later, she assumed the directorship of the teaching and learning center at another university.

As Patrica's story illustrates, particularly about her liberal arts college origins, and as McLeod reiterates in her discussion of WAC specialists as change agents, WAC "aim[s] at improving student writing, but [it does] so by working to change university curricula and faculty pedagogy, which in turn have an effect on student writing" ("Foreigner" 112). How has Patricia been able to act as a change agent in this way, at the same time balancing personal/professional values with her work CCL work? She utilizes three key strategies: putting faculty in familiar roles, focusing collaborative efforts on written products, and initiating research projects that have "currency in the academic marketplace" for faculty participants. The grants, proposals, and reports are products that can motivate faculty. They typically call for the articulation of assessment procedures, provide deadlines, and because grants and proposals are co-written, provides for an agreed-upon division of labor. This pragmatic emphasis also initiates a process of critical reflection that contributes to the production of local and global knowledge and lasting changes in curricular structures, institutional values, and individual pedagogy.[6]

"ROGER": A VETERAN TEACHER WHO (TACITLY) KNOWS THE "ECOLOGIES" OF COLLABORATIVE CONSULTING RELATIONSHIPS

Roger is a veteran adjunct instructor who for the last 13 years has worked in a free-standing composition program at a private, west coast research university with a combined student population of close to 15,000. With the exception of a brief period in the early 1980s, he has been teaching at the university as either a graduate student or part-time instructor since 1972. That makes him, in his own view, something of an "old dinosaur that's been around forever." After receiving an undergraduate degree in English literature, he entered the university to study American literature at the master's level. He taught in the English Department first as a graduate student and then, after completing his Master's, as a part-time instructor. After a brief hiatus, and the formation of a separate, free-standing writing program opened up new opportunities, Roger returned to teaching in the mid-1980s.

Like most full-time instructors in the present program, Roger teaches a 3/3 load based on a 3-year renewable contract. Because of his accumulated experience and because Roger is, by all accounts, a skilled teacher and writer, he is often asked to serve as a consultant to various initiatives, including recent links with the university Honors program and a pilot learning community. He also teaches a sophomore-level writing course designed in collaboration with the School of Management. In any given semester, he also typically teaches a rotation in the WC or a section or two of an upper division professional writing course.

Outside of his teaching, Roger counted among his varied interests playing in a traveling folk and jazz band, "fraternizing with musicians, writers, and artists," and freelance writing in the community—writing poems, music reviews, and such. Once transplanted from his out-of-state home, he's lived in the shadow of the university and never been too far removed from its intellectual "underlife," a word he used to describe the informal aspect of a professional relationship he's cultivated over the years with a close colleague. Together, he and his colleague had spent more than 15 years "processing all sorts of texts" for a science textbook and team-teaching an interdepartmental course based on the text. This notion of underlife struck me as indicative of who Roger is as a compositionist. Because Roger is in many ways *part* of the institutional culture, his case foregrounds how the personal is often inextricably interwoven into the professional dimensions of effective interdisciplinary collaborations. Unlike the prevailing image of the part timer as a transient "free-way flier," Roger is deeply invested in the university community. A great deal of his composition work grows out of his participation in the university underlife where the lines of colleague and friend are blurred amidst poetry readings, dinner gatherings, and other social participation within the community.[7]

His curiosity and insouciance often draws Roger to occasions for interesting conversation, which in terms of his teaching is often in other disciplinary contexts. "I was excited about the Honors learning community," he said, reflecting on one of the cross-curricular teaching appointments he was currently involved in, "because it was actually a chance to be *in view* of another academic course." For Roger, interdisciplinary collaboration is as much about the opportunity to reflect and revise one's own ways of seeing and teaching composition as it is about helping disciplinary experts understand the rhetoricity of their fields:

> You always feel that you're trying to make writing portable and supposedly addressing it in such a way that students can carry what they learn as writers into other contexts. And here suddenly, in person, is the other context. . . . You get to actually be in a dialogue directly with the other course, not just through the students and their writing skills.
>
> One thing that's apparent to me is that our introductory composition courses have a certain agenda about informal writing, shorter texts, writing to learn kinds of activities, writing in a number of different genres, addressing the audiences and purposes of texts. But the courses running parallel in the freshman year, like the philosophy course and anthropology course in the learning community, are demanding the kinds of tasks that we teach in our sophomore level composition course. It raises questions, like "How can I get more second year course-like tasks into my first year course without violating the principles of the course descriptions?" So I do more analysis with my students. And I learned as a tutor-consultant in the writing center too; you can see what kinds of papers people are bringing from other disciplines and what teachers are demanding of them as writers.
>
> So that's a lure of collaboration. As I said, I can get a chance to see how a psychologist reads student work. When there is a disagreement over a paper, I get some insight into how what a psychologist values might be different. . . . I can see the way a psychologist evaluates tests. He's operating much like a general academic reader and not asking of these texts that his students exhibit psychology ways of thinking and knowing. . . . There's some insight there about the other academic courses that the students see the writing course in view of, but the teachers never do. I think that's another dimension, a principle I operate on: What can you actually learn by opening a window on the courses that writing is operating in tandem with?

Here is an instance of Roger's constructive reflection. There is much in the above quoted excerpt bound to the context of our interviews together: He moves back and forth from his perceptions of the composition program's undergraduate writing curriculum; his teaching within a learning community linking writing, philosophy, and anthropology courses; and his experiences evaluating student texts in the course he team-teaches with his psychologist colleague/friend. Roger mediates between his practical experiences and his disciplinary knowledge-base. Through this interplay, he sees connections across these activities and understandings and, through reflection, develops and extends his pedagogical knowledge. Roger values what he learns while he's "in view" of other disciplinary contexts and how it impacts his approach to teaching composition courses and composition theory.

The previous excerpt also shows that Roger sees himself primarily as a teacher, never removing himself completely from considering the implications of his CCL work for his teaching. When engaging in collaborative writing consulting projects, Roger also tacitly assumes a learner's stance, an open eye, an appreciation for the opportunity to expand the horizons of his own thinking about teaching writing. Part of Roger's learner perspective is that he doesn't remove questions of pedagogy from his consultancy work. Roger's appreciation for being "in view" of other courses illustrates this. He talked of these collaborations variously as "new blood" for his pedagogy, or like the design challenges that artists sometimes present themselves with:

> Apparently, in the old days, women got so tired of sewing the same repetitive patterns over and over again that the game came to be somewhat early in the process you designed in a flaw, and then you had to play the game of overcoming it through the rest of the design and make it come out even. . . .
>
> Designing lots and lots of courses and working on your own, some people might be threatened by disrupting that process; but to just have somebody else in there working with you, having the challenge of designing around something else that's going on—not just to build a house, but to build a house around a tree and a rock—it sets up a whole different kind of challenge. One of the great things of teaching with Markos,[8] my psychology colleague, is that you have someone to talk about *exactly* what's happening in your classroom. It's not like you're just talking with another teacher who's teaching a similar course, but it's like you were both at the game. You can go back to the great plays of the day: "What about when so and so said this?" or "What did you think of that confrontation?"
>
> So, I would say one of my interests is in design. It's a chance to have someone else working with you to expand the horizons of the way you design and think about courses. It's a chance to have someone that identifies with the kind of project that you're working on too.

A central factor in Roger's identifying as a teacher and assuming a learner's stance is that teaching has been defined broadly by his program as a scholarly activity that includes the instructional activities of tutoring students, consulting with faculty, and coordinating curricular links between the writing program and other academic units. Roger works in a progressive writing program designed within full view of composition theory and other reformist discourses. The program started as an interdisciplinary academic unit made up of English Department faculty (who had time reassigned to the program), graduate student TAs (mostly from the English Department), and a cadre of writing instructors like Roger. More recently, it has taken on more departmental status with a permanent budget, 10 full-time, tenured composition faculty, 45 to 50 TAs, and 35 to 40 adjunct writing instructors. A small rhetoric and composition graduate program, with about 15 students, was also recently added. The program emphasizes professional development through weekly teacher development groups, cross-curricular liaison activity, administrative work, and scholarly forums such as in-house colloquia and statewide conferences.[9] This result is a reflective culture that fosters scholarly inquiry into composition teaching and the operation of language in its many contexts.

The concern for developing a comprehensive writing curriculum has evolved into a complex web of traditional and nontraditional arrangements. The core of the program is a four-course vertical sequence taught under the aegis of the program, ranging from a required first-year introduction to academic literacies to upper division electives such as advanced writing and technical writing courses. To complement this curriculum, a system of tutoring instruction and faculty consultation has been established that cultivates partnerships between other academic units. This program of "cross-curricular outreach" was purposefully designed to overcome the structural and budgetary limitations of traditional WAC programs. Conceived as a resource to help teachers identify and address specific problems of teaching and learning in partnership with the writing program, it aims to avoid a service model with little commitment from the disciplines.

As Roger described it, WAC at his university exists as a "simple and flexible arrangement which cultivates and receives linkages on a case-by-case, proposal-by-proposal basis." These linkages can come from both within and beyond the writing program, growing out of broad university-wide initiatives, to department needs, to proposals from individual instructors. In this model, several components of traditional WAC programs may be in effect at any given time and change from semester to semester. Writing consultants might be assigned as consultants to whole departments, specific WI courses, writing links/adjuncts, or as co-teachers. "The overall pattern of the activity," according to Roger, "is context driven. Projects are often transient. Budgetary politics and arrangements are varied and complex." A limited number of consultants are budgeted out of the instructional expenses (consultants are released for one instructional section, approximately 10 hours per week), but other resources come from writing program discretionary funds, allocations from other departments, and soft-money grants. At the time of our interview, the writing program staff—including faculty, adjuncts, and TAs—were involved in collaborations with the constituents of more than 20 different academic units.[10]

Clearly, Roger's adjunct work is shaped by this program culture and "cross-curricular outreach" system as much as by his own background and social activity in the broader community. According to Roger, a new faculty member once told him that the writing instructors are the strangest element to adjust to in the program because they have developed as teachers over many years. It was also because they typically had held many positions with "serious administrative responsibilities, managing many aspects of the program":

> We have a different ethos from scholars. Junior faculty who come to the program often have not taught anywhere near the number of years or courses that some of the veteran adjuncts have. Many of the adjuncts are very sophisticated teachers. They don't have the same concentration of scholarly readings as professional scholars, but they've elected to read a lot of things over the years to do develop their practice, and they're aware of lots of material, including theoretical work, which pertains to teaching. Also, some of the veterans have earned their PhD's in English or Education, and they bring that same intellectual momentum to their teaching practice.
>
> The adjuncts also do a lot of the administrative footwork for the program. They act as liaisons with other academic units and programs and head up program projects. The assistant director is an adjunct. The coordinator for staff development is an adjunct. So even in the administrative core there are at least two adjunct instructors. I'm the liaison with Honors, and I don't have anyone watching my every move, saying, "What's going on? What are you doing? What initiatives are going through there?" There's no one above me making the day-to-day decisions. When something significant happens that affects the program or general shape of operations, I know to keep the assistant director informed, so there are no misunderstandings or ugly surprises down the road. Otherwise, I'm trusted to have some professional judgment as a representative of the writing program. At this point, I'm involved in a number of Honors activities, and I'm kind of an auxiliary member of the Honors staff. So I keep our assistant director posted about changes, and I file a report and the end of the year, but outside of that, I don't have someone micromanaging me.

Given the hierarchical nature of the academy, and the prevailing view that adjuncts are often treated as second-class citizens, I asked Roger if he ever felt his status as an adjunct was an issue within the program or across the university:

> My encounters outside the program have always been on a very profes-
> sional, collegial level. I've very seldom felt condescended to as an
> adjunct. The only time it might crop-up is when, on certain program ini-
> tiatives, you realize that you're going to have to submit your work to a
> full time faculty member, and they're going to supervise the effort. That
> doesn't happen too often. . . . So I experience that as my double image
> in my position. In many respects we are treated like professionals.
> Veteran adjuncts are treated for all intents and purposes like faculty. The
> Honors director approaches me as though I were a faculty member in
> the writing program. There isn't a sense of being condescended to at all.
> To be honest, just look down the line and see who my colleagues are and
> who's done what. It's a pantheon of magnificent teachers. It's an honor
> and a privilege to be considered an equal among the veteran adjunct
> staff.

Roger expressed some collective sense among the adjunct staff of being
"strictly not insiders" in terms of being privy to certain program planning
and decision making, but he said that was in the process of being improved.
For the most part, he didn't feel treated as a second-class citizen: "The
emphasis here from day one has been on professionalizing writing instructors." This culture of professionalization can at times lead to a more benign
kind of exploitation, however. "The professional development projects set
up an atmosphere of people needing people to work with. So you can get
hooked," Roger said laughing. "Like when a project director calls me into
her office or something, I'm saying to myself, 'Say no. Say no. No matter
what, say no!' Your plate is full because of all these things and all the links
and everything that people are doing. You've got these initiatives coming
from all directions."

Within this innovative "outreach" environment, Roger was even able to
bring his informal relationship with Markos into the practical realm of
teaching. For 2 years, he and his colleague had been teaching an interdepartmental course offered through both the writing program and the
Psychology Department. The idea for the course grew out of a long time co-
writing relationship between the two. In the mid-1980s, Roger was
approached by his psychologist friend to help turn one of Markos' lecture
courses into a textbook. "I owe my collaboration to the game of squash"
joked Roger, who was recruited through an informal network of squash-
playing friends. Nearly 15 years later, Roger and Markos proposed the
course together because they wanted to involve students in the kind of "discussion, argument, and discovery [they] had come to revel in" as they col-
laborated on researching and writing the textbook.

When finally proposed, the course was welcomed by both departments.
It fit the Psychology Department's need for a WI course, was viewed as an
instance of innovative interdisciplinary teaching, and was considered a basis

for future collaborations. Because of the long history of their relationship, Roger was hesitant to consider it a typical or exemplary collaboration. However, he felt the dynamics of their relationship, when integrated into a student-centered pedagogy, could serve as an effective way to model for students the dialogic process expert academics bring to understanding texts:

> In the classroom, Markos and I used, in flexible and nuanced ways, a klatch[11] of quickly shifting identities to relate to one another. We addressed one another as psychologist and rhetorician, as respected friends, as pranksters and provocateurs, as opponents in debate, as co-authors of a textbook, as American and European, and so forth.

In terms of their pedagogical collaboration, Roger considered it like "taking the show on the road. We had worked for so many years together, and we knew how we talked about texts together. We knew the parameters of what would happen if we disagreed about a text. We knew how we addressed each other." The only question Roger had was how their informal relationship would translate in a classroom context. The familiarity of their relationship came out in his reflections on their "teaching style" together:

> I was very confident and knowledgeable about our style together, and I knew it would be okay, that there wouldn't be any ugly surprises. I knew how we dealt with the whole breadth of conversational things that we might encounter. If I had any anxiety about going into the classroom with him, it was that he's a prankster. He'll concoct something to get me going. The other day before I came into the room, he was saying something to the students, and then I came and asked, "O.K. What are you telling them?" And they all started laughing. He likes to do these little set-ups. . . . And so Markos' invitation is partly impish when he turns to me and says, "What do you think?" Because he's inviting a provocation, like "You want to get something going here, maybe?"

This last part of the conversation is related to my comment during our interview that, when I earlier that day observed their teaching together, Markos invited Roger to respond to Markos' interpretation of a film clip they were analyzing. Because they are so comfortable with one another, what may seem like a power play in one context, in this context Roger referred to it as their own discourse style. It highlights how roles and identities shift in truly dialogic collaborations.

Roger's reflections introduce the possibility of "play" into work, that knowledge construction is social, and as such can at times can be satisfying, enriching, fun—even when on the surface it appears otherwise, as in the case of Roger considering how he and Markos enjoy their particular kind of academic discourse:

We like our ritual combat, Markos and I. We had an incident last year where we were going at each other for something not in any intense way, but Markos was saying, "Oh, good professor [Roger's last name], I have to disagree with you on this point. If what you're saying is true. . ." And I would say, "Yes, but." And we were starting to work it up a little. [Laughing] Then one of the students started getting uncomfortable and tried to smooth over the disagreement. Markos just turned to him and said, "Oh, Ron you're such a sweetie, trying to put ointment on the wounds. It's perfectly alright, Ron. There's nothing you have to be upset about. We do this all the time. There's nothing bad going on here." That's very funny, that the students were trying to step in and mediate between us.

Ultimately, Roger considered his relationship with Markos an instance of true collaboration because, for him, collaboration occurs when the partner does not "detract" from the other's interests, that "the innovations and ideas that the other person brings are valuable and the other person understands them and accepts them as part of his or her style also." When considering Laurel's comments about close-mindedness, Roger's reflections help us further define such a quality of openness and recognize its opposite.

I asked Roger if he considered Markos's pranksterism a way to exert dominance, some exercise of power. Roger was skeptical. Reflecting on power in their relationship set off a dialogue between Roger and me that progressively led to the further construction of Roger's tacit knowledge accumulated over the course of collaborating on many different levels with individuals in many different contexts. Because of the uniqueness of his underlife relationship with Markos, Roger seemed more able to discern the structural dynamics of collaborative relationships that play out in professional, institutional contexts:

Markos and I have a personal relationship, and a personal friendship I would say puts those dynamics you might conceive as power relationships under normal academic conditions in a completely different realm. Power relationships would be foregrounded in cases where I would negotiate links with teachers I don't know very well, like with the anthropology teacher and the philosophy teacher in the learning community. But with Markos, it's not about structural power relationships. If it is a power relationship, it's maybe that Markos is like the dominant member in the friendship. Maybe he would manipulate me more in a friendship than I would, but not always.

So, I think there's just a whole other ecology going on there. I might read such behavior a lot differently from other teachers too, because there is a personal grounding for these kinds of things. . . . You're asking certain kinds of questions that would be really natural to ask of a writing teacher and a psychology teacher collaborating strictly in a professional setting. And I'm suddenly realizing that a lot of these questions don't apply because of all the other dynamics, all the other outside stuff. Behavior that you might see as departmental power-plays in the relationship are really pranksterish provocations that play out in the friendship, like Markos' trying to get my goat or offering for me to challenge him so we can have a little ritual combat or something.

Could it be that Roger takes some of the professional aspects for granted? In other words, he situated his collaboration with Markos in a different realm, a personal friendship, but that friendship is being played out in a classroom context. I asked him if maybe he took some of the professional aspects for granted:

> Yeah, but I guess the significance of that would only be apparent to those present, right? My temptation then would be to say it depends on how the students are seeing it. If it looks like one kind of drama, an interdepartmental or professional power drama, but the two of us actually are perceiving it as different, I guess the next question would be, how are the students seeing it?
>
> I'd also ask where would the impact play out elsewhere. In a way, it plays out in the negotiations between the departments. We have to behave in public according to our professional roles. I am the writing teacher in the eyes of the writing program, and Markos is the psychologist in the eyes of his psychology department. So that dynamic does get read publicly from another perspective. I'm not sure what the implications are. It's a little strange. The way I relate to Markos also has a whole underlife outside of academia. Sometimes we just listen to music. Markos will play me these operatic arias from Charlotte Church and say, "Doesn't she have this beautiful voice?" There's a lot of stuff that we've brought to our professional work and professional relationship that has a whole life of its own. We have to suppress the informalities when we relate to each other when we're in the public eye of our colleagues and students.

Here, Roger articulates his notion of underlife as he locates the power dramas in the context of his interpersonal friendship, and, because of that, his relationship with Markos did not seem as structurally determined as a more formal consulting relationship. But, in the process of constructive reflection, marked by inward question posing and outward responses, Roger too sees that even his personal friendship assumes a public identity as he and his colleague must necessarily represent themselves as professionals within their institution, to their colleagues within their departments, and to some extent, to their students.

So, where he originally did not think his situation with Markos was a useful example of cross-curricular collaboration, Roger began comparing different contexts of consulting familiar to him, either his own or those of his colleagues. He began to develop a rather sophisticated impromptu taxonomy of consulting contexts. The connection that he makes is that they all are very situated and raise particular questions about the role of the writing consultant in those spaces:

> One of the ironies or anomalies is that the link between Markos and I *evolved*; there was nothing in the university, per se, or the academic structure, or the impulse of the WAC links within the writing program that started that collaboration. It came in from a different angle. In that sense, it's anomalous.
>
> The Honors situation I'm in is more typical. The problems there are in the structure of the university. I can't manage that situation. I wouldn't feel that comfortable, for example, going to one of those other teachers one-on-one and saying, "Let's see what we can do more here." I think that they would see that as an imposition. The situation has a different set of rules to it. . . .
>
> There's a link that another adjunct has in a policy studies course where she works with faculty on problems of evaluating papers and what counts as good writing in their courses and how to approach the students as writers. I don't know if she helps with the writing tasks or design of the course, but that's a case where she wasn't the initiator of the link. Rather, the teacher of a large gateway course in policy studies came to the program and said, "We'd be interested in collaborating with a consultant." She's working with a number of teachers who teach the different sections in the course. She's proceeding more as an integral part of the unit. She's going into their space because she was invited. In the learning community, for example, I have a whole course operating in proximity to other courses, but there's still this proprietary sense of the different courses. . . . It's not a situation where students might be bringing in papers from the other courses to be workshopped in my course. . . .
>
> So, when you look at these three situations—my situation with Markos, my situation in Honors, and my colleague's situation in that public affairs class—they all have different flavors and protocols and impulses. They're all different kinds of spaces with different kinds of power structures. I think you're always aware of what's going to give: What can I do here? Who's going to come in my direction, and who's going to back away? I think it's an issue in the learning community: Are we going to be called together to do anything more collaborative before the semester is out? Who should be the convener? So, yeah, there are questions like that. My colleague has questions about how far her powers extend in the public affairs course. What's her authority, and what can she do that's productive? And how receptive are people going to be to what she has to say? She's still feeling her way.

Roger had earlier expressed disappointment that the learning community initiative appeared to be a case of failed collaboration. His high hopes for integrating curricula, partly created from three summer planning meetings that seemed to generate a great deal of enthusiasm and commitment, were dashed once the semester started and the communication stopped:

> The time constraints and schedules precluded it. It's impossible to get us all together. I feel that I don't have a relationship with the other professors, and I'm not the one who controls the access. It's as if the door opened three times, we all got a glimpse, and then we just put it together as we saw it. We've just been running parallel ever since and haven't really been in any kind of collaborative touch with each other. I would see the ideal as being able to say to the philosophy teacher, "You've got a great course, and the kids love it. It's just a terrific opportunity to use writing to help them formulate their thoughts and positions and work out counter positions and for you to evaluate them, the way they're thinking through these problems." But I don't feel that there's enough connection there to do that. Markos is the exactly opposite case. There's already a deep relationship, and I have access to him.

From Roger's perspective the learning community seemed to be facing some institutional barriers to fuller collaboration, whereas his relationship with Markos was much more familiar and unconstrained by such institutional (and interpersonal) barriers:

> I would say there are lots of institutional—I don't know if I would call them "barriers," but *logics* that gravitate against the learning community. Some of them are simply the busy-ness of the people involved. We all had self-contained courses. Teachers suddenly weren't going to redesign their anthropology or philosophy course because a writing course suddenly came from out of the bushes, like "Now I'm going to rethink the way I approach philosophical texts or suddenly put a lot more work for myself into this course because there's a writing teacher on the scene." The courses were already designed, and they're going to go through the way they were conceived. What's going to happen at this point is going to happen; there are no other changes in sight. In the absence of real communication, I talk to my students to see what's going on. So, I guess maybe that's part of the dynamic too, like *que sera sera*, at this point the design moment is over. The courses are all going to fly on their own merits, and the links are going to occur where they might, and the students are going to make choices about how to capitalize on one or the other.

Roger appears very reflective about putting his relationship with Markos in a different context than the learning community interaction he distinguished it from:

In a professional collaboration, some of those other things would develop anyway just through informal contact with teachers. You would come to certain decisions about whether you liked this person or didn't or were comfortable working with them, what their capabilities were; you would develop a camaraderie as you grew comfortable with someone. But Markos and I have had extensive interaction outside the classroom. We've come very *late* to this collaboration, based on a long history of other experiences. So, in some respect, I see it as part of that story rather than the interdepartmental story.

So I think the principles of collaboration in some way follow the institutional logics of how people are put together, under what circumstances and what roles you are to play. Like with Markos, I'm co-teaching within the same space, so we share the classroom. In the learning community, I'm teaching in tandem with two other courses, so I have my own authority as the writing teacher, my own course, my own course design, and command of my area of expertise. My colleague working with the policy studies course, she could be seen as being in much more of a service kind of position, where she's assigned to a course to work with a number of teachers, putting together workshops and such. She's a facilitator, I would say, for writing. So in one context I'm a teacher, in another I'm a co-teacher, and if I were in a context like my colleague's, I would be a consultant.

In the excerpt just quoted Roger uses the interesting notion of "stories," that professional collaborations weave multiple personal and professional/ public stories into a complex interpersonal set of relations that play out in multiple contexts. When these multiple stories are told from the phenomenological perspective of one individual, a researcher may not have access to all of the varied stories that impact a relationship, but through Roger's subjective reflections, one can at least begin to account for them, see that they are part of collaboration. In other words, an observer might read the dynamics of Roger and Markos' classroom interactions as a professional drama of power and control. But, in Roger's case, the personal story took precedence, although at the same time he seemed to take for granted the professional dimensions and how the dynamics of their relationship changed once put into the public realm of a cross-listed WI course. For one, the familiarity of the relationship bred the kind of mutually beneficial collaboration of which Patricia spoke, one premised not on changing the nonwriting specialist, but on mutual inquiry into how discourses operate in a given context. In other collaborations, Roger felt constrained by the institutional logics, less likely to risk the organic play of dialogue he had with Markos. It also reinforces the observation that Mullen et al. and McCarthy and Fishman have made, that collaboration takes a significant about of time to build trust and shared understanding.

Although he initially felt he couldn't "take" anything from his experiences with Markos to the other contexts of, for example, his learning community collaboration, his reflections across these experiences allow him to develop categories based on his experientially based knowledge, make comparisons, and develop loose abstractions to name distinctions occurring in the various categories or, specifically, collaborations. Although he may not have ever consciously transferred his experiences from one context to another, his constructive reflections form the basis for theories that he (and others) might take into future practice. In other words, we can learn from Roger's practical experience. In particular, Roger takes a rhetorical approach to cross-disciplinary collaboration. In reflecting on these dynamics, Roger exhibited a finely tuned, albeit tacit sensitivity to, in his words, the "institutional logics" of writing consulting. Perhaps in part because of his long-term relationship with Markos, Roger seemed particularly attuned to the contextual and structural aspects of any given consultancy.[12] Writing consultants necessarily must identify and assess the institutional logic of the situation so as to better understand their structurally determined role. Of course, this understanding gives academic writing consultants the critical perspective to help them to fill the role more fully or to generate more agency for themselves, so they can revise the role if limiting in any way.

Roger's rhetorical perspective also makes him less likely to perceive potential epistemological conflicts, even though his theoretical awareness might make him cognizant of differing disciplinary perspectives, such as the classic antifoundationalist critiques found in science studies discourse and how they might be perceived as threatening by scientists. He's more likely to understand one's perspective as a disciplinary way of seeing, and has an eye for appreciating and better understanding the perspective that his colleagues bring. And he expects to be changed in the process as well. Roger offered many examples of times he recognized upon reflection where his perspective had been changed by his interaction with Markos, and likewise, how Markos' sensitivity as a "reader of texts" had been heightened. Although clearly an extreme case, the collaboration between Roger and Markos is another instance of the "shared language" that writing specialists and nonwriting specialists co-construct, a language that emerges, for Roger, as a "klatch" of discourses growing out of the shared processing of texts. Roger's rhetorical perspective, when combined with his learner's perspective, and a willingness to embrace these dynamics, makes him less likely to see differences in points of view as conflict, and more likely to see them as productive occasions for dialogue and learning.

"LINDA": A CROSS-CURRICULAR WRITING PROGRAM DIRECTOR WHO HAS LEARNED TO APPRECIATE THE "TIRE-KICKERS"

Reflecting on some of the more difficult collaborations she's experienced over many years directing both a writing center and WAC program, Linda saw significant changes in her approach to interdisciplinary writing consulting:

> When I was first here I was far more threatened and upset by [resistant faculty] than I am now, after the scars have deepened from many lashings over time. And I also feel more confident, much more of an expert. I've come to understand people's positions and their right to them in ways that I didn't when I began. I have a respect for learning overall, and therefore people's disciplinary perspectives overall. And I'm fascinated by those perspectives and what they have to offer me because I'm an inveterate learner. It's not necessary anymore to convert people in that sort of messianic way that I started with. . . .
>
> I guess it's all about the tire kickers, and I've learned to in some ways appreciate them in their niggling and in their picking and in their narrow focus; they often make me think about things that I *wouldn't* have thought about. They cause me to come up with really good arguments. They cause me to look at things that I may not have seen through negative eyes and strengthen my own belief in them, or change them. I worry sometimes—and I say this to students here—that we have this incredibly strong number of positive responses of students that we survey each semester, because I know there's people out there who aren't happy with our writing center. Whether they're exceptions or just came on a bad day, I don't care; I want to hear it. They may actually be seeing something that the rest of us aren't seeing. So, I've kind of come to appreciate that. That's part of the listening, part of the willingness to take yourself out of the middle.

Echoing the values shared by Roger and Patricia, Linda identifies herself as an "inveterate learner." But, here, her reflections are focused specifically on her collaborative practices. She has learned how to collaborate in CCL contexts. After countless collaborations, many resulting in "scars," she has learned patience and understanding, making a reference to the missionary narrative's presumed idealism toward changing faculty. She gives a strong subjective basis for how WAC discourse may have matured from a naïve stance to a more disciplined, professional stance—appreciating what can be learned from seeing other disciplinary perspectives. She has learned to listen. She's even grown to appreciate the "tire-kickers" with whom she must collaborate.

Like Roger, a wealth of experience allows Linda to construct an impromptu continuum with which to describe faculty attitudes. And like Laurel, she groups faculty according to their openness to change:

To me, there are faculty who are easily open and curious and very interested in experimenting with methodologies. Then there are faculty who
are very suspicious, but they'll give it a try—I'm sure there are other
groups of faculty within the range I'm addressing—and then there are
tire-kickers, and the tire-kickers are everywhere. They keep me honest.
. . . There are of course people in academe who don't understand what
this is yet. And I've found that even people who wanted to support
WAC and what comes out of this office, it took them a lot to really
understand what it really was about. They thought they did, but they
didn't. And that was okay, too. That's my patience, the willingness to let
things take their course, kind of an organic approach. I mean you will
drive yourself absolutely crazy, which I did the first three years I was
here. That's part of it, too. It was just so intense starting from scratch,
but you can not approach program development or any kind of program with the idea you're going to get overnight or linear success of the
kind that you might think you deserve or the program deserves.

For the past 12 years, Linda has directed both a WC and the WAC program at a public, urban university of 21,000 students. Nearly one third of the
students are nontraditional, either adults over the age of 25 or minorities.
Many are first-generation college students coming from rural parts of the
state, although every state and many international countries are represented.
As Linda described it, the College of Liberal Arts committee that hired her
at the end of the 1980s first decided to start a WC to support the increased
writing that a WAC program would inevitably generate. Linda and the program were initially affiliated with the College of Liberal Arts, but as the program spread informally to other colleges and its success became known,
both were formally instituted university-wide. The administration and faculty committee planning WAC in the beginning decided to locate the center
as an academic unit outside the English Department. Linda has since been
tenured in the English Department, but looking back, Linda thought her
original location was a wise move, given the institutional politics that she
perceived in her interviews for the position:

I was interviewed by faculty senate people from across the university
because it was considered that I would be serving people across the university, not just the liberal arts college. So I already got a sense of the
politics here, and part of those politics were that everybody was fight-
ing for money and space and staff members, and were I to be located in
a department, then I would be seen as a way for that department to have
gained more staff and more money. So the focus and the animosity
against what I would be proposing would become immediately politi-
cized and the attention would be drawn away from what I considered
the subject, which is writing. So I was very happy that I was not located in a department, for the political reasons I read here, as well as my

own sense of human nature. That is, if it's located in the English department, then it's the English department's business and not anybody else's.

Politically, the university had little support from the state legislature,
creating a culture of fiscal restraint and intense competition for resources.
This condition also contributed to a general, and understandable, resistance
among a faculty increasingly asked to do more with less. The addition of
new work was looked upon skeptically. Linda, hired in an administrative
position outside of any department, was asked to develop a cross-curricular
writing program within this climate. It was not an easy charge, and her
reflections at times conveyed the difficulties she encountered early on, born
of her institutional situation and her own inexperience.

Within this context, Linda steadily managed to build a successful WAC
program with a strong WC at its foundation. The basic model of her program consists of a university-wide, two-course WI requirement. The WC
supports this curricular requirement by tutoring students, sponsoring faculty workshops, linking undergraduate and graduate student tutors to specific WI course, and individualized consulting from either Linda or her assistant.[13] An interdisciplinary committee was also formed to develop criteria
for WI courses and approve individual course proposals. From its original
base of 36 faculty participants, the program grew in 5 years to include more
than 145 faculty who had developed WI courses. But Linda also measures
her accomplishments in more affective ways, by the number of skeptics she
has turned around: "My person in biology who had crossed his arms and
said 'prove it to me' was now teaching a WAC course. He had done such a
good job that biology, which was a real hold-out, soon had instructors on a
waiting list to teach a WAC course, because it was so welcomed and so successful. It became cool to teach WAC."

Linda attributes this success to many factors. As explained previously,
the initial visionaries of the program had the foresight to situate the program
so as to avoid outright turf wars, although there was resistance to a college
initiative led by a nonfaculty member, particularly within the English
Department. The faculty senate had approved the initiative, so officially
there was grassroots support—although they frequently needed reminders,
joked Linda. On the other hand, a resolutely supportive dean helped offset
problems rooted in her administrative status by seating her on several powerful university and College of Liberal Arts committees. Although she was
not located in a department, Linda derived some status/power from a sympathetic dean and core group of faculty.

Although she spoke poignantly about her self-doubt going into the
position, Linda did have a considerable background knowledge of WCs. She
accepted the position after completing her doctorate in American literature.
She had some experience in WC theory and practice, having administered a

WC at her graduate program and developed her professional knowledge through such activities as attending Brown University's first peer-tutoring conference. Her experiences working with individual students, and the challenges and successes that brought, helped lead her toward composition:

> Though my PhD is in literature—I'm one of that generation—I was very interested in writing centers. I was interested in composition, when comp. was forming, but I was really interested in the fact that things I began doing—I'm quite sure out of having the experience in high school, having the personality of a teacher and the mind of one, whatever that means—that I could begin to draw on those experiences and began putting together a series of strategies that seemed to work, but they were different for each student, and that was real clear. The classroom seemed very different from the success was that I was able to achieve in the writing center.

As Linda suggests here, and reiterated repeatedly during our conversations, she "had a life outside academia." After completing her undergraduate degree in English education at the start of the 1970s, Linda taught high school. Toward the end of the 1970s, she went back for an English master's degree. After "a vacation from things," she worked in business in a major midwestern city and "did some other things" like renovate homes for resale. She went back for her doctorate in the 1980s. Linda felt her many careers outside academe ("and I'm not just talking part-time jobs") made a big difference in her cross-curricular administrative and consulting work. This emerged as a significant pattern from our conversations together. Like the practitioners on whom Donald Schön based his theory of reflective practice, Linda drew from a range of practical experiences in her background in the everyday administration of her WC and WAC program. Drawing from her experience in educational contexts, Linda described herself as a teacher "writ large":

> In a sense we're teachers writ large, because what I feel I do is I teach the faculty. When people from outside of here meet me and ask, "What do you do?" I say, "I teach writing; I run two programs, a writing center for students and for faculty who are writing anything, from first-year courses through articles and grants that faculty write; and I *teach faculty how to teach*." So I think there's that. Whatever each of our messianic beliefs are about what we do, we're inveterate teachers who believe very passionately what we do, which is why I think it works. I can't promote things I don't believe in. Over the years, the faculty have done nothing but give positive feedback about how this works.

Linda described her method for "teaching" faculty. Part of it was her patient, learner's approach she described in the earlier passages. Like Patricia, Linda looked for occasions where "changing the teacher" were not the immediate object of the collaboration. Instead, she preferred "working-in ideas," as she put it, "looking for the teachable moments for faculty." In her first semester as director, prior to any workshops, for example, she collected existing assignments from faculty who claimed to use writing in their courses. As she compiled the resources, she included her own commentary suggesting additional ways WAC strategies could be incorporated into the assignments. Echoing Rebecca Howard's discussion of *in situ* workshops, Linda considered presentations about the WC and writing to students in various classrooms as also occasions for educating faculty. Indeed, in her interactions with faculty, she always "looked for the teaching moments," many of which were cast in informal contexts, like lunches, committees on other subjects, questions about student work, unsolicited calls to the center. When the center would begin to see several students from a single course, she would invite the professor to talk with the tutors about the course and his or her criteria for writing assignments. Not only does it help the professors reflect on and articulate their assumptions, but then the tutors also engage them with all sorts of questions. "Those moments are really important for faculty," said Linda. "The faculty come down here and do a presentation, and they really see what we're all about and begin to do the reflectivity that I couldn't have provided in any other ways."

Linda felt that one-on-one interactions with faculty were often the most effective, nonthreatening settings for WAC faculty development. A key support structure in her program was the writing fellows who were assigned to specific WI sections, tutoring students and helping the faculty member with the writing pedagogy. The meetings between her, the tutor, and the faculty member where they discussed roles and responsibilities and went over the syllabus often led to substantive changes. These meetings, which Linda tried to schedule regularly, often led to teaching moments, with everyone focused on course texts like syllabi and assignments. With motivations that resembled Roger's, Linda also attached herself to WI courses in a tutor/consultant role. "By linking myself to different classes, I also get a different disciplinary perspective," she said. "I get my notions kind of pulled out from under me. I have to go re-think things according to a particular discipline. And it makes me see what the [undergraduate and graduate student] tutors are going through too."

It was during these kinds of, in her words, "interactivities" she could apply her "reading" skills to assess the faculty member's specific needs and formulate solutions within the context of that teacher's course:

It's the one-to-one that does it. The sense that someone's there that is really going to listen to them and not tell them what to do, but give them a menu from which they choose items that they feel comfortable with as a teacher, that fits their own personality and the objective of that course and discipline. And I help them translate activities, methodologies into something that is comfortable as well as appropriate for that discipline's ends. That's the spirit and the action with which I'm going to do all this.
. . .

I think those one-to-one situations allow for far more equality than any kind of group collaboration can allow for. The minute you get three or more in a space, the balances begin to change. Then I think it's a matter of, dare I say, personality? Or dare I say gender? Or dare I say knowledge-base? But I can go into some faculty member's office, and I will be the primary listener. I can go to other faculty members' offices, and I will be the primary questioner and speaker, because of their knowledge, because of their reluctance to speak, because of their personality, they're a quiet person—whatever the case may be. I think reading that is part of what makes for a successful collaboration, being a good facilitator. Stimulating talk, of course, when you enter a context is also important, so you can read beyond the surface quiet of it.

I was interested in exploring where exactly these interpersonal skills she characterized as a process of reading, listening, or talking came from. As Linda suggested in the earlier quoted excerpt, she strongly values her intuitive ability to "read" human nature and institutional contexts. Some of this she attributed to her professional training in literary studies. She studied at a small, private university in a major midwestern city, eventually focusing her dissertation on 19th-century American literature:

I'm a good lit. reader, and I know that reading context is what you do. That's one thing about English majors: you read a context, you figure it out, you walk in to it. And, if you're really good, you should be able to mimic that context and still say what you want to say, mimicking it only insofar as they will understand what you are saying.

But Linda also attributed a range of background influences to what she identified as her interpersonal and administrative skills. She considered the influences of her growing up as a middle child, how she learned to "sit back and watch." The sociohistorical time surrounding her upbringing—the 1960s counterculture—also contributed to her sense of social responsibility. "I am an optimist," she said. "I do believe all things are possible. I feel I have a very strong sense of injustice when it comes to people tagging people stupid." She also frequently drew from her business background as she carried out her day-to-day managerial, organizational, and interpersonal tasks.

Linda knew it would take hard work to launch a program. She didn't always paint a glamorous picture. There were many people who wanted the initiative to fail and others who wanted nothing to do with "cleaning up the writing problem." Others didn't want resources being used for WAC. Many traditionalists in the English Department felt threatened by WAC and composition. Some English faculty ignored her credentials. For the first 3 years, she worked always under an air of general skepticism:

> It was always this kind of "prove it to me." I would go into the Art Department and talk to the faculty about writing in the disciplines, why it was necessary, etceteras, and they would be very pretentious as academics can be. I would have chairs come up to me and apologize. They'd say, "Sorry for my faculty. It was really embarrassing to me." And I'd say, "You know, I hate to say it, but I'm used to it. Don't worry about it." I understand that change is difficult. I understood the radicalness of what I was proposing. I knew that it meant pedagogical change. I knew that what they had intended is that I would come in and clean up students' writing and they wouldn't have to do a thing. They never thought of doing anything like that. So when we're talking about academic, cultural, pedagogical change, I knew it was never going to be easy. I wouldn't have known it was going to be as hard as it was, but I was optimistic in a way.

Linda spent the first summer and the first year of the program "talking to anybody and everybody about the program." In addition, although it further exacerbated her workload, anytime asked, Linda joined college committees as a way to get to know faculty and promote the center.

> I probably worked, as I'm sure my family knows, a good 12 to 14 hours a day, for the first three years—a lot of lunches, a lot of one-to-one, a lot of going to departments and colloquia. Probably what signifies that the most is, at some point around the third year, I was getting out of the car and looked down and saw I had two different shoes on. The worst thing was, my first thought was not, "Oh, I have to go home"; my first thought was, "Can I get away with it?" What's worse is that one shoe was open-toed and one wasn't. That's how stressed it was; it was really intense.

This humorous anecdote belies the challenges of such work, often at the expense of personal realms of family and free time. Some of her difficulties she related to inexperience and status, not knowing academic customs and not being in an academic unit. She always considered herself part of the English department, but "they never did." She often felt alienated, "not ever having a sense of place, not ever feeling that I belonged or had a community here with which I could exchange war stories, exchange theories." Although she was liberated somewhat from the pressures imposed by tenure requirements, her early work was shaped by her strong perception that she would be held accountable. She tried to compensate for perceived and real differences in status and knowledge. She was also extremely conscientious:

> I'm not the person that I was then. I had a lot more riding on that position. I was green, and I didn't want anyone to know that. *I was supposed to be an expert in a field that I was new in.* Good grief. No way on *earth* could I let them know about that. I was learning as fast as I could read.

Linda indicates here that at the same time she was drawing from her own practical experiences, she was also integrating disciplinary knowledge on WC and WAC. Spending the first year attending several conferences helped. She also built a strong local and global collegial network—in the later case, tapping into her profession. This helped her draw from what White identifies as one source of the WPA's power.[14] So, while she drew from general interpersonal skills, she also drew from her own field knowledge as well as that of other fields.

In reflecting on the sources of her people skills, she commented: "I think if I was running a catering business and working with clients, I'd be using the same skills I have now. It wouldn't be any different." When I asked what she considered the relationship of interpersonal skills to professional knowledge, she revised her position somewhat:

> Well, I'm going to probably end up contradicting myself just by saying this, but we draw on disciplinary knowledge too. It's not that we ignore it. One of the things we do in here a lot is train our students in terms of learning styles. My colleague is an expert in that. She's licensed to give learning styles inventories. She does that in classes a lot and links it to how to study, how to write, how to process information, how to create an environment that's appropriate. She's taught me great deal about that and we draw on that a lot. Similarly, I draw from my own training in Freudian and Laconian thought, and in interpretation. As I work in other fields, whether I'm taking "Grassroots Organizations" with Randy over in sociology or I'm studying "Cultural Geography" with Jim over in the geography department, because I'm in his class as a tutor or I'm working on articles with them, I'm learning and I'm picking up new research.
>
> That to me is one of the benefits of what I do as a WAC person and a writing center person; I get to see the research that people are working on as they are working on it. I get to take it in and see how it works for me. I get to take it in and translate it into how I might use that to work with my students, how I might talk about tutoring with students. We'll invite the faculty in who are doing interesting research that we

think has implications for what we do here. So, I don't think I'm ignoring that body of research. I'm not becoming an expert in it, but I am drawing on it to become better at the kind of people skills that I need to have in order to create an atmosphere for students where students will want to learn and perform in whatever way they would like to.

So, "people skills" for Linda are not merely a generalizable skill, but rather constructed from a complex interplay of experientially based knowledge, disciplinary knowledge, and applied knowledge from other fields. With this understanding, it is easier to understand the basis for her belief in the centrality of "people skills" in cross-curricular writing program administration:

> You trust a program, but you trust a person. And the personality behind it is what makes the program. You can have a personality with no substance, and you're not going to have a program. You can have a great program and a person with no personality; you're still not going to have a program. I really don't think you can. All the people I know who are enormously successful in WAC and in interdisciplinary activities are people who are people people. Where we got our interpersonal skills, who knows; but that's who we are.

Her diverse background experiences did give her some advantages at what she called "code-switching," seeing how disciplinary constructs often overlap and that some negotiation can create shared languages. This play was "central to any collaboration." She felt she could often readily identify with her colleagues in other fields. She could, for example, call on her business experiences to build her ethos with management and business faculty. But, at the same time, she drew from the interpretive methods she learned in English studies to read/listen to the contexts of collaboration. She drew from interpersonal psychology and learning styles to assess faculty's preferred styles of interacting. Over time, she developed general schema for grouping collaborative styles based on different modes of disciplinary socialization. She approached collaboration from a teacherly perspective, developing systematic methods for "working in" WAC strategies in nonthreatening ways. These strategies were based on the importance she placed "on working with someone and not imposing your view on that person, but if anything, entering into a dialectic with the idea that there's not going to be necessarily a consensus."

Circumstances improved for Linda as she became more experienced. The third year was a watershed year. Her program began gaining momentum as word of mouth spread the program's successes. She made strong allies and friends. WAC became, as she said, hot. It became viewed as a unique programmatic site for interdisciplinary faculty development and collaborative research. This perception contributed to her status, alleviating some of the animosity she felt from some quarters. She eventually negotiated for a tenure-line position in the English Department to secure her status and protect herself from the administrative ax. Many of her early mistakes were because, as she said, she lacked patience and didn't know the slow pace of academic change. Linda does not regret being located outside a department when she started, but her experiences have left her with strong feelings about freshly minted PhDs assuming positions as WPAs. As she put it, "There's just a lot of boundaries you have to walk across very carefully as you move into another person's discipline. If you're not aware that you are operating under assumptions, and we all have to operate under assumptions, then you can get into some very dangerous—I don't want to say dangerous situations—but very sticky situations." It is these sticky situations that academic writing consultants negotiate regularly.

CONCLUSION: INTELLIGIBLE PRACTICES/ INTELLIGENT PRACTITIONERS

In the first profile, Laurel saw her faculty development work as an extension of her WC's mission of improving student literacy. She was not "formally" responsible for faculty development. Yet, for both pragmatic and ideal reasons, it was important for her to educate faculty about the center's resources and about writing-based pedagogical concerns. In this context, she viewed faculty members' "personality" as a major determinant of successful collaborations, particularly their motivation and the degree to which they exercised the power ascribed to their institutional identities (disciplinary, department, individual). But as Laurel's example of the electrical engineer showed, real change often takes considerably more investment of intellectual and material resources than the "informal" consultations she could reasonably provide on a walk-in basis. Laurel began to construct models of effective and failed collaborations and question the limits of her own assumptions of collaboration in her interactions with faculty. Laurel's reflections on the extreme case of the electrical engineer's close-mindedness showed how collaboration that doesn't come "naturally" can be a rich(er) reflective text from which to formulate practical strategies. I revisit the case of the close-minded engineer in chapter 5.

In the second profile, Patricia incorporated her early academic experiences and values into a set of strategies for faculty development that included putting faculty into familiar roles, focusing collaborative efforts on written products, and initiating projects with faculty that have exchange value in the academic marketplace. Consultancy for her often meant working in teams of teacher-researchers. To Patricia, collaboration contributed to a shared sense of identity with faculty in other disciplines. This goes against the belief that compositionists find it difficult or impossible to access other disciplinary cultures (Farris). Patricia was most explicit about her change-agent role. Her reflections on creating resources for faculty development help ground the growth of WAC from a movement into an institutionalized field, or body of specialized knowledge. Through her WAC research and administration, she saw herself as facilitating the development of shared knowledge on the teaching and learning of writing at both local and global levels. For her, distinctions between WAC and WID are "very wrong and misleading," detracting from a shared sense of purpose among writing specialists and the broader academic community.

Roger saw his consulting work as an integral part of his teaching. For him, CCL work put him "in view" of the academic contexts that his first-year composition course partly focused on preparing students for. Writing consulting meant that he could be "in a dialogue directly with the other course, not just through the students and their writing skills." His writing consulting activities always fed back into his own teaching and team teaching activities. Like Laurel, when prompted, Roger began to articulate a sophisticated tacit awareness of how context shapes the "institutional logics" of the various interdisciplinary writing consulting relationships he had been involved in. And although he was reluctant to consider his long-running personal/professional collaboration with Markos a typical or exemplary collaboration, it was apparent as he compared collaborations that his relationship with Markos served as a model for true collaboration. In discussing professional artistry, the knowing-in-action manifested in spontaneous judgments, decisions, and adjustments, Donald Schön noted how artisans can notice flaws in patterns without being able to articulate the pattern's normative principle and how professional athletes can describe irregularities in their game by saying their swing "doesn't feel right" or their shot is "off" (*Educating* 22-26). Like a master craftsman or professional athlete, Roger seemed to use the Markos collaboration to discern how other situations "weren't right."

Like Roger, Linda saw herself as an "inveterate learner" and "teacher." She had "come to understand people's positions and their right to them." Linda's hard-won experience suggested a personal basis to the WAC meta-narrative, that the missionary zeal of the novice is tempered by a more professional inquiry stance of the expert. Partly influenced by her writing center background, Linda felt that the one-to-one interaction was often the most effective and nonthreatening method of faculty development. She had developed, over time, a series of strategies for interacting with faculty members including being patient, stimulating talk, reading the situation, and creating nonthreatening occasions for dialogue. She tended to associate these tactics with commonsensical "people skills," but at the same time often linked them to her knowledge of WAC and other disciplinary perspectives. Through reflection, she could begin to structure and organize her experience in more complex ways. When set against the other profiles, Linda's story of developing WAC in an inimical setting offers a cautionary tale of sorts. It underscores the proposition that interdisciplinary collaborative consulting is complex and doesn't always come naturally, that it requires systematic, conscious attention to be successful. When I asked her if disciplinary knowledge of WAC and composition was enough to be successful, she responded by noting the amount of failed WAC programs and WCs as evidence that more than theoretical knowledge was required.

The participants profiled in this chapter admittedly paid little conscious attention to the social dynamic, ascribing variously to the commonsensical or philosophical models I described in chapter 2. The interpersonal relations between the writing specialists and faculty members were, however, central to their professional activities as teachers, consultants, and researchers. Each of the participants, for example, noted the important roles that personality and interpersonal skills played in their work. When asked to consider the underlying sources and practices related to these concepts, participants seemed to be able to construct from their tacit knowing rather sophisticated understandings of how each reads personality and uses interpersonal skills. They were often inextricably interwoven into their personal/professional lives—as the case of Roger's collaboration, where the lines of colleague and friend were ambiguous at best.

As Schön writes, "The most important areas of professional practice now lie beyond the conventional boundaries of professional competence" (*Educating* 7). Moreover, according to Schön, "we distance ourselves from the kinds of knowledge we need most to understand" (*Educating* 13). Being an effective lawyer, for instance, is more than knowing the law, it requires "skills in trial work, client relations, negotiation, advocacy, and legal ethics" (*Educating* 13). Through the dialogic process of what I call *constructive reflection*, or staged *reflection-on-action*, each of the CCL specialists I interviewed could begin to articulate their tacit knowing-in-action. They could develop impromptu taxonomies of consulting contexts (Roger), faculty attitudes (Linda), and personalities (Laurel). Patricia confidently articulated her "tenants" of collaboration. Being able to articulate their tacit knowledge suggests their practices are systematic and based in practical reasoning, a form of knowing that stands in complement to technical knowledge. In the words of Schön, these processes are intelligent and intelligible. These profiles demonstrate the range of knowledge employed by effective academic writing consultants.

NOTES

1. Following conventional procedures for protecting participants' rights to privacy and protection from emotional or physical harm, all names and institutional affiliations of participants and individuals discussed by participants have been changed to pseudonyms. This is designed to protect participants from fear of reprisals and/or professional harm as a result of information and reflections divulged during interviews and represented in the research report. This is also to protect the rights of individuals discussed by the participants who, because of the study's emphasis on consultanting methods, have no voice of their own in the project.

2. Recall that all identifying information has been changed, even in the details of participants' accounts, to protect participants from emotional or professional harm and allow them to speak freely of potentially sensitive past experiences and politically charged institutional/professional issues.

3. This does not mean the center assumed a passive stance in faculty support, as Laurel was careful to point out. The center was quite pro-active in promoting the center's services. However, without a formal WAC program facilitating local discourse on WAC, the onus falls on the faculty to seek out additional, sustained support, which is why motivation is such a strong factor in Laurel's conception of collaboration.

4. Laurel mentioned how the Internet and her center's Web site make it increasingly easier to meld supporting students with supporting faculty. Increased access to the center's resources makes it possible to both promote the center's main mission of helping students and support faculty through, for example, numerous requests by faculty across the campus on how to use the Web site's many instructional handouts and other research and writing resources.

5. Susan McLeod notes that "whatever the mechanism [for bringing about change], it is imperative that the WAC director be involved and active; those who write about educational innovation emphasize the primacy of personal contact and of personal contact networks in brining about change" ("Foreigner" 113).

6. In distinguishing hierarchical collaborative modes from dialogic modes, Ede and Lunsford comment that hierarchical collaboration tends to be very pragmatic, goal-oriented, and focused on efficiency. It also tends to be controlled by powerful outsiders/managers, conservative, and oppressive. But they refuse to equate dialogic collaboration with "good" collaboration. "Carefully structured and thus hierarchical collaborations" can also lead to productive, mutually beneficial interactions (134-35).

7. During his review of this chapter, Roger reminded me that in referring to his informal relationship with Markos, he was drawing from Robert Brooke's 1987 essay, "Underlife and Writing Instruction." "Underlife activities," as Brooke writes, "are the range of activities people develop to distance themselves from the surrounding institution. By so doing they assert something about their identity" (144).

8. The pseudonym reflects Markos' eastern European background. Although a non-native English speaker, Markos spoke English fluently. He did not, according to Roger, like to compose in English and so recruited a writer to help him with the textbook, to which he promised Roger co-authorship attribution.

9. Each teacher development team consists of 8 to 12 instructors and/or graduate students, who typically range in experience, and one veteran teacher who coordinates the group. "The stipulation," as Roger put it, "is basically to get together with other teachers and talk, and the teachers in the group set the agendas." At the beginning of a semester, the group and individuals within the group determine a professional development project for that term, be it a classroom-based inquiry, a theoretical inquiry, an exploration of the implications of a particular text on their teaching, and so on. Some groups are designed to support particular initiatives like technology or service-learning, others to support those wishing to pursue independent projects. These projects have to be published in some form, be it on a personal Web site or in some other local or global forum. The local forums include conferences, panels, and in-house print and Internet publications focused on composition curriculum and pedagogy.

10. As Roger put it, "the 'base-line' for consulting is the one-release section (10 hours a week) to work in the [WC]. That's what most consultants do. A smaller cadre does WAC work, like my Honors consultancy, which, in a way, is mostly just another consultancy space." He also added that "a number of WAC links" occur as "regularly offered" writing courses associated with other courses.

11. "Klatch" is a German word meaning, "a gathering characterized by informal conversation" (Webster's *New International Dictionary* 3rd. ed. 1971).

12. To Roger, his courses with Markos and in the learning community were "outright teaching." But, administratively, it was often identified as consulting (e.g., when the Psychology Department funded him for a semester). But Roger himself admits to never having "thought in terms of trying to devise a theoretical taxonomy for collaborating across different contexts."

13. The role of the writing center in WAC is often overlooked. C. W. Griffin observes in his 1985 survey of 139 WAC programs that "before most of us had thought about doing faculty workshops or creating writing-intensive courses, the staffs of various writing centers were working not only with the students across the curriculum, but with the instructors as well. . . . The writing center offers training colloquia for faculty, guidance in developing syllabi and instructional practices, courses in peer tutoring, and team teaching and tutorial services" (400, See also Barnett and Blumner; Waldo, *Demythologizing*).

14. According to White, the WPA draws power from institutionally, from her mandate as a "director" charged with improving writing instruction, and personally through her scholarly reputation and academic rank. Another source of power "comes from the profession itself" in the form of professional development, outside evaluators, and evidence from practices elsewhere (11-12). He warns against a WPA putting herself in a weakened position in relation to these sources of power—an argument for WPAs being tenured.

MODELS FOR ACADEMIC WRITING CONSULTING

[We] ought to welcome the problems of collaboration with colleagues in other disciplines. In so doing we can enhance our understanding of the process of discovery and the demands imposed by different writing tasks. We may indeed perform some service—to our students, in helping them become better writers, and to our own discipline, in advancing our claim that the process of writing is, in fact, an important part of the process of learning.
—Odell (49-50)

In our many years of crossing paths in various settings we have been repeatedly struck by the ways in which our experiences raise pedagogical, metarhetorical, ethical, and ideological questions about our projects. At the most obvious level, we have often shared frustrations over our difficulties of "getting through" to practitioners in the professions we study. Even when we believe we have important observations to make about the discourse practices of those we study, we are often ignored, misunderstood, or even treated with downright hostility.
—Segal, Paré, Brent, and Vipond (72)

The epigraphs opening this chapter represent, to a certain degree, historical bookends to WAC practice. In the first passage, published in *College Composition and Communication* (CCC) in 1980, Lee Odell discusses how writing specialists can help faculty in other disciplines better design writing assignments through systematic inquiry into the conceptual processes underlying writing activities in disciplinary classrooms. Observing that faculty are coming to English departments for help understanding the relation-

ship between the process of writing and the process of learning, Odell suggests specific inquiry methods that provide insight into the writing process,
including studying samples of student writing and completing a given
assignment. "When colleagues in various disciplines ask our help in integrating writing into their courses," Odell writes, "we will have to be able to discover—or help our colleagues discover—the specific conceptual demands of
writing they want their students to do" (48-49). This, as Odell notes in the
quoted passage, is a challenging but worthwhile service to not only the university, but also our profession. Although our interest in composition has
evolved from a focus on cognitive writing processes to include the social and
ideological contexts of communication, this work of helping faculty understand the implications of their writing practices and pedagogies continues to
be the mainstay of education-oriented WAC activity. Odell's essay suggests
there can be system to this activity, that writing specialists employ particular research methods.

In the second epigraph, appearing in CCC in 1998, Judy Segal, Anthony
Paré, Doug Brent, and Douglas Vipond write from the discipline-oriented
perspective of professional writing researchers. Their essay explores the limitations of directing knowledge derived from rhetorical inquiry to a primary
audience of other writing specialists, who are often "less than a proper audience" for writing research in workplace and disciplinary contexts (79). But
to direct such knowledge to professionals in other fields, where it can lead
to more substantial reform, is no simple task. Efforts at translating disciplinary knowledge are often, in Segal et al.'s experience, met with various forms
of resistance. Moreover, as composition theory increasingly compels
researchers to examine the relationship between rhetoric and ideology, looking at the political implications of discursive practices, the likelihood that
professionals will ignore or misunderstand these more critical interpretations increases. According to Segal et al., these interpretations may be irreconcilable with some professionals' assumptions about writing or their
socialized professional ideologies. They may even consciously or uncon-
sciously threaten some who are inherently in more powerful positions than
others implicated in such research. But subjecting others to ideological critique risks falling back into naive missionary-like stances of "arrogance and
unreflective manipulation" of foreign cultures (87). The difficulties brought
about from more critical perspectives echo Odell's observation that collaborating with members of other disciplines can be challenging.

When viewed from a historical perspective, the claims of Odell and
Segal et al., separated by nearly two decades, help reinforce the proposition
that writing specialists who work in cross-disciplinary contexts have always
been concerned with knowing better how to collaborate with faculty in
other disciplines, in large part because of the challenges such activity have
always presented. In this chapter, I explore this issue by addressing the ques-

tion of what CCL specialists know and do related to interdisciplinary collaboration. Just what theories and methods are available to guide academic writing consultants? To better understand the CCL specialist's knowledge of how to collaborate, in this chapter I develop a typology of writing consulting models. These models synthesize existing literature on collaboration in CCL contexts and provide additional methods for conducting such work.

A FRAMEWORK FOR WRITING CONSULTING

Table 4.1 outlines four consulting models based on my reading of existing scholarship: the workshop model, the service model, the reflective inquiry model, and the discipline-based research model. The key to this typology is its emphasis on the practice of interdisciplinary collaborative consulting. It can be distinguished from the various "components" or "elements" of WAC, such as WI courses, writing fellows programs, and WCs. Consulting practices are conceivably applied within the context of these various components. In essence, I expand the traditional consulting model of WAC (where a writing specialist confers with a colleague on a one-to-one basis) to include contexts and activities not conventionally considered as consulting. Such a typology helps synthesize the various contexts in which interdisciplinary collaboration occurs—as faculty support, as team teaching, as research. It also helps explicate a conversation on consulting methods and models—what the CCL specialist knows and does. As a set of abstractions, it risks oversimplification and exclusion, but as with all theories (as generalizations), it allows for a more precise discussion of different aims of consulting, roles of the consultant, methods of inquiry, and stances toward faculty. The typology offers a repertoire of approaches to academic writing consulting. Different situations may call for different aims, consulting roles, and stances toward faculty. The theoretical assumptions underlining each model can help consultants recognize when to evoke certain stances and employ certain methods. As I discuss, it is likely the consultant will assume multiple roles throughout the course of a particular consultancy. Many times the situation positions the consultant in certain ways. Being familiar with different models of consulting might also help the CCL specialist strategically steer the situation in more productive directions.

The Workshop Model

It is perhaps universally recognized that the backbone of any WAC program is the faculty development seminar or workshop, "conducted usually by

Table 4.1. Typology of Consultancy Models

	Workshop	Service	Reflective Inquiry	Discipline-Based Research
Aim	Motivate reflection on writing/teaching	Provide instrumental or remedial writing assistance	Improve pedagogy; Produce local knowledge	Understand disciplinary discourse; Produce disciplinary knowledge
Role of consultant	Facilitator	Writing expert	Co-inquirer	Researcher
Methods	Model WAC practices	Application of composition scholarship	Reflective inquiry	Genre studies
Role of faculty	Conduit/collaborator	Subject-area specialist	Co-inquirer	Informant/Collaborator
Examples	Fulwiler; Herrington; Minock; Weiss and Peich	Covington et al.; Lamb; Godwin; Howard	Faigley and Hansen; Kuriloff; Odell; McCarthy and Fishman; Mullin et al.	Bazerman; Freedman and Medway; Paré and Smart; Russell

people with training in teaching writing for people outside of English departments" (Griffin 400). As Walvoord writes, "Throughout the history of the WAC movement, the interdisciplinary faculty workshop has been the basis of the WAC movement, providing the yeast of understanding and commitment that leavens the curricular and programmatic elements of the WAC program" ("Getting Started" 21). The workshop model is thus an important tool in the repertoire of the writing consultant. These workshops typically involve a team of WAC workshop leaders and a group of 15 to 20 volunteer faculty participants. The formats range from 3- to 5-day intensive workshops, usually occurring during campus down times like the summer, and the semester-long seminar that meets once a week over a period of several weeks to a full semester (Faery; Fulwiler, "Writing Workshops," "Showing, Not Telling"; Herrington, "Writing to Learn"; Magnotto and Stout; Minock; Weiss and Peich). The faculty workshop model is not to be confused with WC workshops, such as 20-minute presentations led by writing consultants who visit classrooms. Although the methods are often similar, the latter form can reproduce problematic assumptions, which I discuss in the service model section.

The faculty seminar's underlying aim is usually to addresses some form of "writing crisis" on any given campus or otherwise improve student writing by "showing faculty methods of assigning writing and evaluating student writing, and helping them understand that integrating writing into the curriculum will help students' thinking and learning processes" (McLeod, "Defining" 22). However, as a technology of faculty development, the WAC workshop principally aims to motive faculty toward revising their assumptions and practices regarding writing, teaching, and learning. As Fulwiler notes, good workshops inspire and transform faculty ("How Well" 53). McLeod refers to this as the "affective element" of workshops ("Defining" 23). The WAC specialist assumes the role of a facilitator who creates the context or space for this reflection, introducing composition theory and pedagogy and initiating a dialogue among participants. Based on student-centered approaches to writing instruction—popularized by Fulwiler's "show, don't tell" advice to workshop planners—the academic writing consultant models WAC pedagogical strategies by initiating several group activities, including free-writing, peer review, and group dialogue ("Showing, Not Telling"). Participants also discuss published scholarship on composition theory and pedagogy. Topics include such writing-based concepts as journal writing, peer review, audience analysis, writing for real audiences, revision, formative evaluation, assessment, assignment design, critical thinking, and so on.

The most successful workshop facilitators also generate a shared sense of community among the participants, wherein faculty feel comfortable raising questions and exchanging their own experiences and expertise.

Workshops, according to Fulwiler, are called "workshops" because they are constructive, building community and shared knowledge ("Writing Workshops"). This community-building is considered among the most important outcomes of the workshop (Faery; McLeod, "Defining"; Walvoord, "Conduit"), which until the rise of teaching and learning centers often served as the only institutionally sanctioned site for interdisciplinary dialogue on teaching. Fulwiler claims this sense of community led to significant changes at Michigan Tech in the "general campus atmosphere about writing," in how writing was taught, in teaching methods in general, and in overall faculty performance ("How Well"). In their longitudinal study of three WAC programs, Walvoord et al. found that,

> Faculty often remembered WAC events—workshops, faculty response groups—in terms of community. For many, the WAC community was characterized by safety, liberation, the sort of naming that gave them language for what they were doing, support for their growth, and validation of the importance of teaching. . . . They altered their theories about teaching and learning, acquired new habits of mind, found new confidence and enthusiasm, and changed their roles in relation to students. . . . But few remembered a "true believer" mentality or a top-down presentational mode that compromised community. (137)

The teaching metaphor suggested by Segal et al. is appropriate for the workshop model because WAC workshops have been founded on the principle of participants re-experiencing writing from a student and writer perspective. Through the process of writing, reflection, and dialogue, faculty are not only introduced to relevant theory and practice, but develop empathy for students, learn to value collaboration, and develop an appreciation for the complexity of the writing process.

Many WAC scholars have critiqued the tendency for workshops to assume a training model, where faculty presumably receive one-time training in WAC practices and are then tested for the degree to which they have learned these strategies and use them over time. Walvoord connects this approach to both "conduit" and "convert" models of WAC, pointing to how they problematically define outcomes from the point of view of the WAC administrator and not the faculty themselves ("Conduit"). In these models, faculty are implicitly viewed as the conduit through which WAC strategies are transmitted from the workshop to the classroom, with little room for alteration, or as converts to WAC doctrine. Those who fail to use WAC-defined strategies are either ineffectual or resistant.

According to M. Todd Harper, the WAC workshop has always been caught between the goals of indoctrination and collaboration. Evoking missionary rhetoric, Harper writes: "The resulting relationship between the WAC staff and the participants creates a colonial situation where the views of faculty are silenced" (155). Harper resolves this dilemma by promoting the workshop as a site of both the transmission and construction of knowledge, where faculty exchange experientially based knowledge and co-inquire into their discipline-based assumptions: "The WAC workshop . . . offers a zone of proximal development. It provides faculty an opportunity to share problems within a public forum and to engage in collaborative discussion that at first frames a problem and then seeks a solution for it" (181). The role of the writing specialist is as both facilitator and participant in this process of constructive reflection. The writing specialist assumes dual roles: As a workshop leader, the writing specialist shares principles of rhetoric and composition with participants, but as a colleague, the writing specialist participates in the dialogue. Workshop leaders must acknowledge the experiences and skills that participants posses and allow for the sharing of that knowledge. To foster workshops as "sites of inquiry" not colonialism, Harper suggests strategies such as creating an interdisciplinary committee to organize and conduct workshops, and planning an initial workshop activity that allows the workshop participants to air their questions and concerns.

In a consulting framework, which looks at faculty development practice, the strengths of the workshop model are (a) the nondirective, or facilitator, stance of the writing specialist, and (b) the capacity for dialogue on writing, teaching, and learning among a larger sized group of faculty. The writing consultant might consider what needs or problems can best be addressed in a group setting, using methods that encourage reflection and dialogue. Historically, the group workshop has been used in the first stage of WAC programs as a way to introduce faculty to WAC theory and practice. It has been most often where WAC is first "sold" to faculty. The workshop is also often used as a means to support groups of veteran faculty who have moved beyond the introductory ideas of the initial workshop. These so-called "advanced workshops" serve to keep the conversation going and help faculty integrate additional theories and practices, such as critical thinking, assessment, and computer-aided instruction (Soven, "Advanced"). Semester-long, seminar-like workshops are perhaps the best option for WAC faculty development because the participants can devote extended attention and receive support throughout the development, implementation, and assessment of new curricula, particularly if participants are supported with stipends and course-load reductions.

Techniques developed in the context of the WAC workshop do not have to be confined to the workshop. WAC personnel can initiate workshop-like activities in other contexts. Some techniques developed for workshops might work in, for example, meetings between CCL specialists and departments or committees. Chris Anson, Michael Carter, Deanna P. Dannels, and Jon Rust describe how their Campus Writing and Speaking Program at North Carolina State University partnered with an undergraduate assessment initiative on their campus by applying its faculty development experience to develop a workshop-based training program for people who were charged with assisting individual departments develop specific assessment plans.

The workshop model is limited, however, by its inability to help faculty integrate WAC beyond the activities conducted in the workshop. The need of faculty for additional support has been well established (Gill; Magnotto and Stout; McLeod, "Translating Enthusiasm"; Swilky). Muriel Harris summarizes this view, finding that in the absence of a strong support system, "faculty resist taking on the work themselves":

> There is a falling off of faculty interest when there is not follow through after a workshop. A workshop or intensive training can bring great expectations and can fire teachers up to plunge in, in new and challenging ways. But then, with no follow up and the onset of reality (which is never quite what the workshop might lead the newly inspired to expect), interest wanes. Teachers retreat, fall back to old patterns, and drop out. . . . [The] short seminar approach for faculty training has serious limitations in producing strong follow through. (92)

The strengths of the workshop model contribute to its weakness. Workshops introduce new concepts and practices but because of their short duration can not completely equip the participants with strategies for successfully applying them on a long-term, sustained basis.

The Service Model

When the contexts of consulting move from workshops to small-group, one-to-one, and classroom settings, frequently consulting takes the form of what I call the service model. As I discuss here, I base this model on David Kaufer and Richard Young's discussion of the general skills model of expertise and Edgar Schein's purchase model of consulting. In this model, the collaboration between the writing specialist and the faculty member in the disciplines assumes a traditional view of expertise where the writing specialist is presumed to be the expert on writing and rhetoric, and the faculty member an expert in her discipline or "content area." The need to support faculty beyond the initial workshop has generated several curricular models such as writing consultancies (Blair; Covington, Brown, and Blank; Godwin), WC (Haring-Smith, "Writing Center"); writing fellows programs (Haring-Smith, "Changing"), graduate student assistants/readers (Strenski); and team-taught, linked, and adjunct courses (Graham). Most multifaceted WAC programs utilize many of these components, depending on the type of institution and goals of the program. However, these elements all share the aim of supporting the writing-related needs of faculty, either directly or indirectly. Although many of the methods developed in these models are worthwhile, and although many of these models do lead to significant individual and institutional change, when left uninterrogated, service approaches to consulting risk institutionalizing mere instrumental help to faculty, resulting in little to no significant changes on the part of faculty or department attitudes, assumptions, and practices. Thus, service consulting potentially reproduces the current-traditional assumptions about writing ability and writing instruction that WAC sets out to change.[1]

Kaufer and Young discuss the theoretical complexities they experienced during a pilot collaboration at Carnegie Mellon University designed to assist a biology teacher's efforts to integrate writing into her laboratory course. The central issue that emerged revolved around differing assumptions about language and expertise. From the beginning of the relationship, it seemed the biology teacher, Linda Kauffman, and the writing specialists (Young was supervising Lili Velez, a graduate student consultant) viewed language and its relationship to content differently. The biology teacher initially viewed language from a perspective Kaufer and Young called *Ramistic dualism*, reflecting the classical separation of content from issues of style and form. This view, which James Berlin associates with current-traditional rhetoric, assumes writing to be a transparent medium for communicating pre-existing ideas. The belief that language and content are distinct evolved into the "writing with no content in particular" tradition of writing instruction that assumes that, because writing is an elementary transcription skill, writing assignments can involve any subject area and only generic writing skills need be taught. That is, "pretty much the *same* skills of writing will develop no matter what content is chosen" (78).

Dualist views of language are well suited to what Kaufer and Young identify as a general skills model of expertise: "Dualists . . . separate language and content, leaving the relationship between them unaddressed. Within this school of thought, the division of expertise between the writing expert and the subject-matter expert remains neatly—but usually too simply—demarcated" (90). This division of expertise translates into a division-of-labor relationship where the writing specialist is presumed to possess a general knowledge of writing that is "configurable to any subject matter concerns" and that does "no violence" to disciplinary practices (91). This view, Kaufer and Young argue, conforms to the writing-to-learn approach within WAC, which introduces general language activities like journal writing and collaboration into any educational context. In this model, the writing specialist possesses content knowledge of composition studies scholarship, including knowledge of rhetoric, rhetorical history, the writing process, composition pedagogy, and so on.

This kind of general knowledge, first disseminated in the workshop and further translated in one-to-one consultations, is often well received by faculty uncertain of how to teach writing beyond assigning term papers and grading for mechanics. As Fulwiler writes, "not all teachers know how to integrate writing instruction easily into their pedagogy, nor are they comfortable 'teaching' it outright. Each teacher is already a professional, practicing writer in his or her field, yet few have ever been trained to teach writing to others" ("Showing" 55). Here, the consultant acts as a sounding board, offering advice to faculty as they design and implement writing-based strategies into their existing curricula. The consultant typically reviews course documents such as syllabi and existing writing assignments, interviews the faculty member, and perhaps keeps records and notes in a journal, offering opinions on changes that can be made.[2] The faculty member is assumed to have the freedom to adopt, modify, or reject these suggested methods.[3]

Because faculty can do what they want with the consultant's information, the generalist model of expertise also conforms to what Edgar Schein, who has developed a theory of consulting within the field of organization development, calls the purchase model of consulting:

> The most prevalent model of consultation is certainly the "purchase of expert information or an expert service." The buyer, an individual or manager or organization, defines a need—something he wishes to know or some activity he wishes carried out—and if he doesn't feel the organization itself has the time or capability, he will look to the consultant to fill the need. (*Role* 5)

In the purchase model, the "buyer" defines the need and seeks an outside agent to fill that need or service. In WAC, this need is usually in the form of expert advice on assignment design or assessment and expert services like the reading of student drafts, informational presentations on writing, or course-specific tutoring. (I discuss Schein's theory of consulting in more detail in chapter 5.)

There are problems with the service model. The faculty member figuratively "purchases" the service of the writing expert to fill the need he or she believes he or she cannot or does not want to fill, such as teaching writing, handling the paper load, grading papers. Some WAC programs offer writing specialists (be they trained undergraduate peer tutors, graduate students, or faculty/staff) to help reinforce practices learned in workshops. These writing specialists are also offered as incentives to faculty weary of the demands of writing-based pedagogies. In some WAC programs, such consulting can circumvent faculty development workshops (and hence, faculty involvement) altogether, effectively outsourcing writing instruction to consultancy services. When this happens, writing instruction risks becoming an adjunct to a course or program, not an integral part of it. At the most reductive level, the writing specialist addresses issues of mechanics and style, leaving (or "freeing") the disciplinary faculty member to focus on the "content."

Advanced writing courses (English department courses in social science, science, and technical writing) and curricular components such as writing adjuncts and links (courses taught by writing instructors—usually lower status TAs—that are attached to "content-area" courses) reflect this separation. In her early essay on writing consulting, Catherine Lamb lamented that she often felt her consulting positioned her as the one responsible for writing in a course. She also expressed disappointment "that more people were not willing to make fundamental changes in the function of writing in a course" (298). In service models, even if it seems a department is taking responsibility for writing instruction, that instruction is marginalized in special departmental writing courses, curricular components, and consultancy services. "The danger of using [writing] helpers," writes Susan McLeod, "is that the teacher in charge treats writing as something separate from (and inferior to) the subject matter of the class, something he or she can treat as the helper's responsibility" ("Defining" 23). The conceptual split between form and content is reproduced in such cross-curricular writing instruction structures and practices. As Blair's example (discussed in chapter 1) showed, the service model also potentially contributes to the deprofessionalization of writing specialists, where disenfranchised writing specialists assume marginal roles as adjuncts to the "real work" of the disciplines.

An example of the service model is the "Writing Consultancy Project" at Orange County Community College (Godwin). In it, English Department consultants work with faculty in the college's technical and allied health courses. The consultants "teach lessons and develop materials" through a range of curricular structures, including "credit-bearing writing modules which are prerequisites for designated vocational courses, team-taught writing workshops within the vocational course sequences; special large- and small-group presentations; one-to-one conferences; and supervised work in the project's computer-equipped Technical/Medical Writing Laboratory" (86).

In her discussion of the program, Christine Godwin describes several practices that seem to reflect dualistic assumptions and the problematic separation of form and content. For instance, she lists five "guidelines" designed to "insure that the instructor and consultant work well together":

1. Technical and allied health instructors request consultants.
2. Consultants are specially selected writing instructors who want to work in such a situation.
3. The technical instructor is the expert who leads the consultant.

4. The consultant suggests appropriate writing strategies, which both instructors agree to.

5. Consultants sit in on each section of the technical or allied health course during the first application, and only as needed thereafter. (87)

Godwin describes, for example, how a consultant and a technology instructor collaborate in one course: "In addition to a twenty-minute workshop at the beginning of the weekly electricity lab, the consultant confers with students individually on rough and final drafts of their weekly summaries and supervises their writing in the [writing lab]" (86). In another example, a nursing seminar, the writing consultants teach "sixteen specially designed documentation workshops within the Nursing I-IV course sequence" (86). Godwin asserts the program's goals "foster both a process and product approach," and that the program has been well received by all constituents. Although she discusses a different team-taught assignment that appears highly collaborative, for the most part it is evident that the program's design reproduces many of the assumptions of Kaufer and Young's general skills model of expertise. Guidelines 3 and 5 clearly put the writing consultant in the subordinate position, echoing Blair's deprofessionalization of the writing specialists in Colgate's WAC program. Without evidence of sustained interaction between the writing specialists and the "technical" instructors, and without an indication of shared responsibility for writing instruction, writing seems to be on the periphery compared to the "content" learning.

Service models are not inherently flawed. Together with workshops, they form the basis for the "outreach activities" from which contemporary composition scholarship is disseminated to noncompositionists in academic contexts. Service consulting is claimed to have many advantages, foremost of which is the conspicuous decentralization of writing instruction. Many consultancy programs are housed in the schools and departments they serve. They are cost-effective because the schools typically pay for some or all of the consultants' time and provide the material resources such as classroom and tutoring space, computers, copying, texts, and so forth. Their location and visibility often lead to greater use by students and higher satisfaction from faculty (see, e.g., Covington, Brown, and Blank).

It is the potential of such models to subtly influence faculty that WAC administrators generally cite as an important advantage of this type of support component. Toring Haring-Smith describes Brown University's writing fellows program, which places trained undergraduate peer tutors who serve as first readers of student texts in designated courses ("Changing"). Unlike WC tutors, curriculum-based peer tutors also assume consulting roles as they presumably help faculty design assignments and model ways of responding to student writing. Because these consultants work exclusively with one course, it is assumed they are better positioned to help faculty see connections between writing and discipline-specific learning. "In this sort of nonthreatening atmosphere," Lamb writes, "the possibilities for significant change in the teaching of writing are enhanced" (297). Commenting on the value of these types of consultancy models, Margot Soven observes that rather than receiving the modest help in eliminating the paperload they expected, faculty instead discover that they have "acquired a collaborator, a partner whose influence extends beyond helping students improve their essays. The peer tutor . . . often motivates the faculty sponsor to rethink writing assignments and adopt new methods of responding to student papers" ("Conclusion" 192). These models aspire to create contexts for change.[4]

In another case, Rebecca Howard conceptualizes the "20-minute" in-class workshop as an important vehicle for fostering mutual respect between disciplinary faculty and writing specialists. Skeptical that WAC programs will work unless the intellectual integrity of writing and writing teachers is established, Howard argues that *in situ* workshops—"wherein a writing professor offers occasional composition instruction in courses across the curriculum"—represent "a subtle way of communicating new ideas about ourselves, our discipline, and our pedagogy" (40). These workshops serve as a "forum for subtle, nonconfrontational modification of colleagues' ideas about writing instruction and writing instructors" (40-41). For these workshops to do so, according to Howard, they must (a) address the larger contexts of specific writing events or assignments, for example by not just discussing documentation formats, but why a discipline's documentation style is the way it is; (b) maintain theoretical integrity, or espouse views consistent with writing program goals; and (c) "foster a collegial approach, exchanging expertise with colleagues rather than thrusting ideas upon them" (43-44). As Howard writes, flexible and diplomatic consultancy programs open the door to more substantive and engaged collaborations between writing specialists and disciplinary faculty: "*In situ* pedagogy can provide for pedagogical cooperation between writing faculty and their colleagues, establishing the mutual respect necessary for subsequent mutual endeavors" (45).

Although in theory the consulting practices used to support faculty as they integrate writing-based pedagogical strategies have the potential for generating substantive change, as Howard demonstrates, the practices instantiating these models must be carefully aligned with these theories. Otherwise, they risk reproducing dualist assumptions of language. For instance, although the interaction was perhaps assumed, adding guidelines to Godwin's Orange County Community College Writing Consultancy Project that articulate progressive assumptions about writing and require the consultants and instructors to meet regularly would help reinforce the status of writing in the program. If not, programs and practices founded on the general skills model are unlikely to significantly alter current-traditional assumptions about writing.

REFLECTIVE INQUIRY AND DISCIPLINE–BASED RESEARCH MODELS

The final two consultancy models are based on the assumption that the complexities of WAC faculty development necessitate a more systematic approach. The line between the service model and reflective inquiry and discipline-based research models blurs when assumptions about writing, teaching, and learning compel writing and nonwriting specialists to conduct joint inquiry into how writing functions in a given context. Although inquiry of this nature happens to greater or lesser degrees in the workshop and service models, in the reflective inquiry and discipline-based models, it is accepted as a prerequisite to collaboration. In other words, the methods used are often similar, but as I discuss, the later models are distinguished by their differing assumptions about language and expertise. Service models can directly or indirectly circumvent a research approach on the assumption that existing composition knowledge—be it instruction in documentation formats, assignment design, or writing process—can be applied to most contexts, whereas reflective inquiry and discipline-based research models assume this general knowledge can be applied only after it has been in dialogue with knowledge of the local context.

The last two models partly reflect Bazerman and Russell's distinction between two research traditions associated with cross-curricular writing scholarship: the education-oriented tradition of WAC and the discipline-oriented tradition of WID. Education-oriented research, according to Bazerman and Russell, examines the "roles writing plays in teaching and learning within specific disciplinary and curricular settings"; WID research, on the other hand, takes as the "object of descriptive and interpretive (not prescriptive or normative) study the discourse of other disciplines" (xiv-xv). Unlike Bazerman and Russell, who imply that both WAC and WID research is directed to a composition studies audience, I distinguish between research that is directed primarily to local audiences and that which is directed to the global, disciplinary audience of composition studies. Thus, following the paradigm of teacher-research, which holds classroom-based inquiry by practitioners is a form of rigorous inquiry, I locate such collaborative activity between writing specialists and faculty in other disciplines within the reflective inquiry model of consulting. Research within the discipline-based model does not necessarily target local audiences.[5] This research contributes to the knowledge base of CCL specialists in the form of "content knowledge" of disciplinary discourse, but is limited by the technical rationalist assumption that it can generally be applied to other contexts. Notwithstanding this limitation, these two models demonstrate the variety and interdisciplinarity of research methods used by writing specialists studying writing, locally and globally, in cross-curricular contexts. That is, extant methods in both reflective inquiry and discipline-based research models are of immediate value to those interested in conducting academic writing consulting activity.

Reflective Inquiry Consulting

In this model, the aim of the collaboration is to improve pedagogy within a given local context. The writing consultant and the nonwriting specialist work together as co-inquirers investigating assumptions about language, writing, teaching, and learning. The principle methods of the consultant involve asking questions, conducting rhetorical analysis, and seeking feedback about preliminary assessments and recommendations. The consultant capitalizes on his or her outsider status to help the instructor understand the context of the course, including the instructor's assumptions about (a) disciplinary modes of communication—texts, terminology, methodologies, audiences, purposes, stylistic features, and so on; (b) local curricular goals and course objectives; (c) expectations about student writing; and (d) the individual's approach to the writing process. The consultant also works closely with the nonwriting specialist to evaluate specific writing tasks. Other tools for the consultant include frequent face-to-face and electronic meetings; logs, journals, and written reflections; and written and taperecorded transcripts of interviews with students and teachers. Such inquiry can be extended with focus groups and surveys of multiple people.

The assumptions about language and expertise in this model are grounded in what Kaufer and Young refer to as a monistic approach to language and an interactionist model of expertise. The writing specialists in Kaufer and Young's study quickly learned that the general skills model of expertise didn't fully account for their experiences as consultants. A turning point was when Kauffman, the biology instructor discussed previously, dismissed the writing specialists' suggestion that she add expressive journal writing activities to the students' biology lab notebooks. Kauffman explained that, in accordance with protecting the scientific rigor of experiments, the notebooks had to follow strict conventions that prohibited anything outside of recording data collection and analysis procedures. Young and Velez were dismayed by Kauffman's reply. "The problem for Young and Velez," as Kaufer and Young remark, "was that they began to think that they did not

know enough about the practices in the biology class to make useful suggestions" (80). The writing consultants determined they needed to learn as
much as they reasonably could about languages practices in Kauffman's
biology lab before they could offer useful, lasting interventions. Similar to
the practices described in the service model, they began to collect materials
from the course. However, they also used ethnographic methods to study
the language practices of the course, "using surveys, tape-recorded interviews with Kauffman and the students, taking notes on what went on in lectures and labs, and assembling sets of syllabi, assignments, and student
reports" (82).

According to Kaufer and Young, this research approach conforms to a
situated view of language they refer to as *monism*, that is, that language acts
are a "composite of form and meaning," that "subject matter constrains
writing," and that "subject matter makes a significant difference in the particular writing skills that get learned" (83). Monistic assumptions of language are reflected in the largely tacit tradition of writing instruction Kaufer
and Young refer to as "writing with a specific content." This is how writing
practices have historically been learned in the disciplines. Discipline-specific literate practices have been learned informally, in conjunction with the
acquisition of subject matter knowledge. The problem with this process of
acculturation (and rhetorical education) is that it benefits only those who
can acculturate, or as Kaufer and Young put it, only those who can "overcome an inadequate formal training in writing" (85). WAC programs set out
to demystify the relationship between language practices and disciplinary
conventions. Indeed, that writing specialists necessarily must study the disciplinary and classroom discourses of their colleagues to achieve this end is
nearly a universally accepted premise. This is the view of the learning-to-
write paradigm of WAC, which reacted to early missionary-like attempts to
impose general composition principles without any attention to contextual
factors.

However, this situated position destabilizes the writing specialist's role,
for Kaufer and Velez found themselves in the position of having to claim
that what they could usefully offer Kauffman was access to her own rhetorical expertise. "In such a case," Kaufer and Young admit, "the flow of
knowledge would have been mostly one-way, with Kauffman changing
Velez and Young much more than they changed her. That is, Kauffman
would only come to understand better what it is she already knows" (94).
Contextualist views of expertise, which hold all knowledge is local and contingent, fall short in accounting for the contribution of the writing specialist
(and composition theory) in WAC contexts. But the writing specialists in
the Carnegie Mellon collaboration were making a contribution. As Kaufer
and Young explain,

The interaction seemed to sensitize Kauffman to the existence of general strategies and to the written forms, practices, and reasons behind them. Kauffman came to believe that writing is more than the last and, relatively speaking, less important step in a research project; it is an activity to be valued, studied, practiced, and motivated. And from that perception comes the ability and willingness to create places in the classroom for other rhetorical practices and purposes. (102)

To account for this mutual exchange, brought about as the writing specialists and the biologist explored language practices in Kauffman's laboratory course, Kaufer and Young turn to what they call interactionist theories of expertise. These theories "argue that expertise relies on a complex and so far unspecified interaction between context knowledge and general strategies that are in principle articulable and teachable" (94). In particular, Schön's theory of reflective practice explains the relationship between general knowledge and context-specific knowledge. Instead of the prevailing technical rationalist view, which views practice as the instrumental, top–down application of generalized theory to different situations, Schön argues expert practitioners work from the bottom up, testing a particular situation for its fit to the expert's existing theoretical framework. When the situation doesn't fit the practitioners' existing knowledge—which is nearly always the case, given the complexities of professional practice and contextual variability—the practitioner reflects-in-action, framing the situation as a problem that needs to be solved and adapting exiting knowledge to the particular situation, often in very innovative ways. Hence, the construction of new local knowledge—knowledge that can later, through reflection-on-action, be incorporated into the practitioner's knowledge base for future practice.

"A clear implication of Schön's theory," according to Kaufer and Young, "is to blur the boundaries between insider and outsider knowledge since a reflective practitioner must constantly 'get outside' his or her own context in order to understand it better. And what better way to get outside one's own context than to make use of the perceptions of people who are already on the outside" (98). This changes the consultant and client relationship, encouraging the consultant to elicit a higher level of participation from clients, who need assistance framing and thinking through inevitably unique situations. Kaufer and Young see this as the nature of the relationship between Young, Velez, and Kauffman:

Early on, they defined their relationship according to the value of the distinctive specialties they brought to one another. Each was a specialist to the other and each was, at one time or another, a client. As time went on, the value of what they knew and could bring to each other as outsiders, as nonexperts, began to grow. Velez and Young began to recognize that Kauffman's outside (allegedly naïve) perspective about writing

enhanced their own specialized understanding. Kauffman began to recognize that Velez and Young's outside (allegedly naïve) perspective
about biology, or perhaps more accurately the teaching of biology, could
enhance her own. Who knew what and who was the client for whom
became less important issues. Both sides had a common mission of
deciding what biology students needed to know about uses of language,
and both sides became more reflective about their practice, making the
"sides" themselves less distinct. (98)

Kaufer and Young articulate what it means to, in the parlance of missionary rhetoric, facilitate nonhierarchical exchange in WAC contexts.
Moreover, their interactionist theory of expertise accounts for the specific
expert role of the writing specialist.[6] The writing specialist provides the
stimulus, a dual insider–outsider perspective, general strategies brought
from other contexts, and interpretive techniques. The writing specialist
helps engage the faculty member in a process of reflective practice. Together,
the writing and nonwriting specialist jointly frame "problems to be solved"
in the name of enhancing discipline-specific rhetorical education. Through
this process, the faculty member, and writing consultant, become more "sen-
sitized" to the rhetorical practices of a discipline and, together, they respond
with appropriate pedagogical designs. This view is shared by Kuriloff, who
writes,

> Teaching students to use writing as a tool for learning requires knowl-
> edge about the subject being learned to which writing instructors on
> their own do not have access. Only as a result of collaboration can writ-
> ing instructors and so-called content instructors work together to create
> assignments, develop criteria for evaluation, and help students realize
> the intimate relationship between thinking and writing in any field. . . .
> With a writing teacher asking the right questions and a content instruc-
> tor proposing answers, both teachers learn more than they could possi-
> bly discover alone. (136)

Although Kuriloff's description does not capture as well the dynamic,
two-way exchange theorized by Kaufer and Young, it helps explain the
unique contribution of writing specialists in CCL work. The writing specialist helps the nonwriting specialist "codify disciplinary practices" (Kaufer
and Young 102). This view is consonant with Segal et al.'s notion of "teaching" rhetorical knowledgeability. It also lends theoretical credibility to the
consultant's "sounding board" (Lamb) role, mentioned earlier in the service
model and discussed by Linda in chapter 3.

But, like most theories of collaboration, Kaufer and Young's interactionist model of expertise doesn't offer fully satisfactory practical guidance
on how to, in the words of Haviland et al., "create an intersubjective and

interdisciplinary space where the distinctions between the participants begin to blur as they interchange roles, skills, and knowledge" (49). What techniques did Young and Velez use in their collaboration with the biology professor? What is the method or methods by which the consultant creates this reflective space? What existing methods are at the writing consultant's disposal? Kaufer and Young cite a "progress report" given by Velez and Kauffman at a Carnegie Mellon Teaching Center luncheon as a source of some "insight" into how their collaboration worked:

1. First, we had to learn how to talk to each other: The goals, language, and assumptions we have are not the same. Hours of classroom observations clarified the logic and focus of biology.
2. We had to identify what student assignments already in place might be served better by a different "process."
3. We had to dissect assignments to identify what students were supposed to learn. In the process, we clarified where they had difficulties. We often found there were multiple tasks or goals within a single assignment.
4. By separating multiple tasks or goals from each other, we could redesign assignments so that they more clearly served only one of those goals. We could then set up a series of smaller assignments or activities to build experience or understanding progressively.
5. We promote practice and experience rather than testing.
6. We emphasize both the separate tasks and their integration, but at different stages in the series. For example, in the first semester, the emphasis in lab report requirements might be on good graphic and tabular presentation of data and correct analysis of these data, while in the second semester the task expands to include good introductions to the reports. (88)

These general strategies are helpful. The first point echoes McCarthy and Fishman's emphasis on the complexity of negotiating a shared language within which to proceed. It also echoes Mullin et al., who stress the importance of negotiating roles and responsibilities throughout the collaboration. Kauffman and Velez suggest that a certain lengthy period of ethnographic submersion in the culture is necessary so differing assumptions can be identified and articulated. George Kalamaras took a similar approach during his 2.5-year consultancy to the Biology Department at Indiana University-Purdue University at Fort Wayne, where he assumed a participant-observer role, attending weekly lectures, participating in labs, reading required texts, writing lab reports, and taking the exams. At the same time, Kalamaras was participating in staff-development activities and tutoring students. He attended staff meetings, visited with individuals to discuss teaching methods, gave classroom presentations, and led writing workshops. Velez apparently underwent a similar period of immersion into the culture of biology at Carnegie Mellon. One drawback of such an approach is that it is time consuming and requires substantial resources to support such work.

Kaufer and Young's interactionist model of expertise points to the advantages outsider status has for writing consulting. To borrow Kuriloff's words, the writing consultant does not so much have to become an insider, as she has to know how to "ask the right questions." But how does, as Velez and Kauffman's third point indicates, the writing consultant help "dissect" writing assignments? In an early and often quoted study of student writing in the social sciences, Lester Faigley and Christine Hansen remind us that CCL consulting is fundamentally about assuming a rhetorical approach, one that examines the negotiation of meaning between writers, readers, subject, and context. In addition to knowing general WAC strategies, the writing specialist also knows, in the words of Faigley and Hansen, how to "explore why . . . disciplines study certain subjects, why certain methods of inquiry are sanctioned, how the conventions of a discipline shape a text in that discipline, how individual writers represent themselves in a text, how a text is read and disseminated, and how one text influences subsequent texts" (149).

Other practical methods for rhetorical-based reflective inquiry can be found in Lee Odell, John Dick and Robert Esch, and Huot. These methods are based on naturalistic, qualitative research methods drawn from anthropology and sociology, but at the same time, they are firmly grounded in composition theory. Lee Odell is among the earliest to explore how the writing specialist can help faculty integrate writing. Operating from a write-to-learn framework, Odell identifies perhaps the primary unit of analysis for the writing consultant: separate writing assignments. Consultants should "consider individual writing tasks and try to determine the unique way in which a particular task relates to a writer's attempt to understand a particular subject" (43). Writing consultants should help faculty understand the processes implicit in their writing activities. "When colleagues in various disciplines ask our help in integrating writing into their courses" writes Odell, "we will have to be able to discover—or help our colleagues discover the specific conceptual demands of the writing they want their students to do" (43, 48-49). He suggests three heuristic procedures including (a) having the consultant and faculty member actually write the planned assignment, and afterwards reflect on the experience; (b) examining students' writing, contrasting strong papers with poorer ones; and (c) asking students to compose aloud, allowing for the examination of both their written product and composing process (see also Herrington, "Assignment").

Dick and Esch widen the consultant's scope of inquiry in their "systematic procedure and leading questions to make communication with colleagues in other disciplines more manageable" (179). Dick and Esch recommend that consultants examine the "normative professional [writing] behavior" of a given field, the faculty members' expectations about student writing, and their approach to the writing process. Dick and Esch suggest consultants, who are likely unaware of practices in other fields, first start by investigating the published scholarship of a given field by consulting flagship journals and collecting samples. After reviewing these samples and making preliminary assessments, they interview faculty to help clarify issues of disciplinary terminology, texts, audiences, purposes, stylistic features, and context. Next, they recommend that consultants examine faculty expectations for student writing by studying relevant syllabi and writing assignments, making notes, and raising "detailed, sometimes naïve, questions . . . much as students would" (180). Like Odell, Dick and Esch advocate studying a range of student texts, paying close attention to audience issues because faculty likely never considered the complexity of audience in classroom contexts. This can lead to more creative assignment scenarios that include more transactional, real-world writing. Finally, Dick and Esch focus on examining the nonwriting specialist's writing process and his or her expectations for students' writing processes, the latter of which are often implied in existing writing assignments. Dick and Esch's guiding questions form a good starting point and can be adapted to suit more contemporary issues, such as asking whether an instructor has considered the needs of second-language writers or the availability and suitability of technology in the design and evaluation of writing assignments

In the reflective inquiry model of consulting, seeking feedback from faculty is important to the interactive process. Dick and Esch recommend sharing preliminary research findings with colleagues for "amplification and modification" (180). Such feedback-seeking helps inform both the consultant and the faculty, who gain rhetorical knowledgeability in the process. Information sharing helps build nonwriting specialists' confidence in their ability to plan and carry out writing-based pedagogies: "By helping others make expectations more clear to us, we may also help them make these same expectations more explicit for students" (Dick and Esch 180). Another way of gathering faculty opinion has been the survey questionnaire (Behrens; Bridgeman and Carlson; Harris and Hult; Weiser). For instance, Weiser describes a survey of liberal arts faculty writing assignments, which sought answers to questions about whether or not writing is required in particular courses, the amount of writing, and assignment types and goals. Although Weiser does not specifically address how such surveys can foster dialogue among faculty, clearly such results can be shared and discussed in workshop settings or one-to-one consultations.

Citing the absence of "detailed methods" for gathering information about the range of disciplinary writing encountered by students, Brian Huot describes another feedback-seeking method, the focus group interview (32).

Huot suggests writing specialists conduct qualitative interviews with groups of four to six members of particular schools or departments to gain a better sense of the writing activities of that curriculum and to begin a dialogue between the WAC program and the particular discipline. This method, similar to the qualitative interviewing methodology I described in chapter 3, allows for the dialogic construction of meaning between researchers and participants. As Huot explains, the method involves a primary interviewer who explains the purpose and protocol for the interview, and who asks guiding questions about "what tasks students are being asked to complete, in what order these tasks are assigned within the curriculum, and what skills students need to complete the writing assignments" (34). A secondary interviewer records the responses on a flip chart, overhead, or chalkboard—allowing the interviewees the opportunity to clarify and elaborate their responses. This second interviewer can also ask questions. A third interviewer takes notes, freeing the lead interviewers to concentrate on asking questions and facilitating the dialogue. Immediately following the meeting, the team meets to discuss the interview and to create a report of insights learned from the session. This report is then delivered to the focus group participants, who can then revise or add to it. In Huot's method, feedback is elicited not only after the interview process, but during it as well. Another benefit of this method according to Hout is that it contributes to dialogue among colleagues: "As faculty members talked about courses, writing assignments, and students, other faculty heard such information for the first time. . . . These conversations among faculty fostered interest and participation throughout the university, strengthening the role of writing in their respective disciplines" (33).

Mullin et al. describe additional methods used to facilitate the kind of relationship fostered in the reflective inquiry model, including using initial and recurring face-to-face and electronic meetings; keeping a journal to record questions, reflections, and observations; hand- and taperecording interviews with teachers, students, and (because Mullin was supervising a tutor) the consultant; and collecting written reflections from the teacher and possibly students "to questions posed by the group during meetings" (152). Mullin et al. found that these methods, when coupled with a sincere willingness to negotiate authority and disciplinary assumptions, can foster the "culture of reflectivity" necessary for lasting pedagogical change (169).

Discipline-Based Research Consulting

In the discipline-based research model, the superceding aim is to produce knowledge directed to the global academic community of composition studies. The consultant assumes the customary role of a researcher studying language practices in disciplinary contexts. The writing specialist uses formal research methods with an eye toward choosing methods not only suitable to a particular research problem but also acceptable to the socialized practices of the field. Naturalistic/constructivist research (Russell, "Where Do") and North American genre studies (Russell, "Writing and Genre") are arguably the prevailing research paradigms in cross-disciplinary rhetorical research. In this model, faculty are generally presumed to be participants and influenced by the research. However, discipline-based research predominantly positions faculty in other disciplines as informants who have less active participation in shaping an inquiry beyond providing information of interest to the researcher.

The discipline-based research model tacitly assumes a technical rationalist epistemology. That is, as Schön explains, valid professional knowledge conventionally is thought to involve the "application of scientific theory and technique to the instrumental problems of practice" (*Reflective* 30). Schön adds that "this concept of 'application' leads to a view of professional knowledge as a hierarchy in which 'general principles' occupy the highest level and 'concrete problem solving' the lowest" (24). Technical rationality ignores the procedural skills involved in the framing of practical problems to which technical theories are applied. As I subsequently explain, although discipline-based research involves a certain degree of interaction with faculty, it typically fails to give attention to requisite problem-solving skills that complement technical knowledge. Instead, it assumes that if nonwriting specialists are familiar with a descriptive theory based on an abstraction of their professional discourse, they will somehow know what to do with it. However, discipline-based knowledge must be integrated with attention to the procedural activities of application, which Schön has recuperated in his theory of reflective practice—and which most resembles the reflective inquiry model of consulting I have described. Although the "researcher" role of the writing specialist undermines the certainty with which discipline-based research can be considered a form of consulting, what is lost in this imprecision is gained in the accrual of a sophisticated set of methodological tools. In particular, cultural-historical activity theory and the North American tradition of genre studies offer powerful explanatory lenses. In the following discussion, I briefly review these concepts and concurrent methods. I point to how genre theory can be utilized by writing specialists in CCL contexts, using an example taken from a published case of a writing fellows consulting relationship.

To further tease out the distinction I am making between the reflective inquiry model of consulting, which positions faculty as active collaborators, and the discipline-based research model, which positions faculty as passive informants, I turn to Lucille McCarthy and Barbara Walvoord's models for collaborative research. McCarthy and Walvoord help reconceptualize the relationship between writing specialists and faculty in other disciplines by arguing that "collaborative research in [WAC] is a powerful companion to the usual workshop activities of listening, reading, and discussing" (77). "The theoretical and pedagogical direction given in workshops," they claim, "is a general one."

> There is little in WAC workshops that can specifically tell a college biology teacher, for example, how her or his students are thinking as they write for a particular assignment, nor can workshops tell instructors what problems their students are having or how some students go about solving these problems while others do not. The only way instructors can know how their students are thinking and the only way they can understand how their newly learned teaching strategies influence that thinking is through close observation of their students. Systematic investigation in their own (and others') classroom is, we feel, a central component of writing across the curriculum's second stage. It is through such investigation that teachers will continue to grow after the workshops are finished. (McCarthy and Walvoord 78)

McCarthy and Walvoord's description of three existing models of collaborative research—the focused pair, the reciprocal pair, and the chief researcher with many informants—helps distinguish between generalist and interactionist models of collaboration. These models, presented as a review of existing research, describe different "structural arrangements" of collaborative inquiry. The first model McCarthy and Walvoord describe, the "focused pair" relationship, links a writing specialist with a "teacher from another discipline, and together they study the writing going on in another's classroom" (82). This arrangement is most consonant with traditional WAC consulting models. The second type, reciprocal pair collaboration, involves parallel inquiry into both teachers' classrooms. The third model, the chief researcher with many collaborators and informants, expands to include students. McCarthy and Walvoord define collaborators as "pairs or groups of teacher-researchers who have studied or are presently studying writing, thinking, and learning in various academic contexts" (78). They distinguish informants from collaborators in that informants provide information to researchers while collaborators provide information but also help the researcher plan and carry out the research. Collaborators, unlike informants, fully participate in the design, data collection, analysis, and implementation of the research. WID research, according to critical researchers (e.g., Blyler; Herndl; Segal et al.), tends to position faculty and other professionals as informants. Writing consulting, particularly that which I have associated with the workshop and reflective inquiry models, assumes an active role for the faculty member. In looking to WID research to inform consulting activity, then, the question becomes, in the words of Judy Segal and her colleagues, how better to "inform the informants" (80).

One useful way writing specialists have been codifying the rhetorical practices of disciplines and workplace organizations is through a body of systematic research grounded in cultural-historical activity theory. This research, as David Russell indicates in a comprehensive review essay, "takes as its object the roles writing plays in various activities, particularly those activities in which writing most powerfully mediates work: academic disciplines, professions, and other large and powerful organizations of modern life" ("Writing and Genre" 224). This approach focuses on the way that discourse mediates disciplinary and professional activity. One strand is based on the theoretical category of *genre*, defined as typified rhetorical actions based in recurrent situations. Genre studies looks beyond textual patterns to include the social context surrounding texts. As Russell notes, "Genres are not constituted by formal features, then, but by recurring social actions that give rise to regularities in the discourse that mediates them." The regularities associated with genres are in the words of Bazerman "conventional" and "conservative" in that they provide communities of actors with a certain degree of rhetorical stability in order to facilitate the production of shared knowledge ("Writing and Genre" 224-226). Working from Carolyn Miller's concept of genres as the embodiment of social action, scholars combined methods derived from rhetoric, history, sociology, and philosophy to describe the genres of scientific research articles, other science writing including proposals and popularizations, graduate school writing, psychiatry's "charter document," and undergraduate writing across the disciplines. As Segal et al. write,

> Genres, then, shape thought and action, and suggest to community members what may be thought, said, and done. Community beliefs and values are inscribed in patterns of discourse which, in turn, elicit/evoke/require those beliefs when enacted. (74)

Although these regularities are to some extent determined, they are also dynamic and local. Genres are subject to influence from social structures and human processes. The dynamic quality of genres makes it a challenge to learn how one acquires the knowledge and skill to effectively produce texts within a cultural-historical activity system. But genre theory helps make it possible to identify regularities among texts and formulate principles for informing the instruction and acquisition of literate social activities. The rhetorical practices of any given professional community are often transparent, so bound to its social activity that little conscious thought is given to how language shapes, and is shaped, by that activity. Segal et al. refer to the consciousness of discourse practices that enables one to operate knowledgeably and skillfully within a discursively constituted community as rhetorical knowledgeability or metarhetorical awareness. As Russell concludes, "The tradition of North American cultural-historical research on writing in workplaces and higher education helps practitioners, teachers, and researchers in many areas rethink their activities by making visible what is often currently transparent—their use of inscriptions to mediate their activity" ("Writing and Genre" 233).

In an accessible introduction to genre studies methodology, Anthony Paré and Graham Smart refine the definition of genre as representing "a distinctive profile of regularities across four dimensions: a set of texts, the reading practices used to interpret them, and the social roles performed by writers and readers" (147). This definition, they convincingly assert, "can help researchers explore the full range of social action that constitutes an organization's repeated rhetorical strategies, or genres" (147). Identifying genres by observing their patterns of regularity, in other words, provides a way for researchers to study the influence and acquisition of genre. Paré and Smart describe four interrelated patterns of regularity that constrain genres including regularities in textual features of documents, social roles between writers and readers, composing processes, and reading practices. Because genres are dynamic, it becomes important to consider which features of genres are regular—that is, which are recurrent, repeated rhetorical strategies—and which are irregular, those that cannot be taught, but rather must be acquired through a gradual process of socialization into a given cultural-historical activity system.

Another aspect of genres is inquiry into the ethical and political dimensions of social activity mediated by writing. These questions include why some genres are valorized over others, whose interests are served by their continued use, what worldviews are privileged, and which are suppressed. Aviva Freedman and Peter Medway link these questions to other critical research projects such as feminist and postcolonial cultural studies and critical sociolinguistics, which scrutinize

> the gender and racial ideologies underpinning writing practices, the ways that texts 'position' writer, reader and those represented, and the construction of the Other through writing. They are pregnant with possible conflict not just about theory but about practices affecting real interests such as the flow of power, status, and resources. What, for instance, about the exclusiveness of academic genres? What about the arguably *gendered* nature of scientific discourse? (11)

For Freedman and Medway, the concern of critical genre studies turns from identifying the rhetorical strategies "to consideration of the ends those strategies serve—and hence from rhetoric to ethics" (11). This concern for the political and ethical implications of discourse fits with more critical stances toward WAC, such as advocated by Donna LeCourt.

The theory and methodology of genre studies can offer a coherent system for externalizing the discourse practices within a given classroom context. To offer an example, consider the case of Doug Enders, a graduate student in English who was acting as a writing fellow linked to a WI population geography course taught by geography professor Neil Reid (Mullin et al.). Operating on the assumption that "students may have difficulty meeting a professor's expectations when they enter a discipline like geography from another disciplinary or cultural background and import assumptions that do not belong to the discipline" (Mullin et al. 156), Enders began to question the clarity of a series of writing assignments wherein Reid, the geographer, asked students to "discuss" course issues and texts. Enders wondered, in essence, if "discuss" meant something different in geography than it did in English studies. Ender's concern for disciplinary differences is grounded in the WID approach that eschews colonial stances toward other discourses and instead espouses ethnographic sensitivity to disciplinary differences.

But perhaps had Enders put Reid's expectations about his students' writing in the context of Russell's discussion of undergraduate educational genres, he may have had less difficulty relating to the writing assignments in Reid's class. David Russell's history of cross-curricular student writing helps illustrate the potential of genre studies for informing writing consulting activities in academic contexts. Russell found that

> Genres of student writing have grown up along with the genres of disciplinary practice. The various genres of student writing—essay, research paper, laboratory report, case study, thesis, dissertation—each have a history, which reflects the development of the genres of professional disciplinary practice: scholarly essay, research article, experimental article, case study, and so on. Moreover, traditions of writing instruction have grown up in various disciplines to prepare and select newcomers for their activity systems. ("Writing and Genre" 232)

This awareness of the historical development of student writing in academic settings, coupled with knowledge of genre studies, might have helped Enders better contextualize the problem he and Reid were exploring together. One writing task in particular that Reid describes seems less like "geography" writing and closer to the traditional "documented essay" or research paper that Russell describes, "a comprehensive display of learning on a narrow topic" developed in American universities in the 1860s and 1870s on the German model of "text-dependant scholarship" (*Academic Disciplines* 78-92). For example, Reid expected students to "look at all sides of the issue and present each side carefully" (Mullin et al. 163). He explained to them that their essays "should not be limited to presentation of facts but should discuss ideas and concepts using factual support" and that they "should make use of the readings, suggesting that students draw from the lectures, the videos, and discussions, and synthesize the material into a cohesive, logical, and well-organized essay" (Mullin et al. 163). Another indicator that the course was not discipline-specific is that it appears as if the majority of students were enrolled in the class as "as an elective by those outside the department who need to fill writing-intensive or social studies requirements" (Mullin et al. 154). This suggests the course was a general education elective, geared less toward disciplinary socialization and more toward a detailed, yet nonspecialized introduction to the subject. If this were the case, Reid would likely not expect students to think and write like professional geographers. It may not even be an appropriate goal given the motivation of the majority of students taking the course. There was not an indication in the article that Reid was aiming to teach forms of writing that geographers would likely produce in their daily activity.

On the other hand, questions over disciplinary assumptions are very situated, and thus very appropriate. Enders had indeed brought a certain set of assumptions unique to him about the terminology Reid was using. As the literature on WAC collaboration shows, Enders' questioning of disciplinary assumptions was important and necessary. The pair's discussion over Reid's use of "discuss" in a series of writing assignments helped the instructor realize that he was using the prompt too indiscriminately, obscuring the fact that Reid actually intended more sophisticated tasks for each assignment. (The assignments gradually sought for students to incorporate course texts in their reasoning about the issues.) By asking them to respond to each assignment by "discussing" it, the students had no clear way of seeing and understanding these changing expectations.

At the same time, Enders also seemed somewhat confounded by a belief that disciplinary differences were ever present. That is, Enders experienced some difficulty seeing that Reid's expectation appeared to be that his students exhibit a form of general academic literacy; Reid wanted them to give reasoned opinions supported by evidence from relevant course texts. In his profile from chapter 3, Roger mentioned observing a similar expectation of student writing from his psychology colleague Markos, who was "operating much like a general academic reader and not asking of these texts that his students exhibit psychology ways of thinking and knowing." It appears as if Enders' concerns over disciplinary differences prevented him from possibly helping Reid devise smaller writing activities such as summaries and reviews that could reinforce the students' general academic literacy and help them learn the course texts in preparation for tackling the broader issues of the course. To help negotiate the complexities of the general academic versus discipline-specific literacy binary, Enders could have further pushed Reid to better articulate his goals for the course and each assignment.

This case helps reinforce my argument that the methods afforded by genre studies and cultural-historical activity theory, and the (content) knowledge of different disciplinary and professional discourses developed over the last twenty years, offers another perspective writing specialists can use in their consulting activity—not as prescriptions for practice, but as heuristic generalizations. The case also suggests that the writing specialist's role is to be knowledgeable of this body of knowledge and inquiry methods and to initiate reflection on how well existing rhetorical knowledge fits with the needs of a particular faculty member. Published WID research can serve as another set of explanatory generalizations that writing consultants can draw upon to further facilitate reflection on the functions of writing in particular disciplinary contexts.[7]

The limitation of the discipline-based research model of consulting is that its aim is more focused on producing global rather than local knowledge. With the consultant positioned as researcher and the faculty positioned as informants, the likelihood of substantive interaction is diminished. Judy Segal and her colleagues explore the complexities of actively returning rhetorical knowledge to the professional communities studied. "There is a significant difference between interacting with discourse communities in order to learn about them," they argue, "and actively returning discourse knowledge, interpreted, to the communities we have studied" (73). The problem with discipline-based inquiry, Segal et al. argue, is that it is primarily conducted for the benefit of other composition studies researchers. But the composition community typically has only a theoretical interest in this scholarship. Like the service model, discipline-based research involves little significant participation from the faculty and professionals, who are tacitly positioned as informants. There is only a unidirectional transfer of information—from the disciplines to composition studies. What is often not clear, then, is what is given back to the professional contexts studied, the communities and professionals who stand to benefit most from this knowledge—or whether those in other fields are willing to listen at all.

Segal et al. resolve this tension by articulating an ethical standpoint grounded in critical and social views of rhetorical study that should, if compositionists are to remain consistent with their theories of discourse, compel researchers to, paraphrasing Segal et al.'s colloquial language, stick their necks out into the disciplines and try to return some of what they have learned about professional discourses (80). Segal et al. close their essay with overarching recommendations about how rhetoricians can balance accommodationist and critical approaches by assuming more participatory stances:

> *Gain knowledge slowly and respectfully, ideally with the collaboration or cooperation of the members of the community being studied.* Urging compositionists to work "delicately, from the inside out, with discipline members not only as 'informants' but also as full partners," Segal et al. advocate acknowledging disciplinary com-

plexity and actively seeking out collaboration with nonwriting specialists (84).

Concentrate on problems that the practitioners recognize as significant within their own frame of reference. According to Segal et al., although composition researchers have an obligation to point to problematic discourse practices, it is sometimes possible to "work sideways from problems that practitioners identify to a reframing of those problems in terms that are permitted by a rhetorical focus" (85). This principle of reframing problems as rhetorical issues is central to consulting activity.

Join their conversations. Segel et al. call for compositionists to publish in other disciplinary forums, present at other discipline's meetings, and conduct workshops in workplaces and, I would add, other academic units.

Use the opportunities provided by education. Segal et al. assert that "talking to students may in the long run be our best means of getting a hearing from professionals" (86). They point to WAC programs as a promising site for the kind of action research program they call for, where the lines between disciplines, professionals, and student are blurred. They caution against confusing means with ends, so that WAC programs do not turn into sites where compositionists smuggle in their own "'right thinking' ideas" and turn students into "moles" who would "convert from within" (87).

Don't expect to use what you know to save anyone. Segal et al. learned from their own work that "initiating discussions among practitioners about the implications of professional discourse . . . is necessarily a slow and delicate process. The cultures we study are intricate, dynamic, subtle" (87). They suggest compositionists enter these disciplinary cultures with patience and caution. Resistance can come from those who feel their power threatened by more critical interpretations. But it can also come from incomprehension or from institutional constraints not immediately perceptible by the rhetorician. Consonant with the learning-to-write approach, Segal et al. emphasize that inquiry should begin with respect for "cultural complexity and the beliefs of others" (88).

As general principles, these recommendations are useful. They begin to offer guidelines for how to "tread lightly on other people's paradigms" (Segal et al. 82). The guidelines for more participatory research tend to resemble roles and methods I identify as occurring in the workshop and reflective inquiry models of consulting. Yet, there may be times when it benefits the consultant to assume a more overt role as a researcher, for example, in a situation where conducting research and formulating reports on the efficacy of a pilot WAC initiative is necessary to expand the program and achieve more funding. Here the consultant may want to adopt a collaborative research relationship similar to ones identified by Walvoord and McCarthy. Another example would be consulting at institutions where research is more valued; it might be advantageous to position oneself as a researcher, even though the aims would fall somewhere between the reflective inquiry and discipline-based research models of consulting as I described them.

CONCLUSION

The discussion of consulting models in this chapter was mainly a descriptive effort to synthesize various methods that have been developed and reported on previously. What I hope to be my contribution is bringing these methods together in a way that provides heuristic ways of thinking of about academic writing consulting. One model is not necessarily preferable than the others, for instance. Whereas the service and discipline-based research modes of consulting are more likely to bear negative implications, in certain situations there are advantages to these models. Conversely, when aligned with sound theories of composition and WAC, service models have many benefits. The consulting typology discussed in the chapter provides a repertoire of roles and stances that may be appropriate at given times in a particular situation— or that the consultant can recognize as worth avoiding, as is often the case when others desire narrow service models of support.

Explaining the range of approaches to consulting also helps explain what it means to know "how to collaborate" in the name of enhancing discipline-specific rhetorical education. In particular, to achieve WAC ends, the writing specialist assumes a rhetorical approach, chooses among several methods, perhaps modifying existing methods or creating new ones (see Table 4.2), and uses them as tools to facilitate reflective inquiry into writing practices among particular faculty in specific contexts. When operating in an interactionist framework, the consultant borrows from existing theories (as generalizations) of writing and discipline-specific discourse to help the faculty member contextualize particular pedagogical questions. The consultant does not offer prescriptions, but guiding generalizations whose fit must be tested according to the faculty member's needs and goals.

It is likely that consultants working in service modes use similar rhetoric-based heuristic methods to conduct their work. However, in workshop and reflective inquiry modes, the writing consultant operates out of an interactionist framework, taking an approach that does not preclude the co-con-

Table 4.2. Writing Consultancy Inquiry Methods and Some Sources[a]

Interviewing	• Interview teacher (Odell, Dick and Esch, Kuriloff) • Interview students (Faigley and Hansen) • Conduct focus groups (Huot) • Survey faculty (Weiser)
Analyzing texts	• Examine course documents (syllabi, writing assignments) (Dick and Esch) • Examine student texts (Odell; Dick and Esch) • Examine professional texts (Dick and Esch) • Examine teacher response/feedback (Dick and Esch) • Collect student think-aloud protocols (Odell)
Reflecting	• Write and reflect on student assignment (Odell) • Keep a journal by consultant and instructor for records and reflection (Lamb; Mullin et al.) • Compare goals and expectations of writing specialist and faculty member(s) (Kalamaras; Kuriloff; McCarthy and Fishman; Mullin et al.) • Free-write on consulting relationship/experience (Odell; Mullin et al.)
Observing	• Observe/participate in classes, for example, teachers, student–teacher interaction, collaborative groups, and so on (Faigley and Hansen; Kalamaras; Mullin et al.) • Observe students, for example, learning across classes (McCarthy)

[a]With the exception of the survey, quantitative methods are conspicuously absent from this list. This reflects the prevailing constructivist research paradigm of composition studies. For use of quantitative methods see, for example, Gorman's "Mucking Around" in Young and Fulwiler's *Research into Practice* (1986). Weiss and Peich discuss their use of the Daly–Miller survey of writing apprehension in a faculty workshop. Walvoord observes that quantitative "counting" of Workshop participants and writing-intensive courses, for example, can be useful assessment data, depending on the aim of assessment ("Conduit").

struction of knowledge. That is, service models of consulting tend to reproduce current-traditional form and content dichotomies that, in practice, arrest the active construction of the participating faculty member's rhetorical knowledgeability and, hence, ability to integrate rhetorical education into his or her disciplinary teaching in any sustainable way. The reflective inquiry and discipline-based research models are perhaps best conceived as overlapping categories distinguished by whether the emphasis is on the production of local or global rhetorical knowledge, and whether that knowledge is directed to the local audience immediately affected and invested in the inquiry or the discipline of composition studies and its constituents, an audience interested but nonetheless removed from the immediate context of inquiry. That is, the immediate audience differs between the professionals that have a more pragmatic stake in the research and compositionists interested in the implications of research for theoretical and pedagogical reasons.

Segal et al.'s articulation of an ideological approach to rhetorical study and teaching, one that calls for more action-oriented, participatory strategies, blurs the boundaries between formal discipline-oriented WID research activities and education-oriented WAC activities. In essence, the "research" activities traditionally associated with disciplinary knowledge construction converge with the consulting activities associated with ("mere") teaching and translation of that knowledge. I see this typology of academic writing consulting as mapping the intersection of such scholarly goals in academic contexts. That is, the kind of participatory, action research called for by Segal et al. and others has already been happening for decades locally, in WAC programs across North America, under the guise of faculty development and writing consulting activity.

NOTES

1. *Service* has a special meaning for compositionists. As Sharon Crowley explains, whereas most disciplines have traditionally claimed status through service to the public or to institutions, writing instruction—because of its association with instrumental, even remedial, instruction in formalistic language conventions—has historically been perceived as subordinate, "low" work in relation to other academic labor. The name of this model intentionally evokes composition studies' conflicted "service" ethos.

2. Generic WAC teaching methods have been codified in such texts as John Bean's *Engaging Ideas* (1996), Barbara Walvoord's *Helping Students Write Well* (1987), Andrew Moss and Carol Holder's *Improving Student Writing* (1988), and Art Young's *Teaching Writing Across the Curriculum* (3rd ed. 1999).

3. Faculty teaching in WI programs must often conform to programmatic standards, such as including a percentage of informal writing and allowing for revision of drafts. At the same time, it is considered essential that program guidelines be very loose, otherwise risk discouraging faculty from participation (Farris and Smith 78).

4. See Mullin et al. and Haviland et al. for practical and theoretical discussions of graduate student–disciplinary faculty collaboration. Haviland et al., for instance, discuss a "graduate composition course in WAC offered in conjunc-

tion with a faculty WAC seminar" (52). The graduate students, who also sat in on the faculty seminar, were then paired with those faculty as the later taught a WI course. At the risk of oversimplifying Haviland et al.'s argument, the graduate student "tutor," situated in a middle space between professional and novice, writing specialist and generalist, helps faculty members assume similar stances, thus leading to more productive collaboration. Haviland et al.'s graduate student model also avoids the missionary, colonizer, or handmaiden (i.e., the adjunct status of writing and writing instructors) stances of other WAC models (52).

5.   These are of course tenuous divisions. Often, research undertaken for local reasons eventually finds a global audience (see, e.g., Faigley and Hansen; Huot). But as Phelps points out, reflective inquiry frequently is manifested in such texts as curriculum designs, course policy sheets, and individual lesson plans ("Practical Wisdom"). Traditionally, these texts are not validated as research until they are disseminated globally, in peer-reviewed journals. I explore the implications of these distinctions for CCL work more in chapter 6.

6.   Harper also points to Kaufer and Young's interactionist theory of expertise for explaining the unique contribution of the writing specialist in WAC contexts (see Chapter 2).

7.   For a discussion of how genre theory can work in WAC-related service-learning initiatives, see Jolliffe.

5

THE PROCESS OF ACADEMIC
WRITING CONSULTING

The typology developed in chapter 4 demonstrated *what* the consultant knows and does. In this chapter, I address the question of *how* the consultant does it, or how the writing specialist facilitates a relationship that leads to substantive change, one that helps the nonwriting specialist better understand the role and function of writing in particular settings and avoids its subordination. In other words, this chapter deals with the process of academic writing consulting. Not only did the writing specialists profiled in chapter 3 know how to ask the right questions, but they also appeared to know how to cultivate and maintain effective relationships in CCL contexts. That is, in terms of Schulman's framework of teacher knowledge, these writing specialists seemed to possess skills in addition to their "content" knowledge of rhetorical theory and composition pedagogy; they also seemed to possess a certain procedural knowledge of application, what Schulman calls pedagogical content knowledge, the "blending of content and pedagogy into an understanding of how particular topics, problems, or issues are organized, represented, and adapted to the diverse interests and abilities of learners, and presented for instruction" (8). What are some additional ways that a consultancy framework can help codify this procedural knowledge so that it can be presented as strategies or principles that can guide future practice? I address this question by looking more closely at an episode mentioned in the profile of Laurel from chapter 3. By further applying Edgar Schein's process consultation theory, which I briefly mentioned in my discussion of service consulting in the previous chapter, Laurel's case shows how a consulting framework can help deal with the problem of faculty resistance, a common situation for CCL specialists where the collaboration does not come as easy as when all participants share a collaborative philosophy.

KURILOFF'S FIVE-STAGE MODEL OF WRITING CONSULTING

Dialogue among faculty on teaching is a "natural outcome" of WAC, asserts Peshe Kuriloff, who presents perhaps the most comprehensive "model of consultation that involves collaborative course design and team teaching" (13). Although it is designed as a tool for faculty from different disciplines designing team-taught writing courses, Kuriloff's model has broader applications, particularly for the kind of reflective inquiry promoted by CCL consultants. Like Dick and Esch, Kuriloff provides a set of specific guiding questions to aid collaborative inquiry. In addition, Kuriloff's model encompasses the process of course design by outlining five stages of consultation:

Stage 1: Joint Goal Setting. For Kuriloff, consultation begins with initial meetings focused on answering questions about each participant's assumptions about language, learning goals for the particular course, methods for evaluating that learning, and the type of classroom environment desired (see Table 5.1). Kuriloff stresses the importance of establishing common goals, determining responsibilities, and defining roles. In a team-teaching context between a writing specialist and colleague, "determining who takes responsibility for what in a subject matter-based writing course can raise difficult questions about the relationship between the content of a text and its expression" (145). Role definition—clarifying each instructor's status, understanding the relationship of those roles, ensuring the writing instructor is not "reduced to a grammarian or stylist," and accepting comfortable roles—is essential.

Stage 2: Inquiry and Self-Study. Next, the team examines the function of writing in the given discipline by asking questions such as "What are the forms of writing practiced in engineering?" and "What do those forms reveal about how engineers think?" (see Table 5.1). These questions, which could be asked of any writing situation, are akin to the rhetoric-based heuristics of Dick and Esch, Faigley and Hansen, and Huot that I discussed in chapter 4.

Stage 3: Creating a Context. To help translate the results of inquiry into writing in the discipline, Kuriloff suggests raising questions about the classroom context, including assumptions about discipline-specific learning processes (see Table 5.1). These questions elicit the degree to which students are expected to, for example, write like practicing engineers, or like the example of the population geography course discussed in chapters 2 and 4 (Mullin et al.),

Table 5.1. Guiding Questions for Writing Consulting

Joint goal setting	• What is the relationship between reading and writing? • What should students learn about each? • What kinds of reading and writing should they do? • How should student progress be evaluated? • What type of classroom environment should be fostered?
Inquiry and self-study	• What are the forms of writing used in the discipline? • What do these forms reveal about how practitioners think? • How is new knowledge created? • What type of reasoning, questions, and evidence does the discipline respect? • What kind of language is used?
Creating a context	• What forms of writing are appropriate for student writers? • What audiences should they address? • What purposes should they achieve? • What models should they read? • How do you want students to think? • What is their relationship to knowledge inside their field and outside it?
Implementation	• What will the writing assignments be? • What texts will be assigned? • How will the writing process be emphasized? • In what ways can writing and thinking activities be combined?
Evaluation	• How will success be defined? • What feedback should be collected? • What sources will provide that feedback?

From: Kurlioff (138), with minor syntactical changes to a few questions

demonstrate more general knowledge of the subject. Kuriloff suggests questions similar to Dick and Esch's heuristics, such as "How do engineering students think?" and "What forms and styles of writing are appropriate for them to address?"

Stage 4: Implementation. The insights articulated from the initial conceptualizing during the first three stages are then integrated into a writing-based curricular design, including what the assignments will be, what texts will be assigned, what writing processes will be emphasized, and how writing and thinking activities will be combined (see Table 5.1).

Stage 5: Evaluation. Kuriloff considers questions of course evaluation, including how "success" will be defined, what feedback is desirable, and what are the best ways to collect that data (see Table 5.1). Not only does this help refine the course, but "good record keeping can provide material for public presentation of the experience" (137-148).

Kuriloff doesn't specify how this process is structured over time, but these stages would not be discrete. Rather, they would necessarily overlap and be interrelated to one another. For instance, joint inquiry (Stage 1) during an initial exploratory meeting would likely involve brainstorming answers to questions Kuriloff assigns to all five stages. At that point, it might be determined that more formal, in-depth self-study (Stage 2) and inquiry into the classroom context (Stage 3) might be necessary before (re)considering questions of implementation (Stage 4) and evaluation (Stage 5). Kuriloff's model is built on the collaborative philosophy I described in chapter 2, based on shared authority and consensus. Echoing Roen and Mittan's principles of collaboration, Kuriloff stresses the importance of compatibility: "When collaboration breaks down, generally one person must cede authority to the other or the effort falls apart. Should an impasse occur, you can often transform a collaborative relationship into a simpler consultation" (148). This advice reflects the line I draw between the reflective inquiry and service models of consultation. Moving from "collaboration" to a "simpler consultation" can lead to the subordination of writing and the writing specialist. As I discuss shortly, what is needed is more guidance on how writing consultants might overcome the "impasses" that could lead to simpler consultations/service consulting and, hence, reduced integration of writing, teaching, and learning.

One important aspect of Kuriloff's model is that it incorporates assessment. As Miraglia and McLeod's study of successful WAC programs demonstrated, programs most "enduring," that is, those that are still in existence since 1987, are those that reported engaging in more rigorous assessment activities (54). When approached systematically, the procedures and outcomes of localized classroom inquiry lend themselves to public reports demonstrating, for example, improvements in student writing, the effects of writing on learning, and faculty productivity (Fulwiler, "Evaluating"; Huot and Yancey; Walvoord et al.).

Kuriloff's team-teaching framework provides a useful roadmap for structuring the process of academic writing consulting. But the framework is an abstraction, another theory of collaboration. The writing specialist still must utilize a certain procedural knowledge in the process of applying any generalized model of collaboration. In other words, writing specialists must also know how to manage the process of consulting, a skill that I have suggested is closely related to Schulman's notion of pedagogical content knowledge. In the next section, I return to the case of Laurel to examine the tacit process by which a consultant builds and maintains a collaborative relationship focused on CCL issues.

PROCESS CONSULTATION AND WAC: ADDRESSING THE PROBLEM OF FACULTY RESISTANCE

In the first profile of chapter 3, Laurel reflected on some of her past faculty consultations, pointing to how the faculty member's "personality" shapes whether or not a truly collaborative relationship was formed or a lesser type she called "providing resources." In the absence of a formal WAC program, faculty often came to her WC for help with revising an assignment or questions about how the center can address the writing needs of students. Laurel had fond recollections of her collaboration with the department head of Physical Therapy. He assumed a very nonauthoritarian stance and was very willing to devote his time (and department resources) to improving writing instruction in his department. On the other hand was the case of the electrical engineering professor, who in Laurel's words, "fell off the bad continuum." He appeared very close-minded, and, outside of a stated desire for the WC to grade his students' papers for grammatical errors, he was reluctant to entertain Laurel's many efforts to educate him about the WC's services and about composition pedagogy. He could not hear, for some reason, how Laurel was offering to help him with the perceived problem of poor student writing. She spent considerable time trying to convince him why grading harshly for grammar was ineffective, how working with students' final drafts was ineffective, and how his grading (for grammar) policies were creating hostility among students and even the tutors in the center. In effect, the electrical engineer wanted someone else to take care of writing issues in his course. He was unwilling to consider changing his pedagogy or curriculum, preferring instead to have someone else teach writing. But this is not the aim of WAC. How can a consultancy framework help explain this situation and what might be some alternative strategies for handling it? Although Laurel's case does not occur within the boundaries of a formal WAC program, it is relevant because it involves a scenario common to any WAC program. It is also relevant given that many WAC programs are housed in writing centers (Barnett and Blumner; Waldo, *Demythologizing*).

Foremost, it appears the electrical engineer was adhering to assumptions I have attributed to the service model of consulting. The electrical engineer implicitly made clear divisions between content and form, ideas and their representation, the teaching of "engineering" and the teaching of writing. He may have even outwardly viewed English as a lower status department. In reflection, Laurel admitted that she did not pay close attention to the collaborative dynamic. That is, she didn't pay direct attention to the assumptions each were making about their relationship, about their roles, about the nature of expert relationships in general:

> I thought we had other problems that were more immediately pressing. I didn't think about these things because I kept thinking that what we really needed to do is to talk about what writing really is, but I couldn't find a way for him to listen to me. Feeling defeated about that, I never thought about the issue of collaboration. I felt defeated that we could not talk about the subject that we needed to talk about, i.e., What is writing? How do people learn to write better? And when it became clear that that door was closed, I guess I gave up. . . . Rather than a failed relationship, I didn't do something right because he never understood, and never opened up to thinking about it. And then you have the larger question, When someone tries to teach someone else something or open up the door, who is the failed person, the person who won't listen or the other person who tried to open the door?

Laurel raises questions about who is responsible for the "failure" of the relationship. The less obvious answer is that both Laurel and the electrical engineer contributed in some way to a failure to communicate, or an inability to forge an understanding that could lead to more substantive interaction. The service model of consulting is rooted in traditional assumptions about expertise and the consultant–client relationship. In the general skills model of expertise, the expert possesses a wealth of supposedly applicable technical knowledge that the client does not possess. In the purchase model of consulting, the client assumes there is some need or problem he or she cannot solve and thus requests that an expert fill this gap, in the form of some service or delivery of information—through the application of (someone else's) technical knowledge.

But there are problems with the purchase model of consulting, argues Edgar Schein, who has theorized the process of consultant interventions in the subfield of management studies known as organization development (OD), an applied field in the social sciences that examines how organizations and the working lives of individuals can be improved through planned change interventions. OD draws from such theories and methods as group dynamics, management theory, appreciative inquiry, and industrial and personal psychology. OD professionals acting as consultants to organizations aim to create situations where learning and change can take place among individuals and groups. Much OD theory is geared toward promoting humanistic and democratic values within organizations (Burke; French, Bell, and Zawacki; Van Eynde et al.).[1] In a series of books, Edgar Schein has developed what he calls process consultation, a "philosophy of 'helping,' and a technology or methodology of how to be helpful" (*Revisited* xi; *Role*; *Lessons*). Process consultation is "a philosophy about and attitude toward the process of helping individuals, groups, organizations, and communities" (*Revisited* 1). Schein's theory examines questions about "what the consultant looks for, how the process starts, how a relationship is developed with the client, what kinds of interventions are made, how the process is evaluated, and how it is terminated" (*Role* 4). Because Schein offers a general model for consulting in any context where one person seeks help from another person, I see his theory as having applications for academic writing consulting.

The electrical engineer in Laurel's case seemed to ascribe to the assumptions Schein outlines for the purchase model of consulting. The success of purchase model exchanges, according to Schein, depend on many factors, first and foremost of which is whether the "buyer" of the service has correctly diagnosed her own needs (see Table 5.2). It also depends on a multitude of other contingent factors, including whether the buyer has "communicated these needs to the consultant" and whether she has "thought through the consequences of implementing changes which may be recommended by the consultant" (*Role* 5). According to Schein, the number of contingencies that must go right in this common model help explain "the frequent dissatisfaction voiced by managers with the quality of services they feel they receive" (*Process* 5). The electrical engineer narrowly defined his need as *graders who will read final papers strictly for grammar (and not for content)*. When Laurel, the writing expert, suggested this was not really an effective way to improve student writing, the electrical engineer, in effect, balked. He came looking for expert help, but had not thought through the consequences of what information might be returned to him. He was indeed closed to any suggestion outside his own predetermined intervention.

Schein suggests behavior like this is also attributable to another prevailing model of expertise, what he calls the "doctor–patient" model (see Table 5.2). In this model, which is closely related to the purchase model, the client calls in an expert consultant to examine his or her needs, much like what a patient expects from a doctor. After a period of diagnosis, the consultant is supposed to find out what is wrong, and then, like a physician, recommend a program of therapy. Although this model is very appealing to clients, it is also very problematic. In organizational contexts, the unit or department that is defined as ailing might be reluctant to reveal important details related to the diagnosis because of fear or mistrust. According to Schein, another problem with the doctor–patient model is that the "patient" can sometimes refuse to believe or fail to accept the "prescription" offered by the consultant:

Table 5.2. Edgar Schein's Models of Organization Development Consulting

	The Purchase-of-Information or Expertise Model	The Doctor–Patient Model	The Process Consultation Model
Who defines the problem?	Client determines need that he or she does not see him or herself having the time or know-how to address	The consultant diagnoses problem after soliciting feedback from client	Client and consultant jointly diagnose client's need
What role does the consultant assume?	The consultant acts as the technical expert who fills this need by providing services or information/ knowledge	Consultant acts as doctor applying diagnostic tools to client's situation .	Consultant becomes helper who passes on diagnostic and problem-solving skills to client
What role does the client assume?	The client becomes the passive buyer of consultant's service	Client becomes patient who passively subjects him or herself to consultant's diagnosis	Client becomes active owner, or diagnostician and problem solver, of situation
Whose reality/ epistemology is privileged	The client determines what counts as useful help from his or her perspective	The consultant determines what counts as useful from his or her perspective	Client and consultant agree on what counts as useful help from shared perspective
Limitations	Success depends on many factors, including how well client has defined his or her needs and whether consultant's advice meets expectations of client	Success depends on many factors, including whether or not client accepts consultant's diagnosis and can reasonably implement consultant's recommendations	Success depends on many factors, including whether or not client is willing to take an active role in defining, analyzing, and implementing a solution.

I suspect most companies have drawers full of reports by consultants, each loaded with diagnoses and recommendations which are either not understood or not accepted by the "patient." What is wrong, of course, is that the doctor, the consultant, has not build up the common diagnostic frame of reference with the patient, his client. If the consultant does all the diagnosis while the client-manager waits passively for a prescription, it is predictable that a communication gulf will arise which will make the prescription seem irrelevant and/or unpalatable. (Schein, *Role* 7)

This model also offers insight into the electrical engineer's behavior. It is as if he was confident he knew what was wrong (with his students really), and when the "doctor" didn't prescribe the medicine he expected to receive, he became reluctant—we could even say resistant. But his resistance is, to echo a point made by Debra Swanson-Owens, "natural." Swanson-Owens studied secondary school teachers' natural sources of resistance, the observable discrepancies between WAC programmatic goals and teachers' practice:

[These discrepancies] are appropriate given the presence of particular mismatches between outsider and insider meaning systems. Indeed, teachers' responses seem "resistant" to the extent that they violate outsiders' expectations; at the same time, they are "natural" or appropriate insofar as they reflect teachers' commitments to effective practice as they know it. (72)

The electrical engineer's attitude is thus a conditioned behavior. It is not necessarily a deliberate stance but a role that the faculty member assumes based on prevailing assumptions of expertise, of writing, of the role of writing instructors, and perhaps other factors. Walvoord et al. fault resistance case studies for their implicit presumption that the outsider knows best what good practice is (i.e., WAC orthodox strategies), and the doctor–patient model helps clarify the problematic assumptions researchers make in such studies. Although we must be careful to avoid colonizing stances regarding faculty resistance, for WAC-related faculty development programs to be successful on a long-term basis, they must nonetheless learn how to deal with the "tire-kickers," as Linda (profiled in chapter 3) called them—the middle- and late-adapters, skeptics and naysayers, and otherwise good people who are too busy to imagine change.

Schein's doctor–patient model suggests three possible explanations for the electrical engineer's behavior. First, there was no "common diagnostic frame" built up between Laurel and the electrical engineer. When Laurel suggested grading for grammar was ineffective, the engineer could not seem to get outside of his own assumptions and experiences enough to see alternative practices related to writing instruction. The WAC workshop has traditionally served as the site where this common diagnostic frame is established, but the engineer had no meaningful exposure to WAC. Second, the electrical engineer was assuming a passive stance in the diagnosis of the problem (i.e., "my students' writing skills are broken, you fix them"). He may have been too willing to yield authority to the expert, for likely a complex of legitimate reasons, including lack of knowledge of writing, the size of the course, his overall workload, and possibly other priorities (some of Laurel's comments suggest he was acting as an arm of his department head and perhaps overtly or covertly acting out some departmental political agenda). Third, and closely related to the second point, Laurel's suggestions may not have seemed feasible to the electrical engineer given his current perspective. As Schein writes, "It is often obvious to the consultant what must be done, but the culture of the organization, its structure, or its politics prevents the recommendation from being implemented" (*Role* 15). Because of his workload or a mandated curriculum, he may have been reluctant or unable to see how to significantly alter his current course and the way he teaches it. He may have viewed reading drafts and final papers as too time-consuming (despite his department head's desire to push a writing initiative).

In the absence of the electrical engineer participating in a WAC workshop—which immediately presents itself as one solution (one that wasn't possible given Laurel's limited budget and ambivalent mission)—how might the writing consultant establish a common diagnostic frame from which to address the perceived problem of student writing? Schein suggests that it is the consultant's own attitude and behavior, particularly at the very beginning of a relationship, that contributes to the establishment of what he refers to as a "jointly shared reality in which communication is possible" (*Revisited* 16). In other words, it is up to the consultant to establish a relationship where the client is not positioned in the passive roles that Schein attributes to purchase or doctor–patient models. These roles, as indicated previously, often lead to problematic assumptions on the part of the client as to how the consultant is supposed to act, and what kind of service or information she is supposed to provide. Rather, the consultant must consciously and deliberately attempt to move the relationship into a more mutually participatory framework.

Schein defines this activity as process consultation (see Table 5.2). Process consultation assumes that "neither the client nor the consultant knows enough at the point of initial contact to define the kind of expertise that might be relevant to the situation" (*Revisited* 9). Therefore, the consultant engages the client in a period of joint diagnosis:

> The importance of *joint* diagnosis derives from the fact that the consultant can seldom learn enough about the organization to really know what a better course of action would be for that *particular group* of people with their *particular* sets of traditions, styles, and personalities. However, the consultant can help the manager become a sufficiently

good diagnostician himself, and can provide enough alternatives, to enable the manager to solve the problem. . . . [T]he consultant has a role in teaching diagnostic and problem-solving skills, but he should not work on the actual concrete problem himself. (Schein, *Role* 6)

This statement from Schein is particularly insightful, especially given the familiar metaphorical representation of organizations and disciplines as distinct cultures. Schein echoes the anthropology-influenced WID standpoint that holds writing specialists should, in Christine Farris' words, "work against the 'colonizer' mentality" by "getting inside" disciplinary cultures to gain "local knowledge of how this particular culture functions for these citizens" (115). Schein reinforces the notion, suggested by Farris, that the writing specialist can never truly "know" another discipline. Rather, an interactionist exchange of expertise is necessary to help faculty understand how writing operates in their classrooms and disciplines. Moreover, according to Schein, the goal of consultation is to *teach the process* of diagnosis, so that clients can become sufficiently good diagnosticians themselves. In this way, problems will stay solved longer as the client learns to apply the diagnostic skills to the demands of particular situations. This last point underscores a major limitation of service models of writing consulting as I have described them: Without faculty ownership, WAC provides only partial and short-term fixes to the complex problem of discipline-specific rhetorical education.

Schein defines process consultation as "a set of activities on the part of the consultant which help the client to perceive, understand, and act upon process events which occur in the client's environment" (*Role* 9).[2] In Schein's process consultation model, the client

must learn to see the problem for herself or himself by sharing in the diagnostic process and be actively involved in generating a remedy. . . . The ultimate function of [process consultation] is to pass on the skills of how to diagnose and constructively intervene so that clients are more able to continue on their own to improve the organization. In a sense both the expert and doctor models are remedial models whereas the [process consultation] model is both a remedial and a preventative model. The saying "instead of giving people fish, teach them how to fish" fits this model. (*Revisited* 16, 19)

According to Schein, if clients acquire the diagnostic skills to identify and address perceived problems, they will be more likely to implement appropriate and lasting solutions: "problems will be solved more permanently and the client will have learned the skills necessary to solve new problems as they arise" (*Revisited* 16). "The process consultant may play a key role in helping to sharpen the diagnosis, and to be actively involved in providing alternative remedies which may not have occurred to the client"; however,

according to Schein, the consultant "encourages the client to make the ultimate decision as to what remedy to apply" (*Role* 7).

This model is very much in line with the WID approach, which calls for
critical sensitivity to the situatedness of disciplinary discourse communities.
Like Kaufer and Young's work, it foregrounds the nature of the interaction
between the writing specialist and the faculty member. Although the *ends* are
in line, discussions like those by Kaufer and Young in composition and
Schein in management studies also help articulate *means* as well. Process consultation is, according to Schein, "more of a philosophy or a set of underlying assumptions about the helping process that lead the consultant to take a
certain kind of attitude toward his or her relationship with the client"
(*Revisited* 21). Like WID approaches, Schein's model assumes faculty are
most knowledgeable of their particular needs and goals and that the consultant helps the faculty come to understand the relationship of writing and writing instruction to these objectives. But where WID theory may sometimes
fall short in offering explicit guidance how to accomplish this, Schein's model
helps provide insight into how the consultant can best accomplish the balancing of general composition theory (i.e., remedial interventions) and specific
disciplinary/classroom practices (preventive interventions).

Process consultation suggests that, in a similar situation as the case of
the close-minded engineer, the writing consultant might profit by directing
the relationship into a process mode rather than a doctor–patient mode.
Rather than offering a diagnosis right away—even though she may have a
clearly appropriate recommendation in mind ("grading for grammar is ineffective")—the writing consultant would instead suspend the diagnosis and
suggest that she does not know enough about the situation to offer a feasible solution. This is hard to do, writes Schein, because "when you have a
hammer the whole world looks like a bunch of nails" (Revisited 8). That is,
the consultant is tempted to make premature assessments about appropriate
practice without carefully considering the particular situation or the relationship dynamic. As Schein explains, drawing from a constructivist epistemology, "there is a subtle assumption that there is knowledge 'out there' to
be brought into the client system and that this information, or knowledge,
will be understandable and usable by the client." But knowledge is situated,
or as Schein puts it, any reality apart from that which is constructed between
the client and the consultant is an "elusive concept" (*Revisited* 8). Giving a
diagnosis too soon (i.e., offering a generic WAC strategy) risks establishing
a less-than-effective power relationship (i.e., doctor to patient), and quite
possibly offending or confusing clients, who can presumed to be genuinely
interested in improving their "organization," or classroom. For Schein,

The temptation to accept the power that the other person grants [the consultant] when he asks for advice is overwhelming. It takes extraordinary discipline in those situations to reflect for a moment on what is actually going on (deal with reality) and to ask a question that might reveal more or encourage the other to tell [the consultant] more before [the consultant] accepts the doctor role. . . . The immediate reality is that, at the beginning of any relationship, the consultant does not know what is really being asked or is needed. It is this state of *ignorance* that is, in fact, the consultant's most important guideline for deciding what questions to ask, what advice to give, or in general what to do next. (*Revisited* 8, 10)

Rather than assuming a doctor role, and rush to diagnosis, the writing consultant might recommend an exploratory meeting where they would jointly study the needs of the faculty member (e.g., his or her course/curriculum goals), his or her motivations, perceived problems, tentative solutions, willingness to devote time and energy to research the problem, and so on. Kaufer and Young's discussion of the inappropriateness of expressive journal writing for biology notebooks is another example of a "rushed diagnosis." The consultant and the client must first jointly define what the problem is, based on a shared reality. Only then can they further decide what kind of help is needed. According to Schein, "The consultant must display expertise at giving help and at establishing a relationship with clients that makes it possible to be helpful and that builds a jointly shared reality in which communication is possible" (*Revisited* 16). Linda, the writing specialists profiled in chapter 3, articulated a similar approach that she attributed to her skill in "listening" to faculty and her ability to "read" their needs:

It's the one-to-one that does it. The sense that someone's there that is really going to listen to them and not tell them what to do, but give them a menu from which they choose items that they feel comfortable with as a teacher, that fits that course and discipline. And I help them translate activities, methodologies into something that is comfortable as well as appropriate for that discipline's ends. That's the spirit and the action which I'm going to do all this.

The writing specialist would, in essence, move the faculty member into a workshop or reflective inquiry model described in chapter 4, wherein the writing specialist and faculty member would go through a series of exploratory, heuristic exercises to articulate the faculty member's assumptions about course goals, the function of student writing, and so forth. Instead of talking about "what writing really is," the focus shifts to "what writing really is for the faculty member in that particular situation." Thus, the consultant enacts the same nondirective stance common for workshops

(and, to an extent, discipline-based research). And just as in workshop
modes, the consultant is teaching by modeling the procedural knowledge of
heuristic rhetorical inquiry. This stance is often, because of tacit assumptions
about expertise, not consciously considered outside workshop contexts.
That is, consultations typically are framed, as I've argued, in purchase and
doctor–patient modes. Schein's process model of consultation is consonant
with the reflective inquiry model, where the consultant initiates activities
designed to help faculty in other disciplines get outside their everyday
thinking, frame problems in rhetorical contexts, and articulate the operation
of writing and rhetoric in particular classroom settings. The emphasis shifts
from the writing specialist's transmission of (technical) knowledge, to the
co-construction of situated knowledge between writing specialist and faculty member. This shift, in turn, highlights the development of the faculty
member's procedural knowledge, useful for understanding the rhetoricity of
their disciplinary activity, including teaching. This stance resonates with the
missionary critique in the WAC literature and partly explains why missionary stances are less appropriate.

The notion that writing consultants must first pay attention to establishing a relationship where reality can be "jointly negotiated" is also consonant
with the literature of WAC collaboration that has noted the complexity of
negotiating a "shared language" necessary for collaboratively understanding
writing in disciplinary classrooms (McCarthy and Fishman, "Boundary";
Mullin et al.). This process, as these studies have shown, takes considerable
time to expose assumptions, unravel misunderstandings, and establish a
common analytic framework. It suggests that the consultant avoid expert or
doctor roles and pay attention to developing a common diagnostic framework, even in informal consulting relationships like the casual phone call or
the faculty member who drops in with a question.

As a caveat, Schein states that the minimum underlying condition for
the process model to work is that a person has a sincere desire to improve
some situation and is willing to seek help. Consultants should be cautious of
going forward in situations where the client does not appear willing: "The
spirit of inquiry is an essential characteristic of a potentially successful
client-consultant relationship" (*Role* 81). Clearly, the electrical engineer did
not exhibit this minimum characteristic. And Laurel certainly tried to establish the kind of helping relationship Schein refers to as process consultation.
"I was in my tutor mode," she said.

> I wanted him to think about some things. I kept asking questions, which
> he would not address. He would not respond to the questions I was ask-
> ing about writing in general. If I do a workshop with people, I like to
> have them start by reflecting on their own writing. Once they start
> reflecting on their own writing, you just got them. They begin to think
> about their writing, and they you say, "Well, what about your stu-

dents?" And they say, "Oh yeah, of course." He wouldn't start back there. I would ask those questions face to face, and he would just breeze on with how he's going to send his students in.

Here, Laurel shows herself tacitly transferring workshop methods (and tutoring methods) to her one-to-one consultations. But they weren't working on this faculty member, as she later realized as she reflected on her past action. "I probably took longer [with him] than I should have," she admitted. "I would probably credit that to my lack of perception that we weren't moving anywhere, that I kept up with him. . . . At some point you just have to cut your losses and quit."

To a degree, Laurel's wisdom matches Schein's advice, which is another lesson from this case. Schein recommends that the consultant pay careful attention to the potential client's "degree of openness, spirit of inquiry, and authenticity of communication" during the initial exploratory meeting (*Role* 81). If these essential qualities are lacking, it may not be worth proceeding at that time. As Schein suggests,

> I try to assess the responses I get to some of my questions. If I ask whether the [potential client] is willing to sit down and explore things, I look for a response which indicates genuine willingness. If the [potential client] seems too certain he already *knows* what is wrong [or] if he has me miscast as an expert in something which I am not expert . . . these are all reasons for caution. If I feel the [potential client] merely wants reassurance for some course of action he has already embarked on or wants a quick solution for a surface problem, I will be reluctant to proceed. If none of the barriers described above arises, the exploratory meeting becomes the first major diagnostic step toward the establishment of a relationship. (*Role* 81)

What is unclear from Laurel's reflections is how and when she balanced her expert role, offering technical advice about composition pedagogy, and her process consultant role, asking questions and trying to prompt the electrical engineer into a reflective inquiry model. Schein suggests that how and when the consultant balances these roles—how she balances "remedial" and "preventative" interventions—is important to the establishment of a helping relationship. There will always be times when the consultant will offer educative interventions (offering technical suggestions, general strategies, feedback from observations, coaching, etc.) but according to Schein, the process mode is necessary at the beginning of the helping process because only through joint diagnosis can the consultant help clients define their needs and suggest further inquiry or action.

So, we can never know for sure how the collaboration between Laurel and the electrical engineer may have went had Laurel consciously adopted a different consulting role, or whether the engineer was indeed completely closed to anything Laurel might do. However, as this case and my analysis aims to show, through the process of practical inquiry into academic writing consulting, perhaps it becomes easier to recognize such a type as the close-minded electrical engineer, and maybe by recognizing this type, a writing specialist can begin to more consciously adopt different roles and use different strategies. As Schein's theory of process consultation shows, particularly when compared to the Laurel's case, there can be *system* to helping faculty gain rhetorical knowledgeability—and as such, it can be articulated and taught.

BUILDING THEORIES OF ACADEMIC WRITING CONSULTING PRACTICE

In this and the previous chapter, I used the concept of consulting as a lens to theorize the intellectual work of writing specialists working in cross-disciplinary writing programs. I've tried to suggest the professional dimension of writing consulting, brought about when CCL specialists focus or systematically reflect on the role the collaborative dynamic plays in achieving WAC ends. The consulting models as I've described them are *sources of techniques* for faculty development, and as such, they are not too far off from existing discourse on models of "WAC for faculty" (McLeod, "Defining"). However, the typology in chapter 4 and the discussion of the process of writing consulting in this chapter provide a clearer picture of what the CCL specialist knows and does. The typology, in other words, further articulates the knowledge-base of academic writing consultants. In addition to possessing technical knowledge, consultants also possess a procedural knowledge resembling Schulman's notion of pedagogical content knowledge that enables them to apply abstract consulting principles to specific situations. CCL specialists also know the *process* of academic writing consulting.

The case of Laurel provides insight into the frequently cited consulting skill variously identified as "reading" (Laurel, profiled in chapter 3), "listening" (McCarthy and Fishman, "Boundary"), or "negotiating" (Mullin et al.). This topic warrants further inquiry. In an early discussion of faculty workshop methods, Weiss and Peich reflect on how group theory in social psychology helped explain the seemingly resistant behavior of faculty early in the workshop as a predictable period of general self-orienting behavior. They learned that it takes time for members to feel comfortable, risk disclosure, and communicate freely and that seemingly hostile questions are part of this orienting process. In his process consultation model, Schein speaks of the importance of establishing and maintaining not only the formal contract (which sets the material perimeters of a relationship—duration, place, cost) but also the psychological contract. At the psychological level, Schein writes, "it is important to get out in the open as many misconceptions as possible." The consultant tries to assess the expectations that may "deliberately or unwittingly be concealed by the client. . . . It is important that as many as possible of these misconceptions be revealed early, so they don't function as traps or sources of disappointment later on if and when [the consultant] refuses to go along with something which the client expects of him" (*Role* 85).

Just as OD consultants have techniques for monitoring the maturity and health of group processes, so might the consultant benefit from paying closer attention to building and maintaining the collaborative relationship. In her profile in chapter 3, I noted Patricia's practice of negotiating an actual written contract with colleagues over issues of data, ownership, and voice in situations where they were conducting collaborative research. How might this practice be applied to local classroom inquiry situations? Most WAC programs articulate guiding assumptions that help determine, to some degree, expectations among program participants, but the connection between programmatic goals, faculty development, and particular relationships could be made clearer in the kind of a written agreement that Patricia speaks of. Such policy co-developed by the WAC personnel and faculty might be published in a newsletter, promotional brochure, and/or WAC program Web site. The written agreement would articulate the guiding assumptions of inquiry-based consulting models. A model for such an approach could be human subjects research protocols (Anderson) or ethical guidelines developed in OD consulting contexts (Farrell). The ethical standpoint and practical strategies presented by Segal et al. in chapter 4 provide a good starting point for articulating such a written policy/contract. When translated effectively, such guidelines can also contribute to increasing the sensitivity of the academy to the rhetorical constructedness of discourse, including the recognition of the role rhetoric can play in improving communication within disciplinary contexts. When viewed as an ethical commitment, such policy could also serve as boilerplate information for writing grants and proposing classroom-based inquiry projects, curriculum development pilots, or program assessment. On the other hand, I can also imagine such a policy serving as a lightening rod for criticism and controversy from writing program "enemies" (White). Nonetheless—and this work remains to be done—I think such policy formation and forthrightness would be in line with calls in composition studies to "go public," or to translate and apply composition studies disciplinary knowledge within broader public spheres beyond that of the first-year writing classroom (Anderson; Cushman; J. Harris).

We could also study more closely the skills of, in Schein's words, "diagnosis," or in the words of the WAC specialists profiled in chapter 3, "listening." Schein observes that "it goes without saying that one of the most important things for the consultant to do initially is to listen carefully to the client. Listening is, however, a rather complex activity that can be pursued very actively or passively" (*Revisited* 42). What does it mean to "listen" in CCL contexts? In Linda's profile, listening was a central skill that she variously attributed to her literature training, general people skills, and WAC theory. There is much attention paid in WAC literature to theorizing metaphors of the WAC specialist's role—as missionary, handmaiden, foreigner, anthropologist, ambassador, change agent. Focusing on consulting practice shifts attention to considering metaphors of listening, of reading, of change. In line with critiques of the pathology metaphor of student writing, Schein notes how a focus on "problems" is "itself a metaphor that predisposes us to thinking in deficit, negative, fixing terms" (*Revisited* 56).

The methodologies of active inquiry and appreciative inquiry in OD contexts also have potential applications for academic writing consulting. Appreciative inquiry examines the metaphors of change, focusing on positive models of change such as catalysts, insight, liberation, transformation. Active inquiry works as a technology of active but nonjudgmental listening, a form of open-ended interviewing that seeks to build up the client's confidence, gather information, involve the client in the process of diagnosis, and create a climate of critical introspection. For example, according to Schein, active inquiry involves three levels of inquiry questions: *pure, exploratory/ diagnostic*, and *confrontive*. In pure inquiry mode, the consultant prompts the client to tell the "story" of the situation: "What is the situation? Can you tell me what is going on?" Exploratory/diagnostic questions help "manage the process and content" of the client's story: "How did you feel about that? Why did you do that? What did you do about that? What are you going to do?" Finally, in confrontive inquiry, the consultant shares her own ideas and reactions, but in a way that helps the client think about the situation from a new perspective. This is the "outsider" perspective discussed by Kaufer and Young. Here, the consultant asks such questions as: Could you have done the following . . . ? Have you thought about doing . . .? Have you considered these options . . . ? (*Revisited* ch. 3)

There are also parallels between OD active inquiry and nondirective tutoring methods in writing center theory. Writing fellows often apply similar techniques, but few discussions exist of how such methods work in faculty development interactions. John Thomas Farrell argues—in terms conceptually close to those of this study—that the consulting model is particularly appropriate for, in his context, graduate student tutoring. After noting that humanists generally look upon consulting with skepticism or mystery, Farrell points to the ways codes of ethical conduct for management consultants might usefully address differences between undergraduates' and graduate students' attitudes, motivations, backgrounds and skills. Farrell advances the consulting model as one that aims to establish adult, professional relationships with the graduate students—rejecting both the traditional student–teacher model and the more current collaborative writing teacher model used in writing center discourse. What might similar professional relationships look like in WAC faculty development contexts?

Farrell raises the question of ethical relations. How does the consultant negotiate a critical agenda with the service expectations of the disciplines? As Segal et al. indicate, rhetoricians increasingly agree that understanding the social dimension of writing involves the interrogation of the relationship between discourse and power. These more critical interpretations often seem irrelevant or even threatening to some professionals. Segal et al.'s essay is directed at exploring ways to balance more critical readings and a respect for clients' needs and positionality. Should writing specialists keep their critical agenda hidden from the client? George Kalamaras addresses this issue by characterizing it as a productive *internal tension* for the consultant, a move that essentially conceals the critical agenda from the client. It appears from his essay that these potentially competing agendas were not discussed openly among Kalamaras and the biology department. Is this ethical? How can such a dilemma be resolved? Linda Bergmann makes a connection between differences among WAC/WID approaches and professional ethics. WAC specialists, she argues, must makes ethical decisions about which theories of writing they choose to promote, including the degree to which they accommodate or resist disciplinary discourses. Segal et al. suggest that the writing specialist work first from problems faculty members identify as significant, and help them see their problems in rhetorical contexts. How can the consultant work out these ethical tensions *in practice*? More cases studies of such negotiation could help answer this question.

The frameworks put forth in this chapter are exploratory in the sense that more focused work can illuminate the methodological, epistemological, ideological, social, professional, and personal issues related to the practice of interdisciplinary collaborative consulting. Lee Schulman notes that "one of the frustrations of teaching as an occupation and profession is its extensive individual and collective amnesia, the consistency with which the best creations of its practitioners are lost to both contemporary and future peers" (11). Collecting and interpreting stories and reflections of WAC practice can contribute to our "storehouse" of practitioner knowledge. To add to this knowledge base, as I think we should, we can borrow from scholarship in teacher-research and practical inquiry, which use ethnomethodologies to codify the experientially based, practical wisdom of practitioners. In WAC training programs, such case studies could become a version of Donald Schön's "reflective practicum," a curriculum for developing reflective practice by providing practitioners opportunities to reflect on vignettes and case scenarios (*Educating*). Cases of collaboration, for example, provide grist for the situated performance activities (in-class role-plays) advanced by Shirley Rose and Margaret Finders as a way of providing vicarious experience and developing habits of reflective practice in in-service writing consultants.

But it is not enough to articulate the kinds and sources of consulting knowledge. Any arguments advancing interdisciplinary work must examine the institutional structures and ideologies that constrain such activity, namely the departmentalized structure of the academy and the traditional reward hierarchy valuing research over teaching and service. Chapter 6 examines more closely the question of how academic writing consulting is valued and can be made more valuable.

NOTES

1. For an application of OD theory to WAC/WC program administration issues, see Vaught-Alexander.
2. This definition is from his first book on process consultation. In the most recent book, *Process Consultation Revisited* (1999), Schein expands the definition somewhat: "Process Consultation is the creation of a relationship with the client that permits the client to perceive, understand, and act on the process events that occur in the client's internal and external environment in order to improve the situation as defined by the client" (20). Although this later version highlights the agency and epistemology of the client, the earlier definition is clearer about the contribution, or role, of the consultant.

THE INTELLECTUAL VALUE OF CROSS-CURRICULAR LITERACY WORK

> Let me quote, for example, the letter of one candidate for tenure. He asks, "Can I use material I wrote for money—in one case a 600-page book—as evidence of scholarship? Would my time have been better spent banging out an article this summer rather than working with XYZ Corporation?" The answer, I am afraid, is obvious: in most English departments, writing the refereed journal article would have been a better way to spend his time. Even in an engineering school, the act of writing that 600-page book should have led to further research (that is, funded research), to publication, or to direct impact on his teaching before it became a major issue in tenure review. (Stevenson 353)

While discussing the dynamics of workplace writing consulting, Dwight Stevenson notes how consulting has traditionally been mistrusted in humanities fields: "In engineering, consulting is encouraged because it is expected to lead to research and publication, whereas in English it often is seen as *preventing* research and publication—or as producing publications of unrewardable types" (353). He uses the passage quoted here to illustrate his point. Stevenson is addressing the potential dangers of workplace writing consulting, that writing specialists have to be weary of being lured away from the normal reward system that operates at most academic institutions. As Stevenson admonishes,

> Consulting will compete for the time you need professionally to spend on research and teaching. Make no mistake, consulting is an activity that may be smiled upon by some academic administrators; but it is an activity that ranks significantly below teaching and research in most administrators' minds. No one ever got tenure for consulting. (352)

Stevenson cautions that writing specialists involved in consulting activities should be aware that "consulting is normally seen as an appropriate stimulus to research, publication, and innovative teaching; it is seldom (perhaps never) seen as an alternative to them" (353).

Stevenson's warning has relevance to a discussion of academic writing consulting. The candidate's question from the passage above might reasonably be rephrased as, "Would my time have been better spent banging out an article this summer rather than working with Engineering on their writing proficiency assessment?" The literature of WAC raises issues about the institutionalized barriers to collaboration, namely the faculty-reward system, the departmentalized structure of the academy, and the increasingly heavy workloads of faculty (Ervin and Fox; Holt and Anderson; Kuriloff; Sullivan). According to Pesche Kuriloff, the "department-based authority structure that characterizes most American colleges and universities today restricts many WAC activities to the margins of the curriculum. Formal collaboration and team teaching suffer from marginalization and have proven difficult to institutionalize" (149). Observing that "the *idea* of collaboration has been enthusiastically embraced" in academia, but that the "actual *practice* of genuine collaboration rarely occurs," Elizabeth Ervin and Dana Fox call for the closer examination of the "institutional structures within the academy which suppress collaborative relationships and scholarship" (53). After studying their own experiences and those of their colleagues and mentors, and after looking at the policies in place at the University of Arizona, their home institution, Ervin and Fox conclude that, "while academe has finally acknowledged that collaboration exists, it has not yet recognized its scholarly legitimacy, nor has it developed structures to reward collaborative work" (59). In light of arguments such as these, any discussion of CCL work also has to consider the institutional structures that discourage this type of work and that influence faculty priorities and values.

In this chapter, I examine the extent to which the writing specialists profiled in chapter 3 experienced these institutional barriers in their own professional activity. Specifically, I explore the following questions: How is CCL work assessed/evaluated? How do the CCL specialists fit cross-curricular faculty development activity into the tenure/job expectations of their particular institution? How do CCL specialists describe and document their work? How do they argue the scholarly merit of their work? I do this by first contextualizing considerations of the intellectual character of academic writing consulting within the broader discourse on academic work and contemporary scholarship. After locating CCL work within traditional and contemporary frameworks for assessing faculty work, I focus on the cases of Patricia, Roger, and Linda. I asked the participants to reflect on how they justified their work within their particular institutional context. To supplement this discussion, I collected evaluation documents from Roger and

Linda. Following Ervin and Fox, I also collected documents that shaped or constrained their work, particularly university and department policies. The case studies in this chapter address how the participants constructed their CCL activities within their institution, connecting these reflections to broader discourses on reforming academic scholarship. I close the chapter by suggesting strategies cross-curricular writing specialists can use to describe and document their work.

LOCATING WAC WORK WITHIN THE "USUAL TRIAD"

In the first chapter of their edited collection, *WAC for the New Millennium*, Susan McLeod and Eric Miraglia confront the question of how WAC will fare in a time when colleges and universities increasingly must do more with less. Whether it is from government funds diverted to secondary education or public outcry about the quality of today's college education, exigencies are forcing a climate of fiscal responsibility and academic accountability. Today, the corporatization of the academy is most manifested in the negligible working conditions of what Donald Kennedy calls the "para-faculty," the ever-expanding pool of post-docs, nontenure-line faculty, part timers, and 3-year contracts (48). This corporate outsourcing of academic labor has also been cited as a cause for the market crunches resultant from an overproduction of PhDs in the sciences and, in particular, the humanities. Corporatization is also manifested in the complicated "research" alliances with industry, tuition hikes that exceed annual inflation, and real academic wage compensation at levels equivalent to those of nearly 40 years ago (Finkelstein).

Yet the implications of this paradigm shift are only beginning to be examined by scholars and professional organizations. This collective discourse tends to focus on the subject of faculty work and the quality of academic life—specifically, the inadequacy of the traditional academic system of values and behaviors, as it has evolved from the turn of the century to today, to accommodate today's pressing needs (AACU; Boyer; Kennedy; Kolodny; Readings). The traditional academic system has itself grown over time to incorporate a number of complex and oftentimes conflicting missions, from producing highly specialized disciplinary knowledge (research and publication), to training new specialists (graduate education), to training citizen knowledge workers (undergraduate education), to department and academic citizenship/service (faculty ownership and self-governance). The fallout has been public confusion and criticism, and faculty overload and disaffection. Although American higher education has always embraced these many roles—represented in the "usual triad" of research, teaching, and service—many forcefully argue the trinity has become a hierarchy privileging the production of disciplinary knowledge. Refereed publication has remained the valued criterion for faculty reward and prestige, even at non-doctoral-granting institutions. Never before have productivity expectations been higher for new faculty in research, in teaching, and in service (Boyer; Finkelstein).

To address the effects the publish or perish academic culture has had on, in the main, undergraduate education—but also public perception, graduate mentoring, university governance, faculty morale, and faculty personal lives—arguments have been advanced to broaden the conception of what counts as scholarship to include not only traditional research but also teaching and service work such as administration, community outreach, and faculty development (AAUP Committee; Boyer; Diamond; Glassick et al.). Ernest Boyer's proposed new paradigm of scholarship is well known. Boyer broadened the conception of scholarship to include not only the traditional scholarship of *discovery*—the rigorous production of new knowledge—but also the scholarly activities of *integration*, the synthesis of existing knowledge, putting knowledge in broader contexts, educating nonspecialists; *application*, the practical application of knowledge to address local/social/community problems; and *teaching*, the intellectually reflective instruction, from classroom to collegial contexts, measured by its ability to transmit, transform, and extend knowledge through active learning. Boyer's framework is credited with sparking much formal conversation in separate disciplines about the nature of academic work. The Modern Language Association (MLA) Commission on Professional Service's report "Making Faculty Work Visible" translates Boyer's conception of scholarship into English and composition studies contexts.

An important consideration becomes where to locate WAC consulting work within the recommended frameworks for contemporary intellectual work—or which framework to advocate. Traditional conceptions locate work across the usual triad based on its product and audience (MLA Commission). Although the nature of collaborative research might be clear in this system, other WAC activities such as conducting workshops, overseeing WI courses, or advising faculty in other disciplines become more difficult to locate within the hierarchy. The MLA Commission's alternative model, which recognizes that *type* of work does not necessarily correspond to *quality* of work, variously locates WAC-related activity under teaching, for instance as "professional development," or as service, as applied "internal outreach" citizenship activity (183-184). The Council of Writing Program Administrators' statement on intellectual work articulates five categories of intellectual work specific to writing program administration—program creation, curricular design, faculty development, program assessment and evaluation, and program-related textual production—and four "guidelines" for evaluating this work. In *Scholarship Assessed*, the 1997 follow-up to Boyer's classic *Scholarship Reconsidered*, Charles Glassick, Mary Taylor Huber, and Gene Maeroff offer an overarching set of standards for scholarly work that is derivative of the ideal process of traditional scholarship but, similar to the MLA Commission's recommendations, could be applied to any activity to assess its quality, regardless of the "site," the physical or metaphoric location, of the activity (MLA Commission 172).

Figure 6.1 represents one way to locate WAC work according to the traditional triad of academic labor and the new conceptions of scholarship. The figure's gradient background represents the traditional weight given to research (i.e., refereed publication) and the diminishing value given to teaching and, finally, service. One immediate implication of this map is that the education-oriented activities of WAC specialists typically fall under the categories of teaching and service.

Judy Segal et al. acknowledge that the tenure system prevents more fruitful integration of writing scholarship with the discourse of other disciplines: "In practice, and for many reasons, some of which have to do with getting tenure, we rhetoricians have not always sought to publish our work in the journals of those we really wish would read it" (79). Discipline-based research provides valuable insight, but in the context of academic labor, it is especially worthwhile because of its exchange value in the academic marketplace. To make discipline-based rhetorical inquiry more valued by professionals in other disciplines, Segal et al. propose that rhetoricians spend more time actively "sticking their necks out" into the other disciplines, by joining their conversations, publishing in their forums, and working with them to identify problems that are significant from their disciplinary perspectives. Segal and her colleagues advocate an action research approach that when made public in mainstream journals is really no less valuable than more traditional forms of research. But this activity becomes more closely associated with teaching because it presumably incorporates a pedagogical component in the dissemination of immediately useful local knowledge—materials, reports, proposals, policy revisions, workshops. However, publishing in other professionals' journals, particularly pedagogical journals, potentially diminishes the value of the scholarship in the eyes of writing specialists' promotion and tenure committees.

Only recently has teaching become understood as an activity that extends beyond the boundaries of the classroom. The MLA Commission's report states this most clearly when it argues that the traditional conception of teaching needs to be "expanded, taking into account activities that enrich student learning or enable better teaching, ranging from nontraditional teaching modes (outside classrooms or credit-bearing classes) to teachers' professional development as teachers and their activities in forming and sustaining teaching communities" (183). The report provides 14 sample activi-

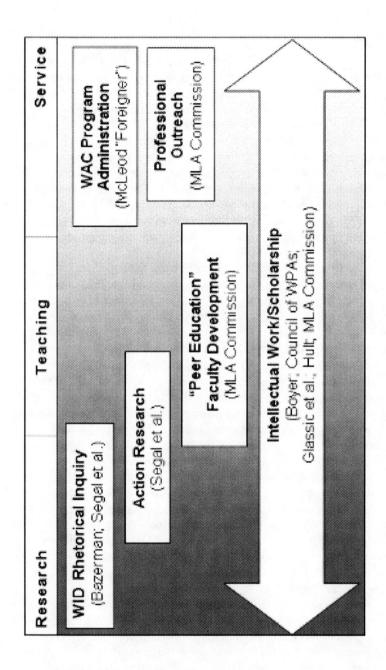

Fig. 6.1. WAC work as research, teaching, service

ties, including co-teaching with others, conducting classroom research projects, designing and implementing the professional development of teaching assistants and professional instructors, and offering faculty or student workshops in areas of one's professional expertise. It is easy to see how the kind of peer education activities of CCL specialists—workshops, curriculum development, consultations—can be considered a form of teaching.

When these teaching activities are closely associated with cross-curricular writing program administration, however, they risk being associated with "mere" institutional service. Susan McLeod's Peace Corps model of WAC, wherein central administrators implicitly believe program development is "simply service" performed by a writing specialist "for the sheer love of it," is an example of this ("Foreigner" 110). As the MLA Commission explains, service has typically been understood as constitutive of "activities required to create, maintain, and improve the infrastructure that sustains the academy as a societal institution" (163). Accordingly, many of the citizenship tasks of applied outreach work and institutional and professional service "have insufficient conceptual demands to qualify as intellectual work, although it may be labor- and time-intensive" (MLA Commission 186). These activities include serving on hiring committees, organizing conferences, advising campus groups, and giving expert opinions. But institutional and professional service, as the MLA Commission argues, does not preclude the possibility of intellectually productive work in this area. Associating any academic work to service often elides the intellectual character of writing program administration, practical application, and other activities that involve the exercise of discipline-specific knowledge and skills. According to the MLA Commission,

> Professional service is distinguished from other sites of faculty work in that it is integrally active or related to practical action; if intellectual work, it has to do with ideas in action—problem definition and problem solving, interpretations of theory in practice and production (and vice versa), invention or design of activities, leadership or major responsibility for enactment of ideas, administration involving responsibility for the actions and welfare of others. (187)

Within this conception, service includes the professional development activities of offering workshops and consultations for faculty, TAs, or students. The MLA Commission adds, "This peer education can also be described under service as 'internal outreach,' and it often exemplifies administration or leadership—of a language or writing program, curricular diversity initiative, or the like" (183-84). This is consistent with discourse on writing program administration. Christine Hult effectively argues against narrow service views of such work, defining the scholarship of writing program administration as "the systematic, theory-based production and oversight of a dynamic program" that is measured in the "day-to-day written work of the administrator" (120, 126). For Hult, writing program administration is more than occasional committee work, it is "a career choice that carries with it a commitment to scholarship" (121).

To consider the intellectual character of CCL work is to understand that, depending on the nature of the particular activity, it can be placed in any of the customary categories and be considered scholarly, as long as it can be subjected to the revised standards for scholarly work. Significant intellectual work, according to the MLA Commission, "should be an outgrowth of professional expertise rather than general knowledge or skills that most educated, intelligent people possess. It must have a public dimension that is amenable to assessment, evaluation, and modification by a critically informed group of peers" (162). According to the MLA Commission, "the quality, significance, and impact of faculty work" is more important than the category of work (162). In the language of the MLA Commission, whether academic work counts as research, teaching, or service "will vary individually, according to the intent and achievement of the unique example being described, and contextually, according to local nomenclature, institutional missions, and purpose" (187). I have been arguing in this study that academic writing consulting is more than the general application of interpersonal or managerial skills, but that it involves the rigorous application of disciplinary expertise. But, as arguments for contemporary scholarship demonstrate, whether academic writing consulting constitutes research, teaching, or service depends on the situation.

Glassick, Huber, and Maeroff assert that only through the development of systematic ways to document and evaluate nontraditional forms of scholarship will such work be admitted into the value system of the academy. The Carnegie Foundation report draws from a wide range of data to create a framework for documenting and assessing faculty scholarship. In examining different standards and criteria used to evaluate faculty work, Glassick et al. claim that "there is a common language in which to discuss the standards of scholarly work of all kinds," and it is rooted in the *process* of scholarly production (35). "When people praise a work of scholarship," Glassick et al. note, "they usually mean that the project in question shows that it has been guided by these qualitative standards: . . . clear goals, adequate preparation, appropriate methods, significant results, effective presentation, and reflective critique" (24-25).

Adequately assessing difficult-to-quantify, nontraditional forms of scholarship begins with recognizing new genres of scholarly production and broadening the scope of what counts as suitable documentation, including portfolios, client/user evaluations, and personal reflections. "Institutions and departments that are serious about expanding the scope of scholarship," assert Glassick and his colleagues, "must acknowledge that scholarly work does not always adorn itself in the traditional cap and gown" (38). Scholarly forms must be opened up to a broader and more diverse spectrum of materials, and they may not be limited to the written word. Conversely, reviewers may not be limited to disciplinary peers, but could include students, clients, nonacademic authorities, and practitioners in the field. For the Carnegie Foundation, the teaching portfolio is the best model for documenting scholarly work. Glassick et al. argue that multiple sources should be considered so as to increase validity and reliability when reviewing non-traditional forms of documentation. Rigorous documentation also promotes better scholarship:

> It takes imagination and discipline to demonstrate that a project had clear goals and was adequately prepared, that it was conducted with appropriate methods and led to significant results, and that it was presented effectively and reflectively critiqued. Thus, documentation to an agreed-upon set of standards can aid the scholar's reflection, informing the revision of old projects, conduct of current ones, and plans for new work. (Glassick et al. 37)

In line with Glassick et al., Christine Hult points to ways the work of writing program administration can be described accurately and evaluated fairly. Given the oftentimes situated knowledge production of writing program administration, Hult criticizes acquiescence to the prevailing faculty reward system:

> Many of us need to share the blame for our currently undervalued work with our higher administrators, since we have too often bought into the hierarchical schemes outlined on our campuses rather than trying to change the premises on which such schemes are based. We need to do a better job of educating our colleagues in academe about the significance of our administrative work and to develop models of evaluation that reflect the complexity of our scholarship. (Hult 127)

For Hult, tenure and promotion cases present an opportunity to make the case for a broadened conception of scholarship: "We can fold into our tenure and promotion documents explicit arguments for the value of the scholarship of administration, categorizing such work as 'scholarly research,' and not 'service'" (127). She recommends that WPAs assemble an administrative portfolio that includes all the various documents produced in the course of administering a writing program, including policy and goals statements, curricular outlines, model syllabi, teacher evaluations, and other in-house publications. Such a collection of evidence should also contain a carefully crafted job description that reflects the complexity of the WPA's work. Hult also recommends that such portfolios include "self-reflective glosses" written by the WPA to help "guide the evaluators through the materials" and connect the work to the "underlying scholarship" (128).

Although there are parallels between writing program administration and WAC faculty development activity, not all writing consultants are WPAs. However, the arguments for establishing the rigor of nontraditional forms of scholarship by Glassick et al., Hult, and the MLA Commission can be brought to bear on justifying the consulting activities of writing specialists. In the next section, I examine how Patricia, Roger, and Linda's CCL work was valued at their particular institutions and how they have argued for its valued. What is immediately apparent is that these three participants represent an interesting, albeit small, range of contexts for assessing scholarly work—a full professor who worked her way up through the institutional ranks, a veteran adjunct instructor, and an associate professor who started her career in an administrative position outside any department but who achieved a tenure-line position within her school's English Department. Following these cases, I conclude by suggesting some strategies writing consultants can use to describe and document their work.

PATRICIA'S COLLABORATIVE SERVICE ETHIC: "MY WORK IS OF A PIECE"

It was apparent to me that Patricia had taken a traditional approach to an academic career, working her way up through the perceived higher education hierarchy—from a small southern college to a major private research university—based on the strength and reputation of her published scholarship. I wondered in what ways this facilitated her career and what, if any, roadblocks she experienced.

Patricia began her reflection looking broadly over her career. Recall from chapter 3 that she began at a small public college. In her words, she started her career "looking like a regular English Department member." She taught at the college while working on her PhD at the nearby university. She received tenure and promotion to the associate level the same year she completed her dissertation in 20th century literature, because she "had been there long enough" and had "done work that was very well received there." In terms of what scholarly activity was valued, "teaching was it." She taught four classes, three of which required different preparations. "It was not a place where publication was a big deal," she said. "Now that was starting to change; there were starting to be, and are now certainly, heavier publication requirements. But at the time, it was a nice bonus if you published."

Patricia was, in her own words, "the poster girl for what you should do to be successful at a small place like that." At the time of her tenure and promotion, she had already begun the WAC work described in chapter 3. She had published an article from her literature dissertation and completed a manuscript of the resource book she developed for her WAC workshops. She received high teaching evaluations and was active in other "highly valued" community and college campus service work, such as receiving a grant for a women's studies program. Her WAC work was "just part" of her service at that point: "It was looked upon favorably in that context, but it would have been equally favorable if I had worked on some other kind of project. There was no particular prejudice against it."

When she moved on to a mid-sized university to develop a WAC program, her tenure-line was in a Writing and Communications Department. She was thus "doing mainstream work" in her department, and "they were very pleased." Her first WAC book was published (and she stopped publishing in literature). The Writing and Communications Department, 2 years old at the time of her appointment, soon afterward became the second highest department in the whole college in terms of enrollment:

> We were booming, we were rolling, we were great. And the people in the department were very, very sympathetic to my work. So, the way I avoided the kind of second-class citizenship that some writing folks get for their research in English departments was to go to a school that had the two as separate departments.

After several years developing writing programs locally and statewide, Patricia moved to a larger public university to run its WAC program. By this time, she had already become a nationally recognized expert on WAC. At the same time, because of the nature of faculty development work, Patricia felt it important to be perceived as a "full, first-class citizen of the faculty." It was essential for her to have credibility among the faculty across campus with whom she would work:

> It was very important to me when I came into this position . . . that I have a position that marked me as a senior member of the faculty, and I held out for the conditions that would get me that, because I felt it was very important for me to have that faculty credibility. I also paid heavy attention to where my office was; that is, it should be in a classroom building and not an administrative building. I also paid attention to the committees I would be on, and so forth. So, I have always sought to look like a faculty member—to *quack* like a faculty member—you have to. Now, given that, anybody who does faculty development, or anything having to do with education, always has lower status in the academy. I do not have the same status here as if I had published in nuclear physics, and I never will, no matter how well I do in my field, because there's a real pecking order of disciplinary status. It doesn't help to be in

a teaching and learning center, and it doesn't help to be a writing center, and it doesn't help to be a woman. But, you know, I've made my piece with that. I chose to be in a field I knew had lower status than if I were to do the next big book on Alexander Pope. I don't want to do the next big book on Pope; I want to do the next big book on teaching or learning. And so, I have always put my values first; it's important for me to work on projects I am interested in. And I have always combined the practical and the theoretical, the practical with the empirical.

Here, discussing both her current and her former positions, Patricia reflects on the importance of maintaining close ties with the mission of teaching and of not losing credibility among faculty through some subtle association with central administration. At the same time, she understands that within the traditional value system of the academy, any activity associated with teaching has less status than research, particularly at larger-sized research-oriented universities. How has she resolved this tension? She has "always put her values first" and connected her interests with work that would carry some currency in the academic marketplace.

Reflecting on how well her work was received at her third institutional location, Patricia commented: "I never got to find out any prejudices against writing across the curriculum there, because I was a tenured full professor. Except to hire me, they had no more decisions to make about me, and I didn't have any more hurdles to cross." Moreover, she was, in her words, "maintaining just a fine publication schedule":

> When that English department underwent an external review, the reviewers berated the department for not using my talents and skills more fully. And the reason they weren't was because I was already too overworked with the WAC center work! In my third year there, I was elected to the executive committee of the department. So, I was one of four or five people in the department of about 45 entrusted with recommending policy decisions at the department. So, I have just finessed the kind of prejudices that some writing and WAC people feel in their own departments.

Understanding and being comfortable with her ability to "finesse" the situation, or to bring about an intended result or change, was important to Patricia. It was particularly important to her at her current position directing a teaching and learning center at a major private research university. There, she accepted a concurrent appointment in both the center and in the English Department. After accepting the position, she found out that an obscure regulation about this kind of appointment denied her departmental or university voting privileges.[1] Although she was angered by this, she did not blame those who hired her. In the absence of what she considered a form of "formal" institutional power—full-time faculty status—she instead resigned herself to accepting the other sources of power she felt she had at her disposal, namely "expert power" and "relational power." Her expert power was clearly derived from her record of scholarship and her experience. And like the case of Linda (from chapter 3), Patricia felt her relational power was derived from her directing the teaching and learning center, where by virtue of her position she sat on several influential university committees: "As long as I'm the director of this center, I can finesse [my power] anyway because I sit on these committees in my position of director. And I have a lot of influence and a lot of power and a lot of respect on campus."

Patricia also exercised relational power through her "actions and interactions with other people."

> I have wonderful organizational and people skills if I do say so myself. I also have colleague skills. These have taken me a very long way. So, as the teaching and learning center director, I have power, but it's low status power. Anything that has to do with teaching at a university is lower status. As a researcher, I've done well, but it's nothing like I've won a Nobel Prize in physics. People assume that somebody in my position probably hasn't done research. But it's there, and when people learn of my work, recognize my work—and the English department reviewed my work—that enhances my power. It will never be like I've won a Nobel Prize in the sciences or am an endowed chair, where everyone knows that because you are the John H. Doe Professor of Physics you must be way up there. That's not immediately apparent in any of the ways that I'm introduced. My colleague skills have won me lots of friends and respect here, but in the academy, those things are always somewhat tipped by your status as a researcher and by the status of the discipline that you're in, and I'm in a low-status discipline. . . . So I didn't win the Nobel Prize in physics, but I'm in a very good place in terms of my own values and my ability to realize them.

Patricia noted that much of her attitude was influenced by where she was at in her career; she was tenured, and despite the hiring glitch, she negotiated a long-term contract that suited her. Her center had overwhelming support from the central administration. She "likes to collaborate," and she "knows how to do it well." These reflections on her relational skills seem directly related to her ability to collaborate and the outcomes of such relationships. She brings a certain kind of ethical standpoint, or set of values, to her work that structures or influences the way she conducts her work, the kind of work she does, the kind of phenomena she observes, and the kind of interpretations she makes:

If I were to go out now on the job market again, what I would have to
say to anybody who would hire me is my career—my work, the body
of my work—is of a piece. My teaching and my administration and my
research are all integrated, and that has been a high value for me.
Something I've really tried to do is to integrate those aspects both in my
live, as I live it on a daily basis and also in my work. I have always tried
to combine the practical and the theoretical. If you want some kind of
"pure research" untainted by any relationship to practice, then I'm not
your person, because that's not at all how I work or how I conceptual-
ize what I do. So, you see, these collaborations have been at the center
of my value system. I have been able—I've been fortunate enough—not
to have to care very much what other people thought about them.

Patricia's career has followed the arguably prototypical path of the academic star. From her small college start to her current position as a director
of a university teaching and learning center, Patricia developed a record of
scholarship and publishing that propelled her to the pinnacle of her field and
then beyond it. She can be counted among the matriarchs who have mapped
the terrain of WAC. Her story would at first not seem to offer any insight
into validating the less-valued teaching or service activities of academic writing consulting. However, she shows her astute awareness of the relative low
status of teaching in relation to more "pure" research. She also understands
the relative low status of English and composition in relation to other, more
valorized fields. Patricia seems to offer precisely the strategies writing specialists need to link their work with how academic labor is traditionally
rewarded. She has demonstrated a remarkable ability to work *within* the
system, melding her personal goals with the outward expectations of her
colleagues and administrators. Patricia has learned how to "finesse" any
subtle or perceived lack of formal power through the exercise of other forms
of power in the academy, namely expert power and relational power.

ROGER'S CROSS-CURRICULAR LINKS: "PART OF THE MIX"

Recall from chapter 3 that Roger's status within his freestanding Writing
Department was that of a well-respected veteran adjunct instructor. He has
often been asked to work as a liaison on especially important projects, such
as the tutoring link with the Honors Program, a special writing course for
the School of Management, or the learning community initiative. And with
his voice being heard often in local presentations, essays, and histories, his
record of service also represents a form of leadership in the department. Two
threads emerged from my conversations with Roger about how his work
was valued at his institution. The first was related to how he and Markos, his

colleague in psychology, negotiated their concept of the Rhetoric of Psychology course into existence, and the second was how Roger represented his consulting activities in performance evaluations within his own department.

In discussing the planning of the team-taught course, Roger spoke of the special "wing-and-prayer arrangements" that had to be coordinated between the two departments. How the team-taught psychology writing course was funded struck Roger as "a lesson in itself about how the institution values this kind of work." It was Markos who first proposed the course to his department, which needed an upper division writing course. Once approved in psychology, Roger had to seek support from his department. For the first 2 years, the writing program funded Roger's participation, with Roger teaching "on load," as he called it, or as part of his regular three-course per semester load. Markos taught the course in addition to his regular load, as an "off-load" experimental course. Because of timing and other curricular initiatives, the Writing Department was unable to fund Roger's continued participation in the course. (Roger described this as a convergence of factors: he missed an important meeting where an important decision was made to devote available resources to a new service-learning initiative.) In the wake of these developments, the Psychology Department funded Roger on a part-time basis. However, Roger was informed that it would be as an off-load arrangement. Because of existing teaching demands, the Writing Department was not in a position to "spare his time," but it was also a way to secure unofficial full-time status (and pay) for Roger. Roger summarized the significance of the semester-to-semester arrangements that enabled the course to continue:

> [The latest arrangement] means the course will continue, somewhat different but still functional. It shows exactly the kind of quirky, wing-and-a-prayer arrangement the system has to come up with to allow a simple concept like this to work. It also shows how tight resources are at the department level.

But the lack of consistent funding also speaks to the precariousness of such nontraditional arrangements. Such curricular initiatives exist as long as the individuals only to disappear soon after them. This fits with David Russell's findings that writing reform movements and nontraditional curricular arrangements have typically failed because of the academy's disciplinary construction and values. Roger's course is reminiscent of the icon principle in WAC, that courses and programs last as long as their energetic and charismatic administrator, but then fade soon after that administrator's retirement or departure. This principle is often considered a key reason why cross-curricular writing programs typically fail to last past the first stage (Walvoord "Future").

In terms of how Roger's participation in such curricular arrangements reflects how his institution values such work, as long as the departments supported the team-taught course materially and ideologically, Roger's work was valuable. His interest and initiative in fostering such cross-curricular links made him more visible to his and other departments, thereby increasing his status. As his experience and reputation increased, so did the likelihood he would be asked to participate in similar initiatives. Roger's difficulties keeping the psychology course within his own normal load were more a result of his department being stretched beyond its own limited resources than any principled resistance to WAC. Such initiatives are increasingly possible nationwide, as calls for undergraduate education reform are making possible such movements as assessment, service learning, teaching with technology, team-teaching, and learning communities. The Psychology Department, for instance, was required to develop its majors' literacy skills and wanted to explore how discipline-specific writing courses could accomplish this. Roger's team-teaching arrangement with Markos and the Psychology Department suggests the microlevel resourcefulness necessary to enact these kinds of progressive institutional arrangements and how such resourcefulness, when linked to programs and goals valued by various institutional constituents, helps improve the status of those involved in such academic labor.

To further understand how Roger's CCL work is valued at his institution, I wanted to focus on his performance evaluations. Roger's department defines teaching broadly as any professional activity that translates its disciplinary knowledge to others. In addition to traditional classroom teaching, the program recognizes as teaching other "specialized help or expertise" directed to students and faculty in various tutoring, linked-course, and team-teaching arrangements. To assess this activity, the department developed a portfolio evaluation system, whereby instructors submit portfolios to a review committee consisting of five experienced, peer-elected instructors. The portfolio evaluations—normed holistic rankings based on articulated criteria—are used as the basis for university-mandated teaching evaluations, workload decisions, merit raises, and hiring decisions.

When I asked Roger how his team-teaching with Markos and consulting for the learning community fit into his evaluation, he replied that there was no "intrinsic value system that would value [his cross-curricular links] more highly than a teacher teaching a regular [composition class]." Of course, I was exploring whether it was undervalued. But he clarified that within the portfolio evaluation system other kinds of program work were understood to be extensions of teaching. This work included such activity as conference presentations, curricular committee work, and working in the professional development/practicum groups. The portfolio represents a teacher's professional activity and development "in all its manifestations."

Indeed, portfolio reviews, which occur every year for teachers with less than 5 years experience and at the end of veteran teachers' tri-ennial contract years, are viewed as an extension of professional development within the department.

According to Roger and policy that I collected from his department, instructor portfolios were to include a three- to five-page reflection on teaching practices, syllabi, student evaluations, peer observations, and samples of student work. Reflective commentary was to accompany each item. The guidelines make provisions for "consultant work" by stating that consultants can represent such work in their teaching reflection or in a discussion of student work samples. The policy further states, "If consultants do not find the means within these components adequate or appropriate for representing their consulting, they may choose to include a letter from a student or a teacher with whom they have worked over time, student evaluations, or a tape or video." Instructors are also invited to include "other items that may provide evaluators a picture of some significant aspect of their professional work," such as articles, case studies, conference presentations, merit awards, a curriculum vitae, or any other "related professional or intellectual work."

Roger felt that the purpose of the portfolio was partly to inform, but also partly to "make visible what you're doing and partly to defend if you think something might be problematic." In keeping with the philosophy of the program, Roger also saw the portfolio as a site for Schön-like reflection-on-action. He viewed it as a place to reflect, to understand, and to begin the continual process of pedagogical redesign. He attributed this somewhat to early anxiety among instructors back when the portfolio system was first being implemented. At first, instructors saw them as "rationales, justifications, and defenses of teaching practices," in light of revisions to the composition curriculum. But making his work "visible" is "more the motive" Roger takes into the task. Roger felt his portfolio was an accurate record, "almost like a journal," of his activities throughout the year. He interpreted an optional section, a category for materials not strictly related to teaching or for extra documentation, broadly:

> I learned to do meticulous record-keeping of everything I do for the writing department because it was always supposed to be accounted for in the portfolio. It's everything you've done for that period. In a sense, it is a good reflective experience. That's what it is designed to do, but it is a lot of work also.

Roger graciously granted me access to his most recent portfolio and resultant two-page evaluation. The portfolio consisted of more than 70 pages of material (not including some syllabi and student work that Roger couldn't account for at the time of our sessions). Because of his veteran contract, it encompassed the last 3 years of his activity. It also included his work with Markos. In the "prefatory matter" of his portfolio, Roger included a required "cover sheet" that answers questions about courses taught and other program activities. He also included four "maps" to guide readers: (a) a list of appointments for the 3-year period, (b) a one-page rationale for the portfolio's organization, (c) a table of contents, and (d) an indexed list of materials (see Appendix A for a facsimile of Roger's prefatory materials).

Although not required, Roger went so far as to document the amount of hourly time he spent on various activities related to his teaching responsibilities. He added additional commentary and contextual cues throughout his portfolio to help guide its reviewers. To further document his special consulting activities, Roger includes copies of the administrative annual reports he was required to submit to the program's outreach director. These short, two-page reports, which required no specified format, informed the outreach coordinator of his activities. They also influenced the program director's "accounting to the college and higher administration." Roger's report on his Honors Program consultancy, for instance, summarizes his principle activities, including meetings with Honors Program coordinators, curriculum meetings with Honors Program instructors, visits to Honors classes, workshops, and student tutorials, and "significant" participation in the production of four student theses. (In Honors, Roger was acting like a writing fellow, but he also participated in curriculum development, making his role more like that of a consultant.) In a "Comments" section, Roger assesses this activity and offers suggestions for improvements to this particular cross-curricular arrangement.

By his own admission, Roger typically includes more materials and supporting documentation than other instructors in the program.[2] His "Response to Student Evaluations," for example, is five manuscript pages long. His reflection on his team-taught course, based on a paper delivered at a professional conference, was more than 15 pages long. To get a sense of how Roger engages in self-analysis, the following are excerpts from his response to student evaluations:

> I found it a shock going through the variety of evaluations. Who are these two Rogers,[3] one who wows whole classes with rave reviews and one who bombs as if willfully? Here are some insights I have into these evaluations that readers may not be able to arrive at themselves and some of the patterns instructive for me. . . .

These evaluations are clearly related to my perceptions of the sound-
ness of course design. Three of the courses in this group were unstable,
experimental, and risky. In one course, I broke completely with my old,
reliable pattern and forced imbalances that called for fresh new solutions. I crashed and burned on this course in the evaluations. On the
other hand, the third experiment, [the psychology course] design
worked very nicely. The Roger in these evaluations is a hero. . . .

Another insight I have is that I have (finally) visibly aged. I am going
gray, my ethos has changed, students respond to me differently as
though I were automatically to be taken seriously. I am now unanimously addressed as "Professor" Roger, and I suspect am being held to
the behaviors of a full professor like my co-teacher Markos. This is a
change for me. I have been going through a transition in my teaching
techniques to try to capitalize on this. . . .

In summary, there are certainly revealing criticisms here that indicate
ways for me to improve. However, I am inclined to caution myself to go
slowly. I have to ask myself if the students are asking for their idea of the
Good Teacher. Could the Good Writing Teacher be an artifact like what
some might consider the Good Writing Course, one that focuses on
grammar and punctuation, or creative writing? And I can't forget that
there is a good Roger here also and ten or so courses that worked.

It is difficult to represent with only excerpts the detail and complexity
of Roger's reflections. A reflective approach is apparent, however. Roger
examines the data—in this case, 3 years worth of student evaluations—and
identifies and interprets the patterns he sees. He integrates reflection on program goals, his own goals, his general pedagogical strategies, discipline-specific pedagogical strategies, and more.

It is clear that Roger's attention to detail was well-received by his portfolio evaluators. He received the highest ranking allowable within the system, "exemplary":

Responses to your portfolio ranged from awe to "confused awe"
because of the thoroughness and complexity of your documentation,
theorizing, reflection, self-assessing. . . . . You scrutinized every component of your teaching materials. . . You scrutinized your student evaluations. . . . You approached syllabi and assignments as if they were
research projects, constantly building, inventing, reusing, and reshaping.
In your Reflection on Psychology 400 which you co-taught, you
defined how you shaped the content of the course into a [writing-inten-
sive] course and explained how necessary it is for instructors collaboratively teaching [writing] courses with teachers of outside disciplines to
play a revisioning role versus the often typically service role and how
the tensions between the demands of the writing course and the psychology course were productive.

The committee also found especially helpful "the very well-prepared glosses contextualizing individual elements." This was consistent with Roger's practice of including summaries of material, especially for longer documents within his portfolio. Conscious of the review committee's huge reading burden, having to intensely pour over any given year's set of portfolios, Roger felt it appropriate to highlight parts of the documents he thought important.

Roger's case is perhaps unusual in that there is a specific place for the kind of cross-curricular activity within his department's conception of teaching. However, his approach to documenting his activities—activities that might variously be considered service or teaching elsewhere—is worth emulating. As he said, he simply "meticulously documents everything."

> It's actually a lot of writing that I try to spread out over the spring semester, writing a reflection, writing reports for the things you did, writing responses to evaluations—if you want, that's an option. You can also write a response to the peer observation, if you want. So you can spend a lot of time pouring over things and reflecting and writing.

This practice is very much shaped by the culture of evaluation and professional development within his program. That is, his Writing Department has aspired to develop an evaluation system that would be sensitive to the talents and approaches of individual teachers but at the same time work to ensure accountability to the needs and goals of the writing program. But Roger also demonstrates how he has personally negotiated this system, seizing on the opportunity to, as Glassick et al. suggest, use formal evaluation as a prompt for reflective self-critique.

LINDA'S CASE FOR TENURE: "LIVING WHAT YOU PRACTICE"

Linda's case offers more insight into the process of negotiating local expectations. In the late 1980s, after completing her PhD in American literature, Linda was hired into an administrative/professional staff position within her university's School of Liberal Arts to direct the WC and develop a WAC program. As a professional staff member, she was required to undergo annual evaluations by her dean. The evaluation procedure for professional staff members never suited her activity, however. From the start of her appointment, Linda spent conscious effort cultivating her scholarly ethos by publishing and teaching. She felt it an important element in gaining credibility among the faculty, and it suited her personal expectation as a trained scholar to publish. Although she was never explicitly required to publish, she felt that developing the perception of being an active professional writer was important to her program's success.

Subsequently, the institutional document Linda was asked to use for annual evaluations had no place to document her research or her teaching activity (she had been approved to teach the tutor-training course as a special topics course in the English Department). So Linda began using the same annual report of professional activities (ARPA) that faculty used. This provided the means to document her research, teaching, and service activities. At that point, she said, she began to "act like a faculty member, even in my own mind." She was evaluated using the ARPA from then on, and as she said, "little did I know it would come into play many years later."

The professional staff reviews continued for 5 years, with Linda receiving excellent evaluations. During this time, she continually promoted her activities within her college and to the university central administration, always tying her reports to the "published missions of the institutions." She would send copies of her ARPA's to the university president and published a comprehensive 5-year report in her WAC newsletter. "It is just so important," she said, "for people like us to be versed in our institutional missions and values; that's how we translate what we're doing into central administration's language. It's a simple WAC/writing principle that we don't practice enough ourselves." She also made sure her personal scholarly achievements were publicized in college and university newsletters. All the while, Linda worked to promote the program's successes and establish the perception of her own efficacy.

After 6 years, the time of a typical tenure-track probationary period, Linda wanted to gain the protection and status of tenure. She wanted to protect herself from what many on her campus considered ambitious administrators who were advancing their own agendas and exercising arbitrary budget cuts. She also wanted a sabbatical. She felt that she had overworked herself to establish the program and that its success warranted some time for reflection and renewal. She began exploring ways this would be possible, at one point proposing to her dean that he create an interdisciplinary humanities department to house the WAC program, American and women's studies, and other interdisciplinary programs. This was, as she explained, in keeping with her philosophy that WAC should not be associated solely with the English Department. With this option a fiscal impossibility, a colleague in English proposed she join the English Department. Yet, the meeting where this idea was introduced was very divisive. "Some allies apologized for weeks to me afterwards, it was so mean-spirited," she recalled. The department voted at that time "not to consider considering" her. Attributing this tactic to her close colleague, she pointed out that this was a slightly better result than a vote not to consider her for tenure. This, as she said, "left it open for the vote to come up at another time."

Linda continued in her professional staff role for 2 more years. There were significant political upheavals in the meantime. The politics were actually "getting very scary" for Linda. The upper administration fell into "disarray." Staff and faculty without tenure were being let go. Programs "languished." The English Department lost its PhD program. When the possibility of her tenure and promotion was again introduced to the English Department, the mood was more sympathetic. The faculty agreed to accept her for a 1-year probationary period in a tenure-track position, which afterward would make her eligible for tenure. A new dean, who was supportive of WAC, proposed using her ("as a guinea pig, I'm always the guinea pig") for a pilot contract system that would require faculty to articulate goals and responsibilities at the start of the year, which would then be used as the basis for evaluations at the end of the year. At this time, a new university vice president for academic affairs was appointed, whom Linda referred to as the "Evil Queen," a reference to her seemingly two-faced support of Linda's quest for tenure.[4] Ultimately responsible for approving her tenure, the Evil Queen "voiced concerns" about budgeting her proposed line (even though Linda was already in the budget as the WC director) and refused to sign off on the contract, claiming it was a liberal arts "thing," but Linda saw this as a calculated move avoiding commitment at that point. In this political climate—a supportive dean, a strong faculty base, a reputation of administrative and scholarly excellence, but a hostile vice president—she prepared for her tenure review.

Linda wanted to ensure that her WAC and WC work would be counted among her scholarly activity and, more importantly, that it wouldn't be held against her. So she sought to put "into contract language" arguments about scholarship of administration and service. Upon her probationary appointment, together with the department chair and her dean, she jointly negotiated a tenure and promotion "statement," or contract that clearly stipulated the criteria and expectations in research, teaching, and service. Her review process was not to be like a full-time faculty member, but rather as an "outside administrator seeking faculty appointment." All of her previous professional activities were to count toward her review. This contract is significant because it clearly articulated the weight of her service activities. In line with Hult's recommendations, the contract lists her service expectations first, before research and teaching: "Linda's[5] . . . original job description and her current revised job description will be submitted with her request for promotion to verify the importance of this area in weighing her case." The contract quoted standard university policy, defining service as "the application of a member's knowledge in the member's professional field to benefit the University, the community, and/or the profession."

The criteria for research and teaching were also included in the contract. In the discussion of her expectations for research, it stated that Linda, "like most English Department faculty, would normally be expected to have published a few refereed articles or a refereed book." Her "conference presentations and grant activities" were also be considered, along with other kinds of "single-authored and (as expected in her discipline) collaborative projects such as accumulated publications, funded and nonfunded research, submitted articles, articles, chapters." Linda purposefully sought to include the recognition of grants and collaborative scholarship. Furthermore, the contract explicitly indicated that, "the level of her research contributions will be limited in quantity because Linda's prime obligation is service." This she felt would protect her, "should I have needed the protection."

The criteria established for evaluating Linda's teaching, or "instructional effectiveness" is also worth noting. The contract again quoted standard university policy to define teaching as "the use of appropriate and productive pedagogical methods." However, the contract recognized that Linda's "contributions in this area go beyond the classroom." Also of significance, Linda purposefully included language that accepted student and faculty testimonials as appropriate measures of her effectiveness:

> Evaluation of the institutional value of Linda's work will be documented by accumulated student and faculty feedback in the form of questionnaires, evaluations, or solicited written assessments from tutors, students, or those faculty who have had opportunities to work with her over a reasonable period of time in which she has served the university. Further feedback will be solicited from the Dean of Liberal Arts and the members of the current Writing Across the Curriculum Committee, who represent a cross-section of the college.

Linda afforded me access to her promotion and tenure documents, including her contract and her promotion and tenure dossier, a thick three-ring binder that included a copy of her vita and a series of narrative statements. It also included copies of her 10 years of ARPAs and resulting merit evaluations. She was required to include statements of her teaching philosophy and research accomplishments. Linda also added two key documents: (a) an opening statement that explicitly addressed the criteria outlined in her contract, and (b) a statement about her administrative service activities. The dossier also contained external review letters from three faculty and a testimonial letter co-signed by the eight-member WAC committee. In keeping with the principle articulated by Glassick and his colleagues, the statements written by Linda outline her philosophies of teaching and administration and highlight what she believes to be the significance of her work in the respective areas. In her "narrative response" to her contract, she explicitly articulated what she believed to be the meritorious ways she had met and exceeded the criteria and expectations set forth in that document. These statements referenced specific work and other documentation that she included in a supplemental file container. The last section of her dossier inventoried the contents of an additional file containing the documentary evidence (see Appendix B for a copy of the table of contents of Linda's dossier). Linda's dossier is a remarkable collection of arguments and evidence.

In her narrative response to her contract, Linda argued how she met the outlined expectations. She foregrounded the fact that it was agreed that evaluative weight was to be placed on her administrative and professional service. To argue her administrative service, she pointed to evidence of the success of her writing center and WAC program and how the program has been incorporated into the university's strategic plan and mission statement. She referenced her APRAs and how her duties and responsibilities rapidly expanded over time given her ability to meet and exceed annual goals. She pointed to the number of faculty publications as a result of her consultations and workshops, the number of approved WI courses, and her activities developing materials for faculty development workshops. She also directed the reviewers to testimonial letters written by current and former deans, the WAC committee, faculty, and students. To establish that she met the criteria for professional service, Linda pointed to her activities with university committees, community outreach, and professional organizations. Her arguments continue like this for her research and teaching. In her research section (identified as "professional activities"), she reiterates that her research "is tempered by my primary responsibility as an administrator of two academic programs." In her teaching section, she lists the courses she taught and co-taught, the students and faculty she tutored, graduate students she mentored, and the dissertation committees she served on. But she also highlights her own broadened conception of teaching: "However, I mostly teach faculty or those who teach others; I do this by conducting faculty development workshops, tutor training courses, in-service meetings with tutors linked to writing intensive sections, and in the outreach workshops linked to the grant projects." Linda's separate administrative, teaching, and research statements then deepen and elaborate on these claims.

As Linda recalled it, her review "sailed through" every administrator and committee. But the Evil Queen tried to deny it. The recommending university committee balked at this suggestion, however, threatening that denial of her case would be grounds for a lawsuit that they would support. She learned that the service, research, and teaching statements were considered very persuasive and important to her approval at all levels of the process. She had even been asked on occasion to share with faculty her strategies for constructing the dossier. Her grant writing and community outreach activities were also extremely valued. Between her curriculum development grants, mentoring projects, and public school initiatives, she was looked on as a "money-making machine," and it would have been politically dangerous for anyone to be associated with those who let her go.

She attributed her institutional success in terms of how well her work was received to the collegial networks she built up. When I asked her if she ever felt her position was indeed threatened, especially early on, she replied:

> I am incredibly optimistic and naïve, even after all these years of cynicism building. I never thought of failure. I never thought I would get fired, initially. It never occurred to me. It wasn't in my vocabulary. It *was* hard not having that academic home, but I learned among the people in biology, art history, geography, and all the other disciplines that there was incredible support and interest in what I was doing. The support of deans, the administration, and really of the president was incredibly important all along. Until the Evil Queen. Then it got scary, which is why I went through the agony of tenure. I never questioned the support of the faculty, just certain administrators that had too much power.
> . . .
> I've always felt both alone and supported. It's an odd position to be it, but it seems that being a writing center/WAC professional, you're always treading across some line: you're being directive/non-directive; you're being an administrator and a faculty member; you're not part of a community, but you're part of every community; you're an outsider, but you're an insider. And that's why we are so very different in many ways. That outsider/insider status is both a plus and it has its downsides. . . . It's like living what we practice in many ways, and that is that you network, you understand, you listen, you adopt, you're flexible, and you build relationships.

When she does feel threatened, she said she begins to network, to rebuild "that faculty base." She commented that, despite surviving through the terms of three university presidents ("five if you count interims"), five provosts or vice presidents, and five or six deans, she never felt a lack of support from the faculty (except for some within the English Department) and from her immediate supervisors. As she said, "You have to build trust and define yourself in your negotiations with colleagues—and I've spent 12 years doing it." Many of the local faculty involved in the review were even surprised to discover that Linda was not a faculty member.

Like Roger, Linda's cross-curricular work earned her respect and status within in her community. When it came time for her tenure evaluation, this hard-earned reputation manifested itself into rich and varied body of documentary evidence, particularly testimonial letters. Of course, Linda strategically constructed her dossier, making sure to include such documentation as part of her overall tenure portfolio. Again, like Roger, Linda's meticulous presentation of her scholarly work persuaded her reviewers that her cross-curricular work (which for over 5 years was conducted in a professional, not academic, position) was of rigorous scholarly nature. As Linda said, she never thought of herself as *not* being a faculty member and as *not* being worthy of tenure. She never thought of WC work or faculty consultations or committee work as *service*, and therefore she constructed it differently: "As long as I chose to reconstruct my job description every year, and as long as I chose to take the staid tenure documents and redefine them by the ways in which I did, they had no alternative but to look at them—to look at me— that way."

CONCLUSION: CONSTRUCTING WAC SCHOLARSHIP

How has the work of these writing specialists been valued and how has it been made valuable? What constitutes these writing specialists' success? There is little doubt that these three individuals can be counted among the overachievers, people extremely dedicated to their professional lives. They excelled according to the existing criteria for evaluating work at their particular institutions with little or no significant prejudice against CCL work. Patricia always sought to bring her work to the broader professional audience, consistently producing work that has exchange value in the academic marketplace, even as she developed useful local knowledge. Roger benefited from his program's progressive conception of teaching, but in part because he valued the opportunity for self-reflection that preparing the teaching portfolio afforded, he took it on himself to carefully document and present his work. Linda's success was similar to Patricia's in that she did more than what was expected of her in terms of research, teaching, and service. However, given the somewhat ambiguous administrative location of her position and the volatile political climate of her institution, Linda strategically negotiated institutional expectations in her contracts that recognized the nontraditional forms of scholarship that were necessary for leading and administering the discipline-based writing program that emanated from her WC. These three writing specialists did not encounter significant problems, largely because they connected their work to accepted forms of academic labor at their institutions.

Patricia's case helps illustrate how to integrate personal professional values with the local expectations of faculty work. It is Patricia's ethic toward collaboration that is most worthy of emulation. She exemplifies the "qualities of a scholar" espoused by Glassick and his colleagues. Although she is conscious of the relatively low status of her work with teaching, learning, and writing, she has "come to peace" with this. She views her work as worthy service that contributes to the "work of the world." She has always been active in terms of campus community service, but she *integrates* this service with her research and teaching. Her intellectual work is manifested in grants, curriculum proposals, writing program administration, and collaborative research. Several "big" books certainly helped her cause, and not every academic may have the gift and drive to be as prolific as Patricia, but she expresses a savvy sensitivity as to what is acceptable within her particular institutional context. Simply put, link what you believe to be important work to projects that have a "payoff in the academic marketplace" for you and your colleagues, which will vary according to the institutional context and career goals of the individual.

Roger shows how meticulous documentation and rigorous reflection helps develop persuasive accounts of one's professional activity. One need not be at an institution where teaching is understood so broadly to accomplish this. Roger most clearly exhibits Glassick and his colleagues' general scholarly standard of self-critical reflection. "All works of scholarship," Glassick et al. write, "be they discovery, integration, application, or teaching, involve a common sequence of unfolding states" that include effective presentation in suitable forums and reflective critique to improve the quality of future work (24). So whether "peer education" be considered teaching or part of one's administrative service duties, through public presentation scholars avail their work to self-reflection and external scrutiny. Reflection also encourages the further application and integration of knowledge into new contexts. "Careful examination and constructive criticism," Glassick et al. add, "enrich scholarly work by enabling old projects to inform new ones. It is precisely the reflection encouraged by these activities that connects separate projects and makes them integral parts of some larger intellectual quest" (35). Although he admitted preparing his evaluation portfolio was time-consuming, Roger appreciated the insights into his own teaching that resulted from writing the various reflections.

At such institutions where academic work is not yet viewed through the Boyer paradigm, and in cases where writing specialists are called on to do traditionally undervalued composition-related work, like WAC faculty development and program administration, arguments will have to made to support one's scholarly activity. As Louise Phelps observes, academic inertia is strong and, despite the increasing weight given to teaching at many institutions, academic values are by and large slow to change ("Rethinking"). Phelps notes that faculty members collectively have the power to change values and practices through the administration of the promotion and tenure system. Yet academics are reluctant to lower the bar in the face of external pressures and continue to socialize new faculty in the traditional academic culture. Not until such institutional structures recognize the broader spectrum of work and "make rewards commensurate with individual talents and highly diverse institutional priorities" will faculty stop feeling like they have to "do it all" ("Rethinking" 13).

Linda's case in particular illustrates how best to balance traditional expectations with the distinctive intellectual character of academic writing consulting, tutoring, and writing program administration. True, Linda's record would speak for itself at any institution, even in more traditional frameworks for assessing academic work. But partly on principle—believing a writing program is the most "public of publications"—and partly for local political reasons—to ensure her tenure approval in a volatile environment—Linda strategically negotiated her own criteria and expectations, making sure that her WC/writing program administration and faculty development work was considered valuable and scholarly.

Linda also argued for expanded forms of scholarly documentation, including student and peer testimonials. What counts as scholarly publication for academic writing consulting can be expanded to include the texts of consulting work—other faculty members' syllabi, reviews of scholarship on disciplinary discourses, and local and global reports of classroom inquiry. Consultants likely employ distinctive genres such as the psychological contract document I discussed in chapter 4, a consultant's diagnosis/feedback report, and workshop materials. Roger's year-end "administrator's report" directed to his writing program's outreach coordinator is another example of a document that manifests his scholarly activity. Glassick et al. propose other new forms of scholarly documentation, such as a statement of responsibilities that reflects expectations negotiated between the scholar and the institution (similar to Linda's promotion and tenure statement), a biographical sketch that lists a scholar's achievements in the relevant areas of the scholar's work (similar to Linda's narrative statements), and selected examples of the scholar's best work, documented according to the standards for assessing scholarly work in "a reflective essay and by rich and varied materials" (43-45).[6] In their own ways, and in light of their particular situations, Roger and Linda each creatively stretched the generic expectations of their institution's evaluation polices and performance expectations.

What I was not initially prepared to learn when I raised the question about the institutional value of WAC work was the participants' perception that their activity in this area was indeed valued and valuable. Granted, it is difficult to generalize across three cases; nonetheless, I found that each participant's CCL work was generally well received at his or her respective institutions. In retrospect, I should have expected that these experts' success would be reflected in their accomplishments as measured by the faculty reward system and indicative of their ability to effectively negotiate this system. These cases suggest that instead of focusing on narratives of frustration and failure, it perhaps can become more productive to focus on stories of successful tactics for arguing scholarly merit. What is insightful, then, in looking at how the work of these accomplished writing specialists was valued, is their strategies for aligning their work with the expectations of their local institutions and broader profession. Better understanding this can help future practitioners reclaim—or locate—the interdisciplinary activities of

CCL specialists within a new paradigm which recognizes that academic writing consulting can be a complex, intellectual activity grounded in specialized knowledge.

NOTES

1. Because her primary appointment was as a professional staff member, she was considered professional staff. Her appointment to the English Department was considered secondary and not a full-time position. Thus, both positions disqualified her from faculty voting privileges.
2. Roger had served on the evaluation committee in the past. He also wrote an analysis of changes in the program's curriculum based on an historical analysis of portfolios stored in the program's public archive.
3. In his reflection, Roger uses last names to refer to himself and his colleague. I have elected to use the pseudonym "Roger" for smoother reading and to be consistent with my use of first-name pseudonyms.
4. As Linda described it, there was tension between the "Evil Queen" vice president and her dean because both applied for the vice president's position. The Evil Queen disfavored those who were considered allied with the Liberal Arts dean, including Linda. "I didn't find out about all of this until way after my tenure, and I'm sure she has her story too," added Linda. This kind of personal politics becomes part of the mix, along with prevailing attitudes about academic work, disciplinary status, gender, and so forth.
5. Again, I have replaced the last name with her first-name pseudonym.
6. Glassick et al. assert that "documentation in depth cannot and should not involve the entire output of a scholar's efforts. A reflective essay, accompanied by rich and varied materials, should focus on selected samples of the scholar's best work. . . . A reflective essay would introduce projects selected, addressing their goals, preparation, methods, and results; presentation of the project; and self-critique and development" (44-45). Roger indicated that one particularly effective strategy the instructors used in portfolio reviews at his institution was to "showcase a particular course and devote a number of pieces to that."

CONCLUSION:
THE FOURTH STAGE OF WAC

Cynthia Lewiecki-Wilson and Jeff Sommers' "Professing at the Fault Lines: Composition at Open Admissions Institutions" evokes the concept of identity to disrupt the way prevailing discourses serve to "structure perceptions so that it is very difficult to see, let alone seriously consider, any possibility of satisfying intellectual work occurring between composition teachers and their students in open admissions programs" (439). Rather than the spaces of predisciplinarity, professional disciplinarity, or even postdisciplinarity that theorists often construct for composition studies, open-admissions colleges are often implicitly constructed as sites "for the discipline of punishment, applied to both students and teachers, and legitimated through metaphors of deficit" (439). To recuperate open-admissions college writing in the historical formation of composition studies, Lewiecki-Wilson and Sommers present descriptive images of writing specialists who teach or have taught at 2- or 4-year open-admissions institutions (440). These images of who open-admissions compositionists really are and what they really do attempt to "reverse" the "normal patterns of thought" about these Other compositionists (440). They ask their mainstream composition audience to "reflect on how such a shift in thinking might change views of the profession and redirect attention to work compositionists need to do for the future" (440). They conclude by arguing,

> The profession should see open admissions composition teaching not as a low-level site merely for the application of knowledge, but as an intellectually productive and transformative site of disciplinary practice. Coming to such an understanding is only the first step, but one that may lead compositionists to undertake and value different kinds of work in

the future. When open admissions composition teaching is seen as central, it becomes clear that working to preserve open admissions programs is as crucial to the future of the discipline as preserving and enlarging graduate programs, and that *translating the practices and theories of the undergraduate writing classroom to colleagues in other departments and the public is as important as conducting research and writing to one another in scholarly journals.* (459; italics added)

Although I by no means wish to co-opt the pressing problem of open-admissions compositionists' material and professional marginalization, I do believe there are parallels in the way WAC is misperceived and ignored within the broader field. Moreover, I concur with Lewiecki-Wilson and Sommers that, as the italicized part of the quoted passage asserts, translating our disciplinary knowledge is as important—or more important, given current pressures to control discourse on literacy by outside constituencies such as legislatures and private education think tanks—than "writing to one another in scholarly journals."

In "WAC Myths and Realities," Susan McLeod and Elaine Maimon respond to what they see as a collective and pervasive misunderstanding of "the WAC enterprise" in mainstream composition studies discourse. Addressing what they call the "still current" view of WAC, McLeod and Maimon single out C.H. Knoblauch and Lil Brannon's "Writing as Learning through the Curriculum," and Daniel Mahala's "Writing Utopias" as exemplifying "a distortion of the history and theory of WAC—promulgating false dichotomies and myths that continue to (mis)inform perceptions of WAC today" (579). They enumerate four such myths perpetuated through the intertextual citation practices of current publications and dissertations that they argue can be traced, in part, back to the Knoblauch and Brannon and Mahala articles:

1. At the beginning of the movement . . . most WAC programs had a reductive focus: "grammar across the curriculum."
2. Writing across the curriculum (WAC) is different from and in opposition to writing in the disciplines (WID), since only the former focuses on "writing to learn" approaches.
3. "Writing to learn" approaches to WAC are superior to those that only focus on learning to write disciplinary discourse, since the latter approach involves only technical correctness.
4. WAC theory in the United States has not challenged the status quo in higher education but has taken forms that "rationalize prevailing institutional divisions and attitudes" (Mahala 786-87), rather than opening up the discussion to competing forms of academic literacy. (574)

McLeod and Maimon refute these assumptions one by one, presenting instead the "realities" of WAC, namely that WAC is a pedagogical reform movement made up of a complimentary WAC and WID approaches, and a programmatic entity made up of many components. Few compositionists today would support the first claim that WAC is merely "grammar across the curriculum," and McLeod and Maimon are "puzzled that it persists" in some quarters. But, despite the turn toward the social perspective in composition, they felt compelled to "speak up in light of the staying power of WAC myths" (574). The beliefs that WID is preoccupied with formalist concerns, that WAC and WID constitute competing theories, and that WAC is a conservative movement have bases in the theory debates of the early 1990s, inspired by arguments such as Mahala's critique, Russell's historical accounts, and Bazerman's landmark "Second Stage" review article. These two approaches, the WAC versus WID "camps" as they have become known in the discourse, have reified into static paradigms that explicitly claim contradictory purposes, understandings of writing, and politics.

In "Missionary Projects and Anthropological Accounts: Ethics and Conflict in Writing Across the Curriculum," Linda Bergmann recounts these contending positions to explore how they shape professional goals and values. The early WAC movement, as Bergmann tells it, focused on translating expressivist composition theory into disciplinary contexts. This writing to learn approach valorized personal expression and personal writing as a means to self-discovery and knowledge acquisition. Student-centered practices such as journal writing and peer collaboration were disseminated in faculty workshops with messianic zeal. "The early discourse on WAC has," according to Bergmann, "a religious fervor and reads like missionary writing" and that "bears a certain resemblance to the enthusiastic community building of the camp meeting or revival" (147). When WAC theory moved into the "second stage," where researchers who adopted constructivist frameworks turned to looking at how writing operates in the disciplines, scholars warned against compositionists assuming "colonizer" or "missionary" stances that assumed our views toward language and reality were superior to those held in other disciplines, as if we were spreading "the Word" on writing, teaching, and learning to the ignorant masses. Scholars argued instead that WAC specialists should assume the stance of ethnographers examining new cultures. As Bergmann writes: "Some WAC practitioners, 'out in the field,' so to speak, like the more anthropologically oriented missionaries of expansionist Christianity . . . have seen that in order to convert the 'natives'—in this case the scientists and engineers—we need to understand their language, their culture, and their practices" (147).

To Bergmann's credit, she admits to exaggerating the difference between the missionary and anthropologist camps and that her use of the religious metaphor is somewhat satirical. But this discourse, what I referred to in chapter 1 as missionary rhetoric, has weighty implications nonetheless:

> The theoretical differences between expressivists and constructivists that could be ignored in the earlier stages of WAC threaten to become ethical differences demanding real choices; despite some common origins, the anthropologist and the missionary have different goals, different professions, and different ethics—and along with them, different codes of behavior and different conceptions of good practice. And thus, I fear, those of us who look at disciplinary writing and the development of expertise as fostering individual growth stand on the other side of a major ethical divide from those of us who see them as opposed to each other. (148)

The key distinction, as Bergmann points out, is that expressivists valorize personal expression above public/transactional disciplinary discourse. Constructivists, on the other hand, hold that personal growth "takes place within disciplinarity, as the student gains proficiency in and understanding of the discourses and practices of a chosen discipline" (147). Only through the process of being socialized into a group, for example American society or academic disciplines, can the individual realize selfhood.

Bergmann's narrative stops short of including "third-stage" arguments critiquing the conservative tendencies of both WAC and WID (Chase; LeCourt; Mahala and Swilky; Tate). In her essay, "WAC as Critical Pedagogy," Donna LeCourt asks WAC to consider its means and ends in relation to writing instruction in other contexts such as first-year writing and advanced composition: "In particular, [those in WAC] seem to have forgotten the concern for alternative literacies and voices Other to the academy that permeates much of our discussion of writing courses in an English department" (390). Following Mahala, LeCourt critiques both WAC and WID's focus on the uncritical initiation, or in her words, the "accommodation" of students into disciplinary/professional discourses (390). LeCourt corrects this approach with her model:

> [A] more open and critical approach to disciplinary discourses would (1) recognize the continual conflicts currently being played out within the discourse, (2) examine the influence of wider social discourses on their construction, and (3) interrogate how a discourse's constitution is both productive and silencing. (393)

In LeCourt's framework, language anthropologists are simultaneously positioned as cultural critics who aim to interrogate disciplinary discourses as they attempt to understand them, so that they can foreground the suppressed perspectives and voices within the disciplines. LeCourt's critical model, based on cultural studies ideological critique, joins other attempts to wrest WAC from its limiting dichotomous construction of writing to learn and learning to write approaches (e.g., Jones and Comprone; Kirscht, Levine, and Reiff; McLeod, "Introduction"; Walvoord, "Future"). When mapped against each other, the perspectives inherent in the three stages of WAC theory might be represented as something resembling Table 7.1.

Despite efforts by theorists to integrate these approaches, there is still evidence that discourse within WAC and the broader field of composition studies has not moved beyond the paradigm wars. As McLeod and Maimon demonstrate, the myths persist. In one of the more recent WAC-related works, *Demythologizing Language Difference in the Academy* (2004), Mark Waldo dwells on the differences between writing to learn and learning to write approaches, determining that "although the two may not be contradictory, they are not complimentary" (11). Waldo wishes to elevate WID over WAC based on the rationale that because writing to learn is grounded in "process-expressivism," developed by composition studies for first-year writing courses, approaches based on this paradigm are incompatible with learning to write because writing to learn approaches "belongs mostly to one discipline. Not shared across the disciplines, it cannot compliment learning to write" (11). Ultimately, Waldo metaphorically wants to "nudge" writing to learn "off the [Ivory] Tower and out of WAC practice" (11). Even though most programs typically incorporate both WAC and WID approaches, the binary logic of the competing paradigms is difficult to escape in the narratives from our field.

In terms McLeod and Maimon would agree with, when reified into static, fixed identities for WAC specialists, the paradigm wars represent a history of WAC misperceptions and false dichotomies. Our professional discourse socializes us to accept these competing positions in many ways. And, as McLeod and Maimon indicate, these false dichotomies, and the tensions they evoke, are instantiated every time the seemingly incompatible traditions are juxtaposed in our official histories and everyday professional conversations. These categories become, like the "buzzwords" or "ideological labels" Kirscht, Levine, and Reiff refer to, subject positions demarcating identity and professional values. Individuals avoid being associated with seemingly retrograde assumptions, as in the case of Bergmann, who admits to switching sides, as it were, after the "discomfort" of at one time "finding herself in the camp of the missionaries" (146). At the programmatic level,

> WAC directors must choose which group we belong to and whose assumptions we share. To put the matter bluntly, at some point WAC directors must face the question of whether WAC programs should seek to teach the discursive practices of scientists, sociologists, and engineers, or to ignore or even attempt to transform them. (Bergmann 150)

Table 7.1 Mapping Three Stages of WAC

	WAC	WID	Critical WAC
Stage	Stage 1	Stage 2	Stage 3
Approach	Writing to learn	Learning to write	Writing critically
Theoretical paradigm[a]	Expressivism	Social constructionism	Social-epistemic
Ideology (what is good)	• Acquisition • Self-discovery	• Socialization • Enculturation	• Agency • Access
Research	Education-oriented	Discipline-oriented	Discourse-oriented
Objects of study	Teaching and learning of writing in disciplinary contexts	Disciplinary rhetorical conventions	Discursive negotiation/construction of: • knowledge • disciplinarity • identity/subjectivity
Pedagogy	Process-based	Genre-based	Cultural studies-based
Disciplines	(Monolithic) Academy	Multiple discourse communities	Sites of: • discursive production and consumption • contestation • action
WAC specialist	Missionary	Anthropologist	Cultural critic
Faculty	"Content-area" instructor	Professional	Collaborator
Student	Learner	• Neophyte • Apprentice	• Agent • Bricoleur

[a]Based on Berlin's histories of contemporary composition studies (Rhetoric and Reality).

Bergmann finds it difficult to avoid suggesting CCL specialists are confronted with anything other than either/or choices, reflecting the limits of still current WAC theoretical discourse. Relying on the notion of ethics as "a group's consensus about ideals," she goes so far as to speculate that "it may be useful to conceive of [the different perspectives] as different professions, or at least, different subprofessions, with distinct values and practices" (149).

The discursive construction of these various and competing roles reflects a disjunction between theory and practice, what Steve Parks and Eli Goldblatt call "the narrow politics of theory debates" (589). These roles become reified into fixed, prescriptive categories, and the maintenance of these categories in the discourse increasingly bears little resemblance to the work of CCL specialists. The still current discourse on WAC promulgates images of CCL specialists that persist in the myths and misperceptions within mainstream composition studies discourse. LeCourt remarks that the most resistance to her efforts at incorporating cultural studies-based rhetorical criticism comes *from other writing specialists* skeptical of disciplinary specialists' willingness to incorporate newer, more democratic practices — and politics — into their teaching (399). As she suggests, "these reactions are based in metaphors about our roles as WAC consultants and the impressions of our colleagues that need to be re-examined" (403).

It was my intention to present a more complete picture of the professional competencies of CCL specialists. More research along these lines could contribute to, in the words of McLeod and Maimon, more "enlightened discussion of what WAC is, what it does, and what it can become" (573). The images of CCL work in chapter 3, for instance, compel us to question the implications of the authoritative narratives of WAC discourse for our practical and theoretical understandings. In place of the missionary rhetoric are concrete representations of WAC practice. The participants in this study were concerned professionals who, through experience and integration of disciplinary and applied knowledge, developed sophisticated, albeit largely tacit, strategies of interacting with faculty members across the disciplines. The profiles go against prevailing conceptions in many ways. Noticeably absent is a missionary zeal often associated with WAC; there are no images of naïve or arrogant colonists looking to make disciplines over in their own ways of thinking. More common was a representation of collaboration as an opportunity to view contexts ordinarily out of the purview of our teaching and research, and to learn about how others approach writing, learning, and teaching. On the other hand, the career trajectories of Patricia and Linda, in particular, speak to the maturation of WAC as a field. Patricia's early nonexpert stances were in part indicative of the newness of composition studies as an academic field of inquiry. She marveled at the steady growth of WAC research, some contributions of which were hers. Linda noted how her early fervor was tempered over time into a respect for peo-

ple's disciplinary perspectives. Even the tire-kickers were for Linda like out-
liers in research data, opportunities to reexamine assumptions and hone
one's own perspective. The individual learning curves represented in their
stories is perhaps a better way to understand and reconcile the missionary
rhetoric of WAC.

Influenced by the teacher-research and professional knowledge movements, both of which seek to recover forms of expert knowing suppressed
by prevailing disciplinary and professional formations, I used the lens of
consulting to explore the knowledge base of CCL specialists. As I argued in
chapter 1, the missionary rhetoric of WAC discourse assumes a paradoxical
stance that has thus far eschewed the expertise of writing specialists in formal WAC programs and other CCL initiatives. This stance has prevented
more systemic inquiry into questions about how writing specialists initiate,
conduct, and assess effective collaborative relationships in CCL contexts;
how they apply theoretical knowledge in day-to-day interactions with faculty and other professionals who seek out our expertise in writing; what
techniques are used when translating our specialized knowledge of composition and rhetoric to nonspecialists; and what methods and models we
should use to guide our CCL work. Foregrounding the professional dimensions of academic writing consulting allows us to examine current theory
and to codify the tacit ways of knowing and doing of experienced consultants, thereby creating new theories of practice to guide our work.

Bergmann is right that as CCL writing specialists we must make ethical
choices. But our concern should not be so self-serving. As a profession, our
choices should be focused outward toward the public and various constituents we serve. Take for instance the following principles of practice outlined by the Organization Development Network, a professional association of OD practitioners.

> The practice of ID is grounded in a distinctive set of core values
> and principles that guide behavior and actions. [These] key values
> include:
> - *Respect and Inclusion*—equitably values the perspective and
>   opinions of everyone.
> - *Collaboration*—builds collaborative relationships between the
>   practitioner and the client while encouraging collaboration
>   throughout the client system.
> - *Authenticity*—strives for authenticity and congruence and
>   encourages these qualities in their clients.
> - *Self-awareness*—commits to developing self-awareness and inter-
>   personal skills. OD practitioners engage in personal and profes-
>   sional development through lifelong learning.

• *Empowerment*—focuses efforts on helping everyone in the client organization or community increase their autonomy and empowerment to levels that make the workplace and/or community satisfying and productive.

I think regardless of the WAC paradigm one identifies with, most would concur that the core values of organization development—respect, collaboration, empowerment—are consonant with WAC's student- and faculty-centered roots. Assuming more of a professional model in WAC theory and practice would allow for more systematic development of ways to translate our disciplinary knowledge in useful and productive ways, with the operative terms of "useful" and "productive" being jointly negotiated between us and our "clients."

As factors such as technology and multimedia, the information economy, and surges in college enrollments continue to call attention to the increased need for professional and public literacies, and as various constituencies come to us for help in the form of grants for assessment and faculty development, in endowments for creating communication institutes and centers, in invitations to sit on panels and other deliberative bodies, we need to study attempts at what Segal et al. refer to as "sticking our necks out" in the disciplines. We should focus our case studies on the negotiation, translation, and application of our field's knowledge. This has to occur, as Christopher Thaiss points out, within the highly localized contexts of individual classrooms, not at the more abstracted level of the "discipline":

> More useful [than WID] in looking at writing cultures in academia might be the notion of "WIC"—or "writing in the course" (analogous to "writing in the workplace"). This concept would allow researchers to observe the richness of each course context without having to fit that context within the arbitrary category of a so-called discipline. ("Theory and WAC" 317)

Thaiss is calling attention to the limitations of overgeneralizing research on disciplinary discourse. For instance, referring to the theoretical premises of WAC paradigms I outlined in Table 7.1, in any given disciplinary context, a student might simultaneously be positioned as "learner" (the student subject position of WAC theory) and "apprentice" (the WID student subject position) with the student subjected to negotiating this tension: Do the student's goals include professionalization (as an apprentice) or are they more short term (learning the course content)? Students variously inhabit these positions, often in conflicting ways. LeCourt names Jim Henry's narratological study of student authorship in an architecture seminar as a promising investigation of the complexity of classrooms as "scenes" of disciplinary discursive activity and negotiation of multiple subjectivity. Thaiss relates such inquiry to the teacher research tradition in composition studies, because it "sees the relationship between the individual teacher and a group of students as the most meaningful locus of study about writing in the academic context" (317). Furthermore, teacher research, as Thaiss observes, positions the teacher as the primary researcher "because the goal of the research is the teacher's knowledge, with the long-range objective being improved teaching and learning" (317).

   I connect my project to teacher research as well. My interest is in understanding the knowledge base of a different sort of teacher practitioner, the academic writing consultant. The consulting lens modifies the object of study in "WIC" research somewhat by adding the role and influence of the writing specialist(s) as a factor worth studying. Other than McCarthy and Fishman and Mullen et al., few have done this in our research. To move beyond the limiting constructions of our own positions as missionaries or accomodationists, I recommend foregrounding our role as rhetoricians, as writing specialists who assume an ideological and ethical responsibility for teaching others the value of rhetorical knowledgeability. To assume otherwise is to ignore our role as change agents authorized (from within and without) to improve literacy—broadly defined—across the curriculum. Part of our effort to reclaim our expertise as rhetoricians must be directed toward developing methods and models for translating our disciplinary knowledge to others. This should be the mission of WAC's fourth stage.

APPENDIX A:
FRONTMATTER TO ROGER'S
EVALUATION PORTFOLIO

I have edited the following frontmatter from Roger's performance evaluation portfolio. I changed full names to pseudonyms, altered course abbreviations and descriptions, and omitted the names of special curricular programs to avoid possibly identifying the actual institution.

Portfolio Cover Sheet

Name: *Roger*
How many years have you taught in the program? *13*
What assignments did you hold over the contract period(s) covered in this portfolio? *See Prefatory Matter, Map 1, Schedule of Appointments*
Did any of these assignments represent wholly new courses or duties for you? If so, which ones? *Yes: WRI 109, Spring 1996 (new course design), WRI 400/PSY 400, Fall 1998 (new course, co-taught in Psychology), WRI 109, Fall 1998 (associated with Honors learning community; I was also new to the [name of special literacy curriculum writing program])*
Did you choose those new assignments, or were they given to you by the program? *Chose the first. Designed and proposed the second. Was invited to teach and accepted the third.*
Did you perform any of your assignments in new ways (like a significantly redesigned version of a particular course)? If so, which ones? *Yes, WRI 109, Spring 1996 was a complete departure from my previous WRI 109, which I had taught successfully for a number of iterations. WRI 400 involved co-teaching with my textbook co-author Markos in the Psychology Department. This was more a writing-intensive content/discussion course than a writing course. WRI 109, Fall 1998 was a [name of literacy curriculum*

writing program] variant taught in an informal dorm setting to a group of students living together.

Map 1: Schedule of Appointments

	Summer 1996 WRI 205 (Dist. Ed.)
Fall 1996 WRI 109 WRI 405 Writing Lab	*Spring 1997* WRI 105 (Dist. Ed.) WRI 209 (Management) Honors consultant
	Summer 1997 WRI 205 (Dist. Ed.)
Fall 1997 WRI 405 WRI 405 Writing Lab	*Spring 1998* WRI 205 WRI 209 (Management) Honors Consultant
	Summer 1998 WRI 205 (Dist. Ed.)
Fall 1998 WRI 400/PSY 400 WRI 109 (learning community) Writing Lab	*Spring 1999* WRI 105 (Dist. Ed.) WRT (Management) Honors Consultant

Map 2
Preface: Organization of this Portfolio

The bulk of this portfolio is organized by course. Amplifying these at certain points are other required portfolio materials. I hope this arrangement will help readers see items like observations and handouts in the context of the courses they were designed for.

Materials are listed, explained, contextualized at the head of each section. Items included for browsing only are marked.

Some of the syllabi, notably the WRI 105s and the WRT 209s contain redundant elements. I have tried to note these on the section head pages, and to mark areas of change in the syllabi schedules—local places where I switched readings or re-wrote policy changes.

If questions arise in the reading of the course evaluations (which range from stellar to dismal), I refer the reader to my response in Part 5

In general, because of the emphases in WRI 209 and the distance education courses, the portfolio is not very effective in portraying collaborative activity among students. I will note here, therefore, that drafts of every significant project are read in peer groups. I also tend to use peer groups in informal classroom exercises, for instance, where students might be asked to straighten out a sample problem text. These are sometimes visible on the course schedules. Two of the handouts emphasize collaborative activity.

Parts 6, 7, and 8 of the portfolio contain material beyond my teaching: Part 6 contains consultant information. Part 7 summarizes my other professional development work, and Part 8 contains my administrative documents written for the program coordinators.

The next item, Map 3, gives a detailed outline of the portfolio contents.

Map 3
Portfolio Outline

Prefatory Material
P.1 Cover Sheet
P.2 Map 1: Schedule of Appointments
P.3 Map 2: Preface
P.4 Map 3: Portfolio Outline
P.5 Map 4: Where Required Materials Can Be Found

Part 1: The Rhetoric of Inquiry Course
1.1 Syllabus WRI 209, Spring 1999
1.8 Syllabus WRI 209, Spring 1998
1.15 Syllabus WRI 209, Spring 1997
1.22 Peer Observation by Nancy
1.24. Handout: Some Rhetorical Characteristics of Scientific Texts
1.26 Sample of Responding to Student Work
1.40 "Researcher," WRI 209 class magazine

Part 2: Observing Language Practices Course
2.1 Approach to Course Design Statement
2.5 Syllabus, WRI 109, Fall 1998
2.16 Syllabus, WRI 105 (Dist. Ed.), Spring 1999
2.29 Syllabus, WRI 105 (Dist. Ed.), Spring 1998
2.42 Syllabus, WRI 105 (Dist. Ed.), Spring 1997
2.55 Syllabus, WRI 109, Fall 1996
2.64 Handout: Debating PC, for 109, Fall 1996

Part 3: The Expert Writing at Work Course
2.41 Syllabus, WRI 405, Fall 1997
3.51 Syllabus, WRI 405, Fall 1996

Part 4: Perspectives on Drug Experience Course
4.1   Syllabus, WRI 400/PSY 400, Fall 1998
4.10 Handout: Peer Responding guidelines
4.11 Reflection, "The Dialogic Instructor"

Part 5: Responses to Student Evaluations
5.1 Response to Student Evaluations

Part 6: Consulting (Tutoring)
6.1 Typical consultant sign-up sheet
6.2 Editing Guide for Honors thesis writers
6.7 Scored Honors editing exercises

Part 7: Professional Development Activities
7.1 Other professional development activities
7.4 Optional Item: Curriculum Vitae
7.6 Optional Item: Classroom observation of another teacher

Part 8: Administrative Reports
8.1 Honors Consultant/Coordinator Report, Spring 1999
8.2 Honors Consultant/Coordinator Report, Spring 1998
8.3 Honors Consultant/Coordinator Report, Spring 1997

Map 4
Portfolio Outline

Cover Sheet	Prefatory matter, p.1
Preface	Prefatory matter, p. 3
Reflection	4.11
Syllabi	Parts 1-4
Three Handouts	1.23, 2.64, 4.10
Teaching Approach	2.1
Classroom Observation	1.22
Student Work	5.1
Tutor Work	Part 6
Optional Items	1.4, 7.4, 7.11

APPENDIX B:
TABLE OF CONTENTS FROM LINDA'S
PROMOTION AND TENURE DOSSIER

I.   Vita (16 pages)
II.   Tenure and Promotion Statement (3 pages)
III.   Supporting Documentation — Narrative: Tenure and Promotion (4 pages)
       a. Letter of Appointment (1 page)
IV.   Supporting Documentation — Administrative Statement (3 pages)
       a. Letter of Support, WAC Committee (2 pages)
       b. WAC Program Description (9 pages)
       c. Writing Center Mission Statement (1 page)
V.   Supporting Documentation — Research Statement (4 pages)
VI.   Supporting Documentation — Teaching Statement (2 pages)
VII.   Annual Report of Professional Activities (ARPA's), 1987-97 (41 pages)
VIII. Annual Evaluations 1987-97
IX.   Outside Reviews
X.   Documentation File Inventory (4 pages)

REFERENCES

Association of American Colleges and Universities (AACU). "Mission Impossible? The Future of Faculty Work." *Peer Review* 1.3 (1999).

AAUP Committee on College and University Teaching, Research, and Publication. "The Work of Faculty: Expectations, Priorities, and Rewards." *Academe* January/February (1994): 35-48.

"ADE Statement of Good Practice: Teaching, Evaluation, and Scholarship." *ADE Bulletin* 105 (1993): 43-45.

Allen, Nancy, Diane Atkinson, Meg Morgan, Teresa Moore, and Doug Snow. "What Experienced Collaborators Say about Collaborative Writing." *Journal of Business and Technical Communication* 1 (1987): 70-90.

Anderson, Paul. "Simple Gifts: Ethical Issues in the Conduct of Person-Based Composition Research." *College Composition and Communication* 49 (1998): 63-89.

Anson, Chris, ed. *The WAC Casebook: Scenes for Faculty Reflection and Program Development.* New York: Oxford University Press, 2002.

Anson, Chris, Michael Carter, Deanna P. Dannels, and Jon Rust. "Mutual Support: CAC Programs and Institutional Improvement in Undergraduate Education." *Language and Learning Across the Disciplines* 6 (2003): 25-37.

Anson, Chris M., John E. Schwiebert, and Michael M. Williamson, eds. *Writing Across the Curriculum: An Annotated Bibliography.* Westport, CT: Greenwood P, 1993.

Austin, Ann E. and Roger G. Baldwin. *Faculty Collaboration: Enhancing the Quality of Scholarship and Teaching.* ASHE-ERIC Higher Education Report No. 7, 1991.

Barnett, Robert W., and Jacob S. Blumner, eds. *Writing Centers and Writing Across the Curriculum Programs.* Westport, CT: Greenwood P, 1999.

Bazerman, Charles. "The Second Stage in Writing Across the Curriculum." *College English* 53 (1991): 209-12.

Bazerman, Charles, and David R. Russell. "Preface: Writing Across the Curriculum as Challenge to Rhetoric and Composition." *Landmark Essays on Writing Across the Curriculum*. Eds. Charles Bazerman and David R. Russell. Davis, CA: Hermagoras Press, 1994. xi-xvii.

Bean, John. *Engaging Ideas: The Professor's Guide to Integrating Writing, Critical Thinking, and Active Learning in the Classroom*. San Francisco, CA: Jossey-Bass, 1996.

Behrens, Laurence. "Writing, Reading, and the Rest of the Faculty: A Survey." *English Journal* 67 (1978): 654-60.

Bergmann, Linda. "Missionary Projects and Anthropological Accounts: Ethics and Conflict in Writing Across the Curriculum." *Foregrounding Ethical Awareness in Composition and English Studies*. Eds. Sheryl Fontaine and Susan Hunter. Portsmouth, NH: Boynton/Cook, 1998. 144-59.

Berlin, James A. "Rhetoric and Ideology in the Writing Class." *College English* 50 (1988): 477-94.

_____. *Rhetoric and Reality: Writing Instruction in American Colleges, 1900-1985*. Carbondale: Southern Illinois UP, 1987.

Blair, Catherine Pastore. "Only One of the Voices: Dialogic Writing Across the Curriculum." *College English* 50 (1988): 383-89.

Blyler, Nancy Roundy. "Research as Ideology in Professional Communication." *Technical Communication Quarterly* 4 (1995): 285-313.

_____. "Taking a Political Turn: The Critical Perspective and Research in Professional Communication." *Technical Communication Quarterly* 7 (1998): 33-52.

Boyer, Ernest L. *Scholarship Reconsidered: Priorities of the Professoriate*. The Carnegie Foundation for the Advancement of Teaching. San Francisco, CA: Jossey-Bass, 1990.

Bridgeman, Brent, and Sybil B. Carlson. "Survey of Academic Writing Tasks." *Written Communication* 1.2 (1984): 247-80.

Britton, James, Tony Burgess, Nancy Martin, Alex McLeod, and Harold Rosen. *The Development of Writing Abilities* (11-18). London: Macmillan, 1977.

Brooke, Robert. "Underlife and Writing Instruction." *College Composition and Communication* 38 (1987): 141-53.

Bruffee, Kenneth A. "Collaborative Learning and the 'Conversation of Mankind.'" *College English* 46 (1984): 635-52.

Bullock, Richard H. "When Administration Becomes Scholarship: The Future of Writing Program Administration." *WPA: Writing Program Administration* 11.1 (1987): 213-18.

Burke, W. Warner. *Organization Development: Principles and Practices*. Boston, MA: Little Brown, 1982.

Burnett, Rebecca E., and Helen Rothschild-Ewald. "Rabbit Trails, Ephemera, and Other Stories: Feminist Methodology and Collaborative Research." *Journal of Advanced Composition* 14 (1994): 21-51.

Chase, Geoffrey. "Accommodation, Resistance, and the Politics of Student Writing." *College Composition and Communication* 39 (1988): 13-22.

Council of Writing Program Administrators. "Evaluating the Intellectual Work of Writing Administration." *WPA: Writing Program Administration* 22.1-2 (1998): 85-104.

Covington, David H., Ann E. Brown, and Gary B. Blank. "An Alternative Approach to Writing Across the Curriculum: The Writing Assistance Program at North Carolina State University's School of Engineering." *WPA: Writing Program Administration* 8.3 (1985): 15-23.

Crowley, Sharon. "Composition's Ethic of Service, the Universal Requirement, and the Discourse of Student Need." *Composition in the University: Historical and Polemical Essays*. Pittsburgh, PA: University of Pittsburgh Press, 1998. 250-66.

Cushman, Ellen. "Opinion: The Public Intellectual." *College English* 61 (1999): 328-36.

Debs, Mary Beth. "Reflexive and Reflective Tensions: Considering Research Methods from Writing-Related Fields." *Writing in the Workplace: New Research Perspectives*. Ed. Rachel Spilka. 238-52.

Diamond, Robert M. "The Tough Task of Reforming the Faculty-Rewards System." *Chronicle of Higher Education* 11 May 1994: B1-3.

Dick, John A. R., and Robert M. Esch. "Dialogues Among Disciplines: A Plan for Faculty Discussions of Writing Across the Curriculum." *College Composition and Communication* 36 (1985): 178-82.

Durst, Russel K., and Sherry C Stanforth. "'Everything's Negotiable:' Collaboration and Conflict in Composition Research." *Ethics and Representation in Qualitative Studies of Literacy*. Eds. Peter Mortensen and Gesa. 58-76.

Ede, Lisa, and Andrea Lunsford. *Singular Texts/Plural Authors: Perspectives on Collaborative Writing*. Carbondale: Southern Illinois University Press, 1990.

Ervin, Elizabeth, and Dana L. Fox. "Collaboration as Political Action." *Journal of Advanced Composition* 14 (1994): 53-71.

Emig, Janet. *The Composing Processes of Twelfth Graders*. Urbana: National Council of Teachers of English, 1971.

Faery, Rebecca Blevins. "Teachers and Writers: The Faculty Writing Workshop and Writing Across the Curriculum." *WPA: Writing Program Administration* 17 (1993): 31-42.

Faigley, Lester, and Kristine Hansen. "Learning to Write in the Social Sciences." *College Composition and Communication* 36 (1985): 140-49.

Farrell, John Thomas. "The Writing Center Professional and Graduate Students: Developing an Ethical Paradigm." Paper presented at the annual meeting of the Conference on College Composition and Communication. Milwaukee. March 27-30. ERIC ED 399 546.

Farris, Christine. "Giving Religion, Taking Gold: Disciplinary Cultures and the Claims of Writing Across the Curriculum." *Cultural Studies in the English Classroom*. Eds. James A. Berlin and Michael J. Vivion. Portsmouth, NH: Boynton/Cook, 1992. 112-23.

Farris, Christine, and Raymond Smith. "Writing-Intensive Courses: Tools for Curricular Change." *Writing Across the Curriculum: A Guide to Developing Programs*. Eds. Susan H. McLeod and Margot Soven. Newbury Park, CA: Sage, 1992. 71-87.

Finkelstein, Martin. "Academic Careers in 2000 and Beyond." *Peer Review* 1.3 (1999): 4-8.

Fish, Stanley. "Anti-Professionalism." *New Literary History* 17 (1985): 89-127.

Fontana, Andrea, and James H. Frey. "Interviewing: The Art of Science." *Collecting and Interpreting Qualitative Materials*. Eds. Norman K. Denzin and Yvonna S. Lincoln. Thousand Oaks, CA: Sage, 1998. 47-78.

Foucault, Michel. "What is an Author?" *Power/Knowledge: Selected Interviews and Other Writings, 1972-1977*. Ed. Colin Gordon. New York: Pantheon Books, 1980. 101-20.

Freedman, Aviva, and Peter Medway. "Locating Genre Studies: Antecedents and Prospects." *Genre and the New Rhetoric: Critical Perspectives on Literacy and Education*. Eds. Aviva Freedman and Peter Medway. Bristol, PA: Taylor and Francis, 1995. 1-20.

French, Wendell L., Cecil H. Bell, Jr., and Robert A. Zawacki, eds. *Organizational Development: Behavioral Science Interventions for Organization Improvement*. 4th ed. Englewood Cliffs, NJ: Prentice Hall, 1990.

Fulkerson, Richard. "Composition Theory in the Eighties: Axiological Consensus and Paradigmatic Diversity." *College Composition and Communication* 41 (1990): 409-29.

Fulwiler, Toby. "Evaluating Writing Across the Curriculum Programs." *Strengthening Programs for Writing Across the Curriculum*. Ed. Susan McLeod. San Francisco: Jossey-Bass, 1988. 61-75.

——. "How Well Does Writing Across the Curriculum Work?" *College English* 46 (1985): 113-25.

——. "Showing, Not Telling, at a Writing Workshop." *College English* 43 (1981): 55-63.

——. "The Quiet and Insistent Revolution: WAC." *The Politics of Writing Instruction: Postsecondary*. Eds. Richard Bullock and John Trimbur. Portsmouth, NH: Boynton/Cook, 1991. 179-87.

——. "Writing Workshops and the Mechanics of Change." *WPA: Writing Program Administration* 12.3 (1989): 7-20.

Fulwiler, Toby, and Art Young, eds. *Programs that Work: Models and Methods of Writing Across the Curriculum*. Portsmouth, NH: Boynton/Cook, 1990.

Galegher, Jolene, Robert E. Kraut, and Carmen Egido, eds. *Intellectual Teamwork: Social and Technological Foundations of Cooperative Work*. Hillsdale, NJ: Lawrence Erlbaum, 1990.

Gebhardt, Richard C. "Evolving Approaches to Scholarship, Promotion, and Tenure in Composition Studies." *Scholarship and Academic Advancement in Composition Studies*. Ed. Richard C. Gebhardt and Barbara Genelle Smith Gebhardt. Hillsdale, NJ: Erlbaum, 1997.

Gere, Anne Ruggles, ed. *Roots in the Sawdust: Writing to Learn Across the Disciplines*. Urbana, IL: National Council of Teachers of English, 1985.

Gill, Judy. "Another Look at WAC and the Writing Center." *Writing Center Journal* 16 (1996): 164-78.

Glassick, Charles E., Mary Taylor Huber, and Gene I. Maeroff. *Scholarship Assessed: Evaluation of the Professoriate*. An Ernest L. Boyer Project of the Carnegie Foundation for the Advancement of Teaching. San Francisco, CA: Jossey-Bass, 1997.

Godwin, Christine M. "The Writing Consultancy Project." *Writing Across the Curriculum in Community Colleges* (New Directions for Community Colleges, No. 73). Eds. Linda C. Stanley and Joanna Ambron. San Francisco, CA: Jossey-Bass, 1991. 85-90.

Gorman, Margaret E. "Mucking Around." *Writing Across the Disciplines: Research into Practice*. Montclair, NJ: Boynton/Cook, 1986. 228-34.

Graham, Joan. "Writing Components, Writing Adjuncts, Writing Links." *Writing Across the Curriculum: A Guide to Developing Programs*. Eds. Susan H. McLeod and Margot Soven. Newbury Park: Sage, 1992. 110-33.

Griffin, C. W. "Programs for Writing Across the Curriculum: A Report." *College Composition and Communication* 36 (1985): 398-403.

Hanson, Kristine. "Face to Face with Part-Timers: Ethics and the Professionalization of Writing Faculties." *Resituating Writing: Constructing and Administering Writing Programs*. Eds. Joseph Janangelo and Kristine Hansen. Portsmouth, NH: Boynton/Cook, 1995. 23-45.

Haring-Smith, Tori. "Changing Students' Attitudes: Writing Fellows Programs." *Writing Across the Curriculum: A Guide to Developing Programs*. Eds. Susan H. McLeod and Margot Soven. Newbury Park: Sage, 1992. 175-88.

_____. "The Writing Center and Tutoring in WAC Programs." *Writing Across the Curriculum: A Guide to Developing Programs*. Eds. Susan H. McLeod and Margot Soven. Newbury Park: Sage, 1992. 154-74.

Harper, M. Todd. "Revolution or Colonialism: The Role of English Departments in the Writing Across the Curriculum Movement." Diss. University of Louisville, 1998.

Harris, Ilene B. "New Expectations for Professional Competence." *Educating Professionals: Responding to New Expectations for Competence and Accountability*. Eds. Lynn Curry, Jon Wergin, and Associates. San Franciso: Jossey-Bass, 1993. 17-54.

Harris, Jeanette, and Christina Hult. "Using a Survey of Writing Assignments to Make Informed Curricular Decisions." *WPA: Writing Program Administration* 8 (1985): 7-14.

Harris, Joseph. "Public Scholarship." *College Composition and Communication* 50 (1998): 151-52.

Harris, Muriel. "A Writing Center without a WAC Program: The De Facto WAC Center/Writing Center." *Writing Centers and Writing Across the Curriculum Programs*. Eds. Robert W. Barnett and Jacob S. Blumner. Westport, CT: Greenwood P, 1999. 89-104.

Haviland, Carol Peterson et al. "Neither Missionaries Nor Colonists Nor Handmaidens: What Writing Tutors Can Teach WAC Faculty about Inquiry." *Writing Centers and Writing Across the Curriculum Programs*. Eds. Robert W. Barnett and Jacob S. Blumner. Westport, CT: Greenwood P, 1999. 45-58.

Healy, Dave. "The Deprofessionalization of the Writing Instructor." *WPA: Writing Program Administration* 16 (1992): 38-49.

Herndl, Carl G. "Teaching Discourse and Reproducing Culture: A Critique of Research and Pedagogy in Professional and Non-Academic Writing." *College Composition and Communication* 44 (1993): 349-63.

Herrington, Anne J. "Writing to Learn: Writing Across the Disciplines." *College English* 43 (1984): 379-87.

_____. "Assignment and Response: Teaching with Writing Across the Disciplines." *A Rhetoric of Doing: Essays on Written Discourse in Honor of James L. Kinneavy.* Eds. Stephen Witte, Neil Nakadate, and Roger D. Cherry. Carbondale: Southern Illinois University Press, 1992: 244-260.

Holt, Mara, and Leon Anderson. "The Way We Work Now." *Profession 1998.* New York: MLA, 1998. 131-42.

Howard, Rebecca M. "In Situ Workshops and the Peer Relationships of Composition Faculty." *WPA: Writing Program Administration* 12 (1988): 39-46.

Hult, Christine. "The Scholarship of Administration." *Theorizing and Enacting Difference: Resituating Writing Programs Within the Academy.* Eds. Joseph Janangelo and Christine Hansen. Portsmouth: Heinemann, 1997. 119-31.

Huot, Brian. "Finding Out What They Are Writing: A Method, Rationale, and Sample for Writing-Across-the-Curriculum Research." *WPA: Writing Program Administration* 15 (1992): 31-40.

Jolliffe, David A. "Writing Across the Curriculum and Service Learning: Kairos, Genre, and Collaboration." *WAC for the New Millennium: Strategies for Continuing Writing-Across-the-Curriculum Programs.* Eds. Susan H. McLeod, Eric Miraglia, Margot Soven, and Christopher Thaiss. Urbana, IL: National Council of Teachers of English, 2001. 86-108.

Jones, Robert, and Joseph Comprone. "Where Do We Go Next in Writing Across the Curriculum?" *College Composition and Communication* 44 (1993): 59-68.

Kalamaras, George. "Effecting Institutional Change through Writing Across the Curriculum: Ideology and Inner Dialogue." Paper presented at the annual meeting of the Conference on College Composition and Communication. Boston. March 21-23. ERIC ED 332 220.

Kaufer, David, and Richard Young. "Writing in the Content Areas: Some Theoretical Complexities." *Theory and Practice in the Teaching of Writing: Rethinking the Discipline.* Ed. Lee Odell. Carbondale and Edwardsville: Southern Illinois UP, 1993. 74-104.

Kelly, Harold H. *Personal Relationships: Their Structures and Processes.* Hillsdale, NJ: Lawrence Erlbaum, 1979.

Kennedy, Donald. *Academic Duty.* Harvard, MA: Harvard UP, 1997.

Kirsht, Judy, Rhonda Levine, and John Reiff. "Evolving Paradigms: WAC and the Rhetoric of Inquiry." *College Composition and Communication* 45 (1994): 369-80.

Kirsch, Gesa E. *Women Writing the Academy: Audience, Authority, and Transformation.* Carbondale: Southern Illinois University Press, 1993.

Knapp, Mark L., and Gerald R. Miller, eds. *Handbook of Interpersonal Communication.* 2nd ed. Thousand Oaks, CA: Sage, 1994.

Knoblauch, C. H., and Lil Brannon. "Writing as Learning Through the Curriculum." *College English* 45 (1983): 465-74.

Kolodny, Annette. *Failing the Future: A Dean Looks at Higher Education in the Twenty-First Century.* Durham, NC: Duke UP, 1998.

Kuriloff, Peshe C. "The Writing Consultant: Collaboration and Team Teaching." *Writing Across the Curriculum: A Guide to Developing Programs.* Eds. Susan H. McLeod and Margot Soven. Newbury Park: Sage, 1992. 134-53.

Kvale, Steinar. *InterViews: An Introduction to Qualitative Research Interviewing.* Thousand Oaks, CA: Sage, 1996.

Lamb, Catherine E. "Initiating Change as a Writing Consultant." *College English* 45 (1983): 296-300.

LeCourt, Donna. "WAC as Critical Pedagogy: The Third Stage?" *Journal of Advanced Composition* 16 (1996): 389-405.

Lemke, Alan, and Lillian Bridwell. "Assessing Writing Ability: An Ethnographic Study of Consultant-Teacher Relationships." *English Education* 14 (1982): 86-94.

Lewiecki-Wilson, Cynthia, and Jeff Sommers. "Professing at the Fault Lines: Composition at Open Admissions Institutions." *College Composition and Communication* 50 (1999): 438-62.

Magnotto, Joyce Neff, and Barbara R. Stout. "Faculty Workshops." *Writing Across the Curriculum: A Guide to Developing Programs.* Eds. Susan H. McLeod and Margot Soven. Newbury Park: Sage, 1992. 32-45.

Mahala, Daniel. "Writing Utopias: Writing Across the Curriculum and the Promise of Reform." *College English* 53 (1991): 773-89.

_____ and Jody Swilky. "Resistance and Reform: The Functions of Expertise in Writing Across the Curriculum." *Language and Learning Across the Disciplines* 1.2 (1994): 35-62.

Maimon, Elaine. "Beaver College." *Programs that Work: Models and Methods for Writing Across the Curriculum.* Eds. Toby Fulwiler and Art Young. Portsmouth: Boynton/Cook, 1990: 137-62.

_____. "Collaborative Learning and Writing Across the Curriculum." *WPA: Journal of Council of Writing Program Administrators* 9 (1986): 9-15.

_____. Preface. *Writing Across the Curriculum: A Guide to Developing Programs.* Eds. Susan H. McLeod and Margot Soven. Newbury Park, CA: Sage, 1992. ix-xiv.

_____. "Writing Across the Curriculum: Past, Present, and Future." *Teaching Writing in All Disciplines.* Ed. C. Williams Griffin. San Francisco, CA: Jossey-Bass, 1982. 67-74.

McCarthy, Lucille P. "A Stranger in Strange Lands: A College Student Writing Across the Curriculum." *Research in the Teaching of English* 21 (1987): 233-65.

McCarthy, Lucille P., and Stephen M. Fishman. "Boundary Conversations: Conflicting Ways of Knowing in Philosophy and Interdisciplinary Research." *Research in the Teaching of English* 25 (1991): 419-68.

_____. "A Text for Many Voices: Representing Diversity in Reports of Naturalistic Research." *Ethics and Representation in Qualitative Studies of Literacy.* Eds. Peter Mortensen and Gesa E. Kirsch. Urbana, IL: National Council of Teachers of English, 1996. 155-76.

_____, and Barbara E. Walvoord. "Models for Collaborative Research in Writing Across the Curriculum." *Strengthening Programs for Writing Across the Curriculum.* Ed. Susan H. McLeod. Newbury Park, CA: Sage, 1988. 77-89.

McLeod, Susan H. "Defining Writing Across the Curriculum." *WPA: Writing Program Administration* 11 (1987): 19-24.

_____. "The Foreigner: WAC Directors as Agents of Change." *Resituating Writing: Constructing and Administering Writing Programs.* Eds. Joseph Janangelo and Christine Hansen. Portsmouth: Boynton/Cook, 1995. 108-16.

_____, ed. *Strengthening Programs for Writing Across the Curriculum*. WAC Clearinghouse Landmark Publications in Writing Studies: <http://wac.colostate.edu/aw/books/mcleod_programs>. 2000. Originally Published in Print, 1988, by Jossey-Bass, San Francisco.

_____. "Translating Enthusiasm into Curricular Change." *Strengthening Programs for Writing Across the Curriculum*. Ed. Susan H. McLeod. WAC Clearinghouse Landmark Publications in Writing Studies <http://wac.colostate.edu/aw/books/mcleod_programs/>. 2000. Originally Published in Print, 1988, by Jossey-Bass, San Francisco. 5-13.

_____. "WAC at Century's End: The Ghost of Fred Newton Scott." *WPA: Writing Program Administration* 21 (1997): 67-73.

_____. "Writing Across the Curriculum: An Introduction." *Writing Across the Curriculum: A Guide to Developing Programs*. Eds. Susan H. McLeod and Margot Soven. Newbury Park: Sage, 1992. 1-11.

_____, and Elaine Maimon. "Clearing the Air: WAC Myths and Realities." *College English* 62 (2000): 573-83.

_____, and Eric Miraglia. "Writing Across the Curriculum in a Time of Change." *WAC for the New Millennium: Strategies for Continuing Writing-Across-the-Curriculum Programs*. Eds Susan H. McLeod, Eric Miraglia, Margot Soven, and Christopher Thaiss. Urbana, IL: National Council of Teachers of English, 2001. 1-27.

_____, Eric Miraglia, Margot Soven, Christopher Thaiss, eds. *WAC for the New Millennium: Strategies for Continuing Writing-Across-the-Curriculum Programs*. Urbana, IL: National Council of Teachers of English, 2001.

_____, and Margot Soven. "What Do You Need to Start—and Sustain—a Writing-Across-the-Curriculum Program?" *WPA: Writing Program Administration* 15.1-2 (1991): 25-33.

_____, and Susan Shirley. "Appendix: National Survey of Writing Across the Curriculum Programs." *Strengthening Programs for Writing Across the Curriculum*. Ed. Susan H. McLeod. WAC Clearinghouse Landmark Publications in Writing Studies <http://wac.colostate.edu/ books/mcleod_programs/appendix.pdf>. 2000. Originally Published in Print, 1988, by Jossey-Bass, San Francisco. 103-30.

McNenny, Geraldine, and Duane H. Roen. "The Case for Collaborative Scholarship in Rhetoric and Composition." *Rhetoric Review* 10 (1992): 291-310.

Miller, Richard. "'Let's Do the Numbers': Comp Droids and the Prophets of Doom." *Profession* (1999): 96-105.

Minock, Mary. "A(n) (Un)Certain Synergy: Rhetoric, Hermeneutics, and Transdisciplinary Conversations about Writing." *College Composition and Communication* 47 (1996): 502-23.

Miraglia, Eric, and Susan H. McLeod. "Whither WAC? Interpreting the Stories/Histories of Enduring WAC Programs." *WPA: Writing Program Administration* 20 (1997): 46-65.

MLA Commission on Professional Service. "Making Faculty Work Visible: Reinterpreting Professional Service, Teaching, and Research in the Fields of Language and Literature" *Profession* 1996. New York: MLA, 1996. 161-216.

Mortensen, Peter. "Going Public." *College Composition and Communication* 50 (1998): 182-205.

Mortensen, Peter, and Gesa E. Kirsch eds. *Ethics and Representation in Qualitative Studies of Literacy.* Urbana, IL: National Council of Teachers of English, 1996.

Moss, Andrew, and Carol Holder. *Improving Student Writing: A Guidebook for Faculty in All Disciplines.* Dubuque, IA: Kendall-Hunt, 1988.

Mullin, Joan, Neil Reid, Doug Enders, and Jason Baldridge. "Constructing Each Other: Collaborating Across Disciplines and Roles." *Weaving Knowledge Together: Writing Centers and Collaboration.* Eds. Carol Peterson Haviland et al. Emmitsburg, MD: National Writing Centers Association Press, 1998. 152-71.

Murphy, Christina. "The Writing Center and Social Constructionist Theory." *Intersections: Theory-Practice in the Writing Center.* Eds. Joan A. Mullin and Ray Wallace. Urbana, IL: National Council of Teachers of English, 1994. 25-38.

Nelson, Cary, ed. *Will Work for Food: Academic Labor in Crisis.* Minneapolis: Minnesota UP, 1997.

North, Stephen. "The Idea of a Writing Center" *College English* 46 (1984): 436-46.

Odell, Lee. "The Process of Writing and the Process of Learning." *College Composition and Communication* 31 (1980): 42-50.

O'Neill, Peggy, Ellen Schendel, and Brian Huot. "Defining Assessment as Research." *WPA: Journal of Writing Program Administrators* 26 (2003): 10-26.

Organization Development Network. "Principles of Practice." 1 May 2004 < http://www.odnetwork.org/principlesofpractice.html>.

Paré, Anthony, and Graham Smart. "Observing Genres in Action: Towards a Research Methodology." *Genre and the New Rhetoric.* Eds. Aviva Freedman and Peter Medway. Bristol, PA: Taylor and Francis, 1995. 146-54.

Parks, Steve, and Eli Goldblatt. "Writing Beyond the Curriculum: Fostering New Collaborations in Literacy." *College English* 62 (2000): 584-606.

Peritz, Janice. "When Learning is Not Enough: Writing Across the Curriculum and the (Re)Turn to Rhetoric." *Journal of Advanced Composition* 14 (1994): 431-54.

Phelps, Louise. "Practical Wisdom and the Geography of Knowledge in Composition." *College English* 53 (1991): 863-85.

_____. "Rethinking the Meaning of Faculty Overload." *Peer Review* 1.2 (1999): 12-13.

Ray, Ruth. *The Practice of Theory: Teacher Research in Composition.* Urbana, IL: National Council of Teachers of English, 1993.

Readings, Bill. *The University in Ruins.* Cambridge, MA: Harvard University Press, 1997.

Reiss, Donna, and Art Young. "WAC Wired: Electronic Communication Across the Curriculum." *WAC for the New Millennium: Strategies for Continuing Writing-Across-the-Curriculum Programs.* Eds. Susan H. McLeod, Eric Miraglia, Margot Soven, and Christopher Thaiss. Urbana, IL: National Council of Teachers of English, 2001. 52-85.

Roen, Duane H. "Writing Administration as Scholarship and Teaching." *Academic Advancement in Composition Studies: Scholarship, Publication, Promotion, Tenure.* Eds. Richard C. Gebhardt and Barbara Genelle Smith Gebhardt. Mahwah, NJ: Lawrence Erlbaum, 1997. 43-55.

Roen, Duane H., and Robert K. Mittan. "Collaborative Scholarship in Composition: Some Issues." *Methods and Methodology in Composition Research*. Eds. Gesa Kirsh and Patricia A. Sullivan. Carbondale and Edwardsville: Southern Illinois University Press, 1992. 287-313.

Rose, Shirley, and Margaret Finders. "Learning from Experience: Using Situated Performances in Writing Teacher Development." *WPA: Journal of Writing Program Administrators* 22 (1998): 33-52.

_____, and Irwin Weiser. *The Writing Program Administrator as Researcher: Inquiry in Action and Reflection*. Portsmouth, NH: Boynton/Cook, 1999.

Russell, David R. "American Origins of the Writing-across-the-Curriculum Movement." *Writing, Teaching, and Learning in the Disciplines*. Eds. Anne Herrington and Charles Moran. New York: Modern Language Association, 1992. 22-42.

_____. "Where Do the Naturalistic Studies of WAC/WID Point? A Research Review." *WAC for the New Millennium: Strategies for Continuing Writing-Across-the-Curriculum Programs*. Eds. Susan H. McLeod, Eric Miraglia, Margot Soven, and Christopher Thaiss. Urbana, IL: NCTE, 2001. 259-98.

_____. "Writing Across the Curriculum and the Communications Movement: Some Lessons from the Past." *College Composition and Communication* 38 (1987): 184-94.

_____. "Writing Across the Curriculum in Historical Perspective: Toward a Social Interpretation." *College English* 52 (1990): 52-74.

_____. "Writing Across the Curriculum in 1913: James Fleming Hosic on "'Co-operation'." *English Journal* 75.5 (1986): 34-37.

_____. "Writing and Genre in Higher Education and Workplaces: A Review of Studies That Use Cultural-Historical Activity Theory." *Mind, Culture, and Activity* 4.4 (1997): 224-37.

_____. *Writing in the Academic Disciplines, 1870-1990: A Curricular History*. Carbondale and Edwardsville: Southern Illinois University Press, 1991.

Sandler, Karen Wiley. "Starting a WAC Program: Strategies for Administrators." *Writing Across the Curriculum: A Guide to Developing Programs*. Eds. Susan H. McLeod and Margot Soven. Newbury Park: Sage, 1992. 47-57.

Schein, Edgar H. *Process Consultation: Its Role in Organization Development*. Reading, MA: Addison-Wesley, 1969.

_____. *Process Consultation: Lessons for Managers and Consultants*. Reading, MA: Addison-Wesley, 1987.

_____. *Process Consultation Revisited: Building the Helping Relationship*. Reading, MA: Addison-Wesley, 1999.

Schön, Donald A. *Educating the Reflective Practitioner: Toward a New Design for Teaching and Learning in the Professions*. San Francisco: Jossey-Bass, 1987.

_____. *The Reflective Practitioner: How Professionals Think in Action*. New York: Basic Books, 1983.

_____, ed. *The Reflective Turn: Case Studies in and on Educational Practice*. New York: Teachers College Press, 1991.

Schulman, Lee S. "Knowledge and Teaching: Foundations of a New Reform." *Harvard Educational Review* 57 (1987): 1-21.

Segal, Judy, Anthony Paré, Doug Brent, and Douglas Vipond. "The Researcher as Missionary: Problems with Rhetoric and Reform in the Disciplines." *College Composition and Communication* 50 (1998): 71-90.

Seidman, Irvin. *Interviewing as Qualitative Research: A Guide for Researchers in Education and the Social Sciences.* 2nd ed. New York: Teachers College Press, 1998.

Shaughnessy, Mina P. *Errors and Expectations: A Guide for the Teacher of Basic Writing.* New York: Oxford UP, 1977.

Showalter, Elaine. "Presidential Address 1998: Regeneration." *PMLA* 112 (1999): 318-27.

Smith, Louise. "Opinion: Why English Departments Should 'House' Writing Across the Curriculum." *College English* 50 (1988): 390-94.

Soven, Margot. "The Advanced WAC Workshop." *Journal of Teaching Writing* 12.2 (1994): 277-86.

_____. "Conclusion: Sustaining Writing Across the Curriculum Programs." *Writing Across the Curriculum: A Guide to Developing Programs.* Eds. Susan H. McLeod and Margot Soven. Newbury Park: Sage, 1992. 189-97.

_____. "Curriculum-Based Peer Tutoring Programs: A Survey." *WPA: Writing Program Administration* 17.1-2 (1993): 58-74.

Stevenson, Dwight W. "The Writing Teacher in the Workplace: Some Questions and Answers about Consulting." *Writing in Nonacademic Settings.* Eds. Lee Odell and Dixie Goswami. New York: Guilford, 1985. 345-89.

Stygall, Gail. "Certifying Knowledge: Options for WPAs." Unpublished essay, 1998. 33 pp.

Sullivan, Patricia A. "Revising the Myth of the Independent Scholar." *Writing With: New Directions in Collaborative Teaching, Learning, and Research.* Eds. Sally Barr Reagan, Thomas Fox, and David Bleich. Albany: State University of New York P, 1994. 11-30.

Sullivan, Patricia, and James E. Porter. *Opening Spaces: Writing Technologies and Critical Research Practices.* Greenwich, CT: Ablex, 1997.

Swanson-Owens, Deborah. "Identifying Natural Sources of Resistance: A Case Study of Implementing Writing Across the Curriculum." *Research in the Teaching of English* 20 (1986): 69-97.

Swilky, Jody. "Reconsidering Faculty Resistance to Writing Reform." *WPA: Writing Program Administration* 16.1-2 (1992): 29-33.

Tate, Gary. "A Place for Literature in Freshman Composition." *College English* 55 (1993): 317-21.

Thaiss, Christopher. "Theory in WAC: Where Have We Been, Where Are We Going?" *WAC for the New Millennium: Strategies for Continuing Writing-Across-the-Curriculum Programs.* Eds. Susan H. McLeod, Eric Miraglia, Margot Soven, and Christopher Thaiss. Urbana, IL: National Council of Teachers of English, 2001. 299-326.

_____. "Writing Across the Curriculum." *Theorizing Composition: A Critical Sourcebook of Theory and Scholarship in Contemporary Composition Studies.* Ed. Mary Lynch Kennedy. Westport, CT: Greenwood P, 1998. 356-64.

Trimbur, John. "Consensus and Difference in Collaborative Learning." *College English* 51 (1989): 602-15.

_____. "Writing Instruction and the Politics of Professionalization." *Composition in the Twenty-First Century: Crisis and Change.* Eds. Lynn Bloom, Donald A. Daiker, and Edward M. White. Carbondale: Southern Illinois University Press, 1996: 133-45.

_____, and Lundy A. Braun. "Laboratory Life and the Determination of Authorship." *New Visions of Collaborative Learning.* Ed. Janis Forman. Portsmouth, NH: Boynton/Cook, 1992. 19-36.

Van Eynde, Donald F., Judith C. Hoy, and Dixie Cody Van Eynde, eds. *Organization Development Classics: The Practice and Theory of Change—the Best of the OD Practitioner.* San Francisco: Jossey-Bass, 1997.

Vaught-Alexander, Karen. "Situating Writing Centers and Writing Across the Curriculum Programs in the Academy: Creating Partnerships for Change with Organizational Development Theory." *Writing Centers and Writing Across the Curriculum Programs.* Eds. Robert W. Barnett and Jacob S. Blumner. Westport, CT: Greenwood P, 1999. 119-40.

Waldo, Mark. *Demythologizing Language Difference in the Academy: Establishing Discipline-Based Writing Programs.* Mahway, NJ: Lawrence Erlbaum, 2004.

_____. "Inquiry as a Non-Invasive Approach to Cross-Curricular Writing Consultancy." *Journal of Language and Learning Across the Disciplines* 1 (1996): 6-22.

Walvoord, Barbara. "From Conduit to Customer: The Role of WAC Faculty in WAC Assessment." *Assessing Writing Across the Curriculum: Diverse Approaches and Practices.* Eds. Kathleen Yancey and Brian Huot. Norwood, NJ: Ablex, 1997. 15-36.

_____. "The Future of WAC." *College English* 58 (1996): 58-79.

_____. "Getting Started." *Writing Across the Curriculum: A Guide to Developing Programs.* Eds. Susan H. McLeod and Margot Soven. Newbury Park: Sage, 1992. 12-31.

_____. *Helping Students Write Well: A Guide for Teachers in All Disciplines.* New York: Modern Language Association, 1986.

_____, et al. *In the Long Run: A Study of Faculty in Three Writing-Across-the-Curriculum Programs.* Urbana, IL: National Council of Teachers of English, 1998.

Weiser, Irwin. "Local Research and Curriculum Development: Using Surveys to Learn About Writing Assignments in the Disciplines." *The Writing Program Administrator as Researcher.* Eds. Shirley K. Rose and Irwin Weiser. Portsmouth: Boynton/Cook, 1999. 95-106.

Weiss, Robert, and Michael Peich. "Faculty Attitude Change in a Cross-Disciplinary Workshop." *College Composition and Communication* 31 (1980): 33-41.

Weiss, Robert S. *Learning From Strangers: The Art and Method of Qualitative Interview Studies.* New York: The Free Press, 1994.

White, Edward H. "Use It or Lose It: Power and the WPA." *WPA: Writing Program Administration* 15 (1991): 3-12.

Williams, Julia. M. (2001). "Transformations in Technical Communication Pedagogy: Engineering, Writing, and ABET Engineering Criteria 2000." *Technical Communication Quarterly* 10 (2001): 149-67.

Yancey, Kathleen Blake. *Reflection in the Writing Classroom.* Logan: Utah State University Press, 1998.

Yancey, Kathleen Blake, and Brian Huot, eds. *Assessing Writing Across the Curriculum: Diverse Approaches and Practices.* Norwood, NJ: Ablex, 1997.

Young, Art. *Teaching Writing Across the Curriculum.* 3rd ed. WAC Clearinghouse Landmark Publications in Writing Studies: <http:// wac.colostate.edu/ aw/books/young_teaching>. 2002. Originally Published in Print, 1999, by Prentice Hall, Upper Saddle River, New Jersey.

Young, Richard. "Impediments to Change in WAC Programs." *Composition in Context: Essays in Honor of Donald C. Stewart.* Eds. W. Ross Winterowd and Vincent Gillespie. Carbondale: Southern Illinois University Press, 1994. 126-38.

Zawacki, Terry Myers, and Ashley Taliaferro Williams. "Is It Still WAC? Writing within Interdisciplinary Learning Communities." *WAC for the New Millennium: Strategies for Continuing Writing-Across-the-Curriculum Programs.* Eds. Susan H. McLeod, Eric Miraglia, Margot Soven, and Christopher Thaiss. Urbana, IL: National Council of Teachers of English, 2001. 109-40.

AUTHOR INDEX

A

AAUP Committee on College and University Teaching, 154, *197*
Allen, N., 154, *197*
Anderson, L., 33, *197*
Anderson, P., 147, *197*
Anson, C., 6, 18, 103, *197*
Association of American Colleges and Universities, 44, 153, *197*
Atkinson, D., 33, *197*
Austin, A.E., 43, *197*

B

Baldridge, J., 4, 40, 41, 44, 51, 56, 80, 100(*t*), 109(*n*4), 115, 117, 123-124, 128(*t*), 132, 144, 146, 190, *205*
Baldwin, R.G., 43, *197*
Barnett, R.W., 84(*n*13), 135, *197*
Bazerman, C., 4, 26, 100(*t*), 110, 120, 156(*t*), 183, *197-198*
Bean, J., 6, 106(*n*2), *198*
Behrens, L., 117, *198*
Bell, C.H., 137, *200*
Bergmann, L., 20, 149, 183-184, 185, 187, 188, *198*
Berlin, J.A., 35, 105, 186(*t*), *198*
Blair, C.P., 20, 21, 23, 104, 107, 108, *198*
Blank, G.B., 100(*t*), 104, 108, *199*

Blumner, J.S., 84(*n*13), 135, *197*
Blyler, N.R., 9, 120, *198*
Boyer, E.L., 43, 153, 154, 156(t), *198*
Brannon, L., 182, *202*
Braun, L.A., 35, *208*
Brent, D., 14(*n*3), 26, 27, 97, 98, 102, 114, 120, 121, 125-126, 129, 147, 149, 155, 156(*t*), 189, *207*
Bridgeman, B., 117, *198*
Bridwell, L., 38, *203*
Britton, J., 17, *198*
Brooke, R., 70(*n*7), *198*
Brown, A.E., 100(*t*), 104, 108, *199*
Bruffee, K.A., 36, *198*
Bullock, R.H., 44, *198*
Burgess, T., 17, *198*
Burke, W.W., 137, *198*
Burnett, R.E., 36, *198*

C

Carlson, S.B., 117, *198*
Carter, M., 103, *197*
Chase, G., 184, *198*
Comprone, J., 185, *202*
Council of Writing Program Administrators, 44, 154, 156(*t*), *198*
Covington, D.H., 100(*t*), 104, 108, *199*
Crowley, S., 105(*n*1), *199*

211

Cushman, E., 13, 147, *199*

D

Dannels, D.P., 103, *197*
Debs, M.B., 49, *199*
Diamond, R.M., 44, 154, *199*
Dick, J.A.R., 37, 116-117, 128(*t*), 132, 133, *199*
Durst, R.K., 35, 40, *199*

E

Ede, L., 10, 12, 32, 34, 35, 39, 41, 45, 68(*n*6), *199*
Egido, C., 33, *200*
Emig, J., 17, *198*
Enders, D., 4, 40, 41, 44, 51, 56, 80, 100(*t*), 109(*n*4), 115, 117, 123-124, 128(*t*), 132, 144, 146, 190
Ervin, E., 32, 36, 43, 152, 153, *199*
Esch, R.M., 37, 116-117, 128(*t*), 132, 133, *199*

F

Faery, R.B., 101, 102, *199*
Faigley, L., 100(*t*), 110(*n*5), 116, 128(*t*), 132, *199*
Farrell, J.T., 147, 148-149, *199*
Farris, C., 2, 20, 37, 92, 106(*n*3), 141, *199*
Finders, M., 44, 150, *206*
Finkelstein, M., 153, 154, *199*
Fish, S., 23, *200*
Fishman, S.M., 4, 38, 39, 40, 41, 44, 59, 80, 100(*t*), 115, 128(*t*), 144, 146, 190, *203*
Fontana, A., 49, *200*
Foucault, M., 32, *200*
Fox, D.L., 32, 36, 43, 152, 153, *199*
Freedman, A., 100(*t*), 122, *200*
French, W.L., 137, *200*
Frey, J.H., 49, *200*
Fulkerson, R., 35, *200*
Fulwiler, T., 4, 15, 19, 36, 100(*t*), 101, 102, 106, 134, *200*

G

Galegher, J., 33, *200*
Gebhardt, R.C., 44, *200*
Gere, A.R., 67, *200*
Gill, J., 104, *200*

Glassick, C.E., 44, 154, 155, 156(*t*), 158-159, 160, 170, 173, 176, 177, 178, 178(*n*6), *200*
Godwin, C.M., 100(*t*), 104, 107-108, 109, *201*
Goldblatt, E., 187, *205*
Gorman, M.E., 128(*t*), *201*
Graham, J., 104, *201*
Griffin, C.W., 84(*n*13), 101, *201*

H

Hansen, K., 22, 44, 100(*t*), 110(*n*5), 116, 128(*t*), 132, *201*
Haring-Smith, T., 2, 104, 108, *201*
Harper, M.T., 102-103, 114, *201*
Harris, I.B., 47, 50, *201*
Harris, Jeanette, 117, *201*
Harris, Joseph, 147, *201*
Harris, M., 104, *201*
Haviland, C.P., 109(*n*4), 114-115, *201*
Healy, D., 22, *201*
Herndl, C.G., 120, *201*
Herrington, A.J., 100(*t*), 101, 116, *201*
Holder, CV., 6, 106(*n*2), *205*
Holt, M., 152, *202*
Howard, R.M., 86, 100(*t*), 109, *202*
Hoy, J.C., 137, *208*
Huber, M.T., 44, 154, 155, 156(*t*), 158-159, 160, 170, 173, 176, 177, 178, 178(*n*6), *200*
Hult, C., 44, 117, 156(*t*), 157-158, 159-160, *201*, *202*
Huot, B., 5, 18, 22, 36, 110(*n*5), 116, 117-118, 128(*t*), 132, 134, *202*, *205*, *209*

J

Jolliffe, D.A., 125(*n*7), *202*
Jones, R., 185, *202*

K

Kalamaras, G., 4, 27, 37-38, 115, 128(*t*), 149, *202*
Kaufer, D., 37, 104, 105, 108, 111-114, 115, 116, 142, 148
Kelly, H.H., 33, *202*
Kennedy, D., 153, *202*
Kirsch, G.E., 9, 45, *202*
Kirsht, J., 37, 185, *202*
Knapp, M.L., 33, *202*

Knoblauch, C.H., 182, *202*
Kolodny, A., 153, *203*
Kraut, R., 33, *200*
Kuriloff, P.E., 4, 18-19, 36, 42-43, 100(*t*), 114, 116, 128(*t*), 132-134, 152, *202*
Kvale, S., 49, 50, 52, *203*

L

Lamb, C.E., 37, 100(*t*), 107, 109, 114, 128(*t*), *203*
LeCourt, D., 20, 27, 122, 184, 187, 189, *203*
Lemke, A., 38, *203*
Levine, R., 37, 185, *203*
Lewiecki-Wilson, C., 7, 8, 181-182, *203*
Lunsford, A., 10, 12, 32, 34, 35, 39, 41, 45, 68(*n*6), *199*

M

Maeroff, G.I., 44, 154, 155, 156(*t*), 158-159, 160, 170, 173, 176, 177, 178, 178(*n*6), *202*
Magnotto, J.N., 101, 104, *203*
Mahala, D., 23, 182, 184, *203*
Maimon, E., 3, 4, 15, 19, 20, 31, 35, 36, 182, 183, 185, 187, *203*
Martin, N., 17, *198*
McCarthy, L.P., 4, 38, 39, 40, 41, 44, 51, 59, 80, 100(*t*), 115, 119-120, 127, 128(*t*), 144, 146, 190, *203*
McLeod, A., 36, 37, *205*
McLeod, S.H., 4, 5, 15, 18, 19, 27, 60-61, 61(*n*5), 68, 101, 102, 104, 107, 134, 146, 153, 156(*t*), 157, 182, 183, 185, 187, *203*, *204*
McNenny, G., 33, 36, *204*
Medway, P., 100(*t*), 122, *200*
Miller, G.R., 33, *204*
Miller, R., 3, *204*
Minock, M., 28(*n*4), 100(t), 101, *204*
Miraglia, E., 5, 134, 153, *204*
Mittan, R.K., 32, 134, *206*
MLA Commission on Professional Service, 44, 154, 155, 156(*t*), 157, 158, 160, *204*
Moore, T., 33, *197*
Morgan, M., 33, *197*
Mortensen, P., 9, 13, *205*

Moss, A., 6, 106(*n*2), *205*
Mullin, J., 4, 40, 41, 44, 51, 56, 80, 100(*t*), 109(*n*4), 115, 118, 123-124, 128(*t*), 132, 144, 146, 190, *205*
Murphy, C., 31, 40, *205*

N

Nelson, C., 13, *205*
North, S., 9, 55, *205*

O

O'Neill, P., 5, *205*
Odell, L., 97, 98, 100(*t*), 116, 117, 128(t), *205*
Organization Development Network, 188, *205*

P

Paré, A., 14(*n*3), 27, 97, 98, 100(*t*), 102, 114, 120, 121, 122, 125-125, 129, 147, 149, 155, 156(*t*), 189, *205*, *207*
Parks, S., 187, *205*
Peich, M., 100(*t*), 101, 128(*t*), 146, *208*
Peritz, J., 20, 37, *205*
Phelps, L., 110(*n*5), 177, *205*
Porter, J.E., 9, *207*

R

Ray, R., 8, 9, 24, 52, *205*
Readings, B., 153, *205*
Reid, N., 4, 40, 41, 44, 51, 56, 80, 100(*t*), 109(*n*4), 115, 118, 123-124, 128(*t*), 132, 144, 146, 190, *205*
Reiff, J., 37, 185, *203*
Reiss, D., 5, 18, *205*
Roen, D., 32, 33, 35, 134, *204*, *205*, *206*
Rose, S., 44, 149, *206*
Rosen, H., 17, *198*
Rothschild-Ewald, H., 36, *198*
Russell, D.R., 3, 15, 16, 17, 18, 22, 26, 28(*n*2), 37, 43, 100(*t*), 110, 119, 121-122, 123, 165, 183, *198*, *206*
Rust, J., 103, *197*

S

Sandler, K.W., 21, *206*
Schein, E.H., 104, 106, 131, 136, 137, 139, 140-141, 141(*n*2), 142-143, 144, 145, 146, 147, 148, *206*
Schendel, E., 5, *205*

Schön, D., 24, 47, 48, 85, 92, 93, 113, 119, 149, *206*
Schulman, L.S., 25, 26, 47, 131, 135, 146, 149, *206*
Schwiebert, J.E., 18, *197*
Segal, J., 14(*n*3), 26, 27, 97, 98, 102, 114, 120, 121, 125-126, 129, 147, 149, 155, 156(*t*), 189, *207*
Seidman, I., 51, *207*
Shaughnessy, M.P., 62, *207*
Shirley, S., 18, *205*
Showalter, E., 13, *207*
Smart, G., 100(*t*), 122, *205*
Smith, L., 23, 24, *207*
Smith, R., 2, 106(*n*3), *199*
Snow, D., 33, *197*
Sommers, J., 7, 8, 181-182, *203*
Soven, M., 2, 4, 5, 36, 103, 109, *204, 205, 207*
Stanforth, S.C., 35, 40, *199*
Stevenson, S.W., 151, 152, *207*
Stout, B.R., 101, 104, *203*
Stygall, G., 33, *207*
Sullivan, P.A., 9, 32, 152, *207*
Swanson-Owens, D., 38, 139, *207*
Swilky, J., 23, 38, 104, 184, *207*

T

Tate, G., 184, *207*
Thaiss, C., 5, 15, 189-190, *207*
Trimbur, J., 22, 34, 35, *207*

V

Van Eynde, D.C., 137, *208*
Van Eynde, D.F., 137, *208*
Vaught-Alexander, K., 137(*n*1), *208*
Vipond, D., 14(*n*3), 26, 27, 97, 98, 102, 114, 120, 121, 125-126, 129, 147, 149, 155, 156(*t*), 189, *207*

W

Waldo, M., 37, 84(*n*13), 135, 185, *208*
Walvoord, B., 4, 6, 21, 27, 36, 38, 42, 59, 101, 102, 106(*n*2), 119-120, 127, 128(*t*), 134, 139, 166, 185, *204, 208*
Weiser, I., 44, 117, 128(*t*), *208*
Weiss, R.S., 52, 100(*t*), 101, 128(*t*), 146, *208*
White, E.H., 89(*n*14), 147, *208*
Williams, A.T., 5, 18, *209*
Williams, J.M., 5, *208*
Williamson, M., 181, *197*

Y

Yancey, K.B., 18, 36, 46-47, 48, 134, *209*
Young, A., 4, 5, 6, 18, 106(*n*2), 200, *205, 209*
Young, R., 37, 38, 104, 105, 108, 111-114, 115, 116, 142, 148, *202, 209*

Z

Zawacki, R.A., 5, *209*
Zawacki, T.M., 18, 137, *209*

SUBJECT INDEX

A

Academic literacy, 15-19, 24, 124, 132-133, 182
Academic reward system, 42-44, 153-160, 177-178
Academic writing consulting, 4, 7, 10, 11, 19, 24-25, 36, 40, 45, 81, 93, 99, 127, 131, 134, 137, 146, 148, 150, 152, 158, 190
Action research, *see* participatory research
Active inquiry, 148
Activity theory, *see* genre studies
Advanced writing courses, 37, 107
Antiprofessionalism, 23
Appreciative inquiry, 136, 148
Assessing faculty work, 152-160, 171-178
  portfolio evaluation, 159-160, 166-170, 176, 179
Assessment, 5, 12, 18, 103-104, 106, 134, 166
Attitudes, faculty, 93
  close-mindedness, 57-58, 76, 91, 135
  openness to change, 58-59, 76, 83, 144-145
  tire-kickers, 82-83, 139
Authorship, 32-33

B

British recitation system, 16

C

Code-switching, 90
Collaboration theory, 4, 10, 31-36, 53-54, 114-115, 135
  commonsense/traditional model, 11, 32-34, 42, 58, 93
  collaborative philosophy model, 11, 34-36, 41, 56, 59, 93, 131, 134
  consulting model, 11, 36-44
  dialogic model, 12, 34-36, 39, 75, 94
  hierarchical model, 32, 59, 94
Collaborative research, 33, 36, 41-43, 65-66, 119-120, 127, 147, 152, 177
  barriers to, 42-44, 152, 155
Communications movement, 16
Constructive reflection, 47-50, 54, 60, 70-71, 77, 81, 93
Consulting models, 37, 99
  discipline-based research model, 110, 118-128
  doctor-patient model, 137-140, 142-144
  process consultation model, 140-146, 150

purchase model, 104, 106, 136-137,
    140, 144
reflective inquiry model, 110-120,
    126-128, 134, 143
service model, 104-110, 114, 125,
    127-128, 131, 134, 136, 141
workplace model, 11, 151
workshop model, 21, 37-38, 62-65,
    99-104, 120, 126-127, 139-140, 143-
    146
Contracts, for faculty collaboration, 66,
    146-147
Correlation movement, 16
Cross-curricular literacy, defined, 3, 14
Cross-curricular outreach, 71-73, 108,
    157
Current-traditional rhetoric, 105, 110,
    128
Curriculum-based peer tutors, see
    writing fellows

D

Disciplinarity, views toward, 22-23, 28,
    39-41, 81-82, 116-117, 123, 132-133,
    165, 181

E

Ethnographic methods, 37-41, 112, 115,
    123
Expertise, denial by writing specialists,
    20-24, 28
Expertise, models of
general skills model, 104-106, 108,
    136, 120
interactionist model, 111-114, 120,
    127, 141

F

Faculty development, goal of WAC, 19
Faculty resistance, 4, 8, 34, 38, 42, 84,
    102, 126, 131, 139, 146
Faculty reward system, 12, 32, 152-160
Finesse, 162, 164
Focus-group interview method, 117-118

G

Genre studies, 100, 119, 121-125
German research model, 16
Grant writing, 63-65, 68, 147, 176
Group theory, 146

I

Identity, professional, 13
Informed consent, 52, 94
Interpersonal psychology, 33, 147
Interpersonal skills, 32, 87, 89-90, 93,
    163
    see also people skills
Interviewing, qualitative method, 49-52,
    118

K

Klatch, 75, 81, 95

L

Language across the curriculum
    movement, 17
Language, views toward
bellatristic, 16
monism, 111-112
ramistic dualism, 14, 105, 136
transparent, 16
Learning communities, 3, 5, 18, 28, 70,
    78-79, 81, 95, 166
Learning to write, 18, 112, 126, 182, 185-
    186
Listening skills, 39, 87, 90, 143, 148, 146
Literacy crisis, 17

M

Missionary approach to WAC, see
    missionary rhetoric
Missionary rhetoric, 10, 20-22, 27, 92,
    98, 102-103, 112, 114, 123, 144, 183-
    188, 190
Myers-Briggs personality type scale, 33

N

National Writing Project, 8, 14, 18, 21
National Writing Across the
    Curriculum Conference, 5
National network of WAC programs, 18
Naturalistic research, 39-40, 116, 119
Nonwriting specialist, defined, 14

O

Open-admissions colleges, 7-8, 9, 17,
    181-182
Organization development, 106, 136,
    147, 150, 188-189

P

Participatory research, 9, 27, 125-126, 129, 159
Peace Corps model of WAC, 60-61, 157
Personality, 32-33, 38, 55-60, 91, 93, 135
People skills, 31-33, 89-90, 93, 148, 163
Play, 75-76
Power, and collaboration, 12, 39-40, 76-81, 92, 152
Practical inquiry, 8-9, 24, 47, 51, 146, 149
Practical reasoning, 93, *see also* reflection-on-action
Practice theory, 50
Practitioner knowledge, 149, *see also* teacher knowledge
Process consultation theory, 11, 131, 137-146, 150
Professional artistry, 92
Professional knowledge, *see* teacher knowledge
Professionalization of writing teachers, 13, 21-27, 74, 188
deprofessionalization, 21, 107-108

R

Reflection-in-presentation, 47
Reflection-on-action, 47-48, 50, 93, 167
Reflective practice, 12, 85, 113-114, 119
Reflective practicum, 149-150
Reflective turn, 24, 46
Research paper genre, 106. 123-124
Rhetorical knowledgeability, 3, 14, 20, 114, 117, 121, 128, 146, 190
Rhetoric of inquiry movement, 37

S

Scholarship, new model of, 43-44, 154-158
Service learning, 5, 13, 130, 166
Situated performance activities, 150
Still-current WAC discourse, 65, 182-183, 187
Surveys, of faculty, 117, 128

T

Teacher development groups, 72, 74, 95
Teacher knowledge, 15, 25-27, 47, 131, 149
Teacher research, 8-9, 24, 40, 44, 110, 120, 149, 188, 190

Team-teaching, 69, 71, 74-81, 133-144, 152, 165-166
Technical rationalism, 93, 113, 119
Technology and WAC, 18, 94, 103, 117, 147, 166, 189
Transcribing interview data, 52

U

Underlife, 69-70, 76, 94

W

Workshops, for faculty, *see* consulting models
Writing Across the Curriculum (WAC), Clearninghouse, 5-6
critical approaches to, 98, 122, 125, 149, 184-187
history of, 3-4, 15-20, 22-23, 62-64, 67-68, 92, 182-190
teaching guides, 6, 129
Writing apprehension survey, Daly-Miller, 128
Writing assignment design, 97-98, 115-117, 123-125
Writing center, 37, 46, 53-61, 82, 82-85, 95, 104, 108, 135, 148, 150, 170, 172, 176
Writing center workshops, in situ, 86, 109
Writing consultancies, 37-38, 104, 107-109
Writing fellows, 2-3, 20-21, 40-41, 86, 104, 108, 123-125, 129-130, 148
Writing intensive courses, 1, 17-18, 20, 40-41, 72, 74, 80, 84, 86, 123-124, 129, 165, 174
Writing in the classroom (WIC), 189-190
Writing in the disciplines (WID), 4, 6, 18, 26, 67, 88, 92, 110, 120, 123, 125, 129, 141-142, 149, 182-185
Writing links/adjuncts, 18, 72, 78, 84, 104, 107
Writing program administration, 3, 18-19, 21-24, 28-29, 36, 44, 88, 90, 147, 154-155, 157-160, 165-166, 176
Writing to learn, 17, 37, 105, 116, 182-183, 185-186

Printed in the United States
71284LV00003B/130-135

9 781572 736337